COMPLEXITY, MANAGERS,
AND ORGANIZATIONS

ORGANIZATIONAL AND OCCUPATIONAL PSYCHOLOGY

Series Editor: PETER WARR
*MRC/SSRC Social and Applied Psychology Unit, Department of Psychology,
The University, Sheffield, England*

A list of books in this series is available from the publisher on request.

COMPLEXITY, MANAGERS, AND ORGANIZATIONS

SIEGFRIED STREUFERT

Department of Behavioral Science
The Pennsylvania State University College of Medicine
Hershey, Pennsylvania

ROBERT W. SWEZEY

Behavioral Science Research Center
Science Applications International Corporation
McLean, Virginia, and
The George Washington University
Washington, D.C.

1986

ACADEMIC PRESS, INC.
Harcourt Brace Jovanovich, Publishers

Orlando   San Diego   New York
Austin   Boston   London   Sydney
Tokyo   Toronto

ACADEMIC PRESS, INC.
Orlando, Florida 32887

United Kingdom Edition published by
ACADEMIC PRESS INC. (LONDON) LTD.
24–28 Oval Road, London NW1 7DX

Library of Congress Cataloging in Publication Data

Streufert, Siegfried.
    Complexity, managers, and organizations.

    Bibliography: p.
    Includes index.
    1. Executive ability.   I. Swezey, Robert W.
II. Title.
HD38.2.S77   1986   658.4'09   85-28784
ISBN 0–12–673370–8 (alk. paper)

PRINTED IN THE UNITED STATES OF AMERICA

86 87 88 89   9 8 7 6 5 4 3 2 1

Contents

3

The Place of Complexity in Organizational Science

4

Complexity Theory: The Cognitive Structure of Individuals in the Organization

5

Complexity Theory: The Structure of Information Processing in Organizations

6

The Measurement of Differentiative and Integrative Complexity

7
Research Data on the Behavioral and Organizational Effects of Dimensionality

8
Physiological and Health Implications of Complexity and Other Managerial Styles

9
Contributions of Complexity Theory to Organizations

APPENDIX
Measurement via the Time–Event Matrix

Preface

The competent functioning of managers and the success of organizations is a concern not only for executives and scientists, but for society itself. It is, therefore, not surprising that a multitude of research projects on these topics has been completed and that thousands of relevant articles and books have been published. Nonetheless, researchers have not yet been able to resolve the mystery of the highly successful organization and have not yet developed an adequate prescription for executive excellence. We believe that the earlier lack of success in capturing these qualities is, at least in part, due to the approach that has been used. Most previous theories and research efforts on executive performance and on organizational functioning have looked only at the surface of managerial and organizational success.

Take, for example, questions of executive competence. We have spent years considering *what* successful executives do and what their less successful brethren do. We have studied the *content* of their thoughts and actions. We have not been alone. Following the observations of Peters and Waterman in their book *In Search of Excellence,* a host of popular books on executives and organizational functioning has appeared. Again, most of them have chosen the same approach. Typically, they have asked what competent executives or organizations do, what decisions they make or do not make, and what they do differently than managers and organizations that fail.

Unfortunately, the concern with the "what" of excellence is not sufficient. While it considers the *content* of executive or organizational functioning, it does not reveal the underlying *processes* that create that content. Without question, a concern with the content of, for example, executive or organizational decisions can be important and useful. However, it is rarely useful in and of itself. Content-based conclusions may not even apply universally: Where task demands and organizational characteristics differ widely across settings, diverse decisions, diverse leadership styles, and so forth, may well be optimal. In other words, prescriptions drawn from excellence in one organization may be quite inappropriate in another.

A different approach is needed. We need theory that is more universally applicable, that is, that can point toward optimal managerial and organizational functioning across a wide range of settings, task demands, and constraints. Such an approach is employed in this book. Rather than emphasizing the content of managerial and organizational functioning, we focus primarily on the processes that generate the content. We are concerned with structure, with managerial information processing, and with the processing of organizational input into output. Our approach is based on complexity theory, which is extensively presented and reviewed in chapters that focus on managers and organizations. Subsequent chapters of this book are concerned with data collection methods and with findings from two decades of relevant research. Last, but not least, the book also considers the physiological implications of managerial excellence, based on some research data that link executive excellence and disease.

Acknowledgments

Complexity theory is not new. While its beginnings were greatly different from the theory presented in this book, early theorists such as Kelly or Bieri made it all possible. Early conversations of this book's senior author with Harold Schroder and O. J. Harvey were vital to the initial development of our theory. Michael Driver and Peter Suedfeld have contributed many of their thoughts and insights in earlier and later years. Susan Streufert, coauthor of the 1978 theory on cognitive complexity, has added many valuable concepts.

The present volume grew out of theory and data developments that were made possible by a number of research projects which were primarily funded by the Office of Naval Research and the U.S. Army Research Institute for the Behavioral and Social Sciences. That support is gratefully acknowledged. Without it, the advances contained in this volume would not have been possible.

A number of researchers who participated in these projects should be acknowledged. Among them are Eleanor Criswell, Elaine Davis, Ann Denson, Rosanne Pogash, and Ken Unger. The thoughts of the sponsors of our research efforts have generated valuable progress in theory and research efforts. We would especially like to express our appreciation to Owen Jacobs, Bert King, John Mietus, John Nagay, Judith Orasanu, and Bob Sasmor.

We thank those scientists and executives who provided specific comments on this book project while the manuscript was in the planning phase, while it was being written, and after completion of earlier drafts. Among them are Alexander Kliger, Glenda Nogami, Susan Streufert, and, of course, the editor of this Academic Press book series, Peter Warr. Without Peter Warr's recommendation, this book would probably never have been written. His comments on the initially submitted manuscript have, in our view, greatly improved this volume.

Finally, we thank Elizabeth Spataro for her excellent clerical work, and for the time she took beyond working hours to get the manuscript to the publisher.

1

Introduction

Within any given period of time, some organizations will flourish, others will subsist, and yet others will collapse. To some extent, the fortunes of organizations are determined by outside (e.g., market-based) forces. In good part, however, an organization's future is a product of its internal functioning. What are the internal characteristics of organizations that survive, even in the face of adversity? What are the characteristics of those that fail, even in a favorable environment? Answers to those questions are of considerable importance.

In *In Search of Excellence,* Peters and Waterman (1982) have discussed various successful private-sector organizations. When we decided to write the present volume, *In Search of Excellence* had not yet appeared. We had, however, collected considerable data that are relevant to both organizational and managerial success. Where Peters and Waterman consider the same organizational phenomena with which we had been concerned, our data-based perspective is often in agreement with their observational conclusions.

Our views are highly relevant to their concerns with *how* organizations and people in organizations function. Peters and Waterman imply that there are major differences in *how* corporate decision makers think, *how* organizational information is processed, *how* organizations provide environments that permit creativity to emerge, and *how* decisions are made and carried out.

Our views and data are less relevant to the views of Peter and Waterman where those authors describe the effects of corporate belief systems and attitudes, for example, *what* employees of successful organizations think and how those thoughts may be translated into action. On initial thought, any differences between ''what'' and ''how'' may appear trivial. On second thought, however, this difference takes a considerable importance. The question ''how?'' concerns the *structure* of information processing and information flow within an organization. That structure has major impacts on what is accomplished, how it is accomplished, and possibly most importantly, on what is not accomplished.

Structural information-processing is the central topic of a variety of theories known collectively as complexity theories (e.g., Bieri, 1955; Schroder, Driver, and Streufert, 1967; Scott, 1962). These theories address the structural dimensions that underlie the flow, processing, and use of information. In its more recent form (Streufert, 1978; Streufert and Streufert, 1978), complexity theory focuses on *differentiation* (the number of dimensions that are relevant to an information-processing effort), and *integration* (the relationships among these dimensions). The theory also considers the impact of the *environment* on information flow and processing. As Scott, Osgood, and Peterson (1979) have suggested, that environmental impact may vary across diverse cognitive (or organizational) *domains* where differing degrees of dimensionality may exist.

This book applies complexity theory both to individual managers acting in a decision-making capacity, and to the structure and functioning of organizations. It describes and predicts both how information is processed through an organization and how inputs result in outputs. Our focus is on the processes that occur between input and output: (1) the dimensions along which information that has an impact on an organization, (2) how new information is related to other new or established (stored) information, (3) how and when modifications of organizational and individual management behavior occur, and (4) how a final organizational output is derived.

The processing of information through the organization and through the cognitive structure of individuals within the organization is described as dimensional differentiation and integration. Differences in the degree of managerial and organizational differentiation and integration can have a decisive impact on how an organization functions. They can, in some cases, spell the difference between organizational survival and organizational extinction.

This application of complexity theory to organizations occurs at an opportune time. As discussed by Peters and Waterman, strictly quantitative approaches to organizational analysis have often failed. New theory is needed. The theory we provide is concerned with the cognitive and organizational processes that underlie and predict managerial and organizational behavior. We deal with the processes that underlie many of the observations made by other organizational scientists and observers of the organizational environment, such as Jaques and associates (e.g., Jaques, 1976) and Peters and Waterman. However, as the reader will see, we do not *always* agree with the assumed cognitive or organizational foundations of those observations.

In this book, we explore reasons why organizational science has not previously considered a structural complexity approach to organizational analysis. Is the vocabulary necessary to employ these concepts missing? Have we merely failed to assemble existing concepts into a meaningful theoretical structure? Given the necessary terminology, how can complexity theory best be applied to organizations? What existing data bases can provide answers to questions about organizational structure or organizational management? What data are suggestive of future research?

Questions such as these are addressed in this book. Our approach toward answering these questions differs in at least two ways from the more strictly quantitative techniques for solving organizational problems: Our approach derives measurement from observations rather than from pre hoc probability estimates, and it views rationality in a nonhierarchical fashion.

DESCRIPTIVE VERSUS PREDICTIVE ANALYSIS

Scientists have a bias toward predictive theory. Certainly that bias can be justified because inferences about causality are not possible (at least not with any reliability) from mere descriptions of events. The sciences that are concerned with organizations (and with people in organizations) are no exception. Many organizational scientists believe that sufficient efforts will allow discovery of invariant numerical relationships among observable events and that these relationships, once established, will hold over time. Where research fails to find such relationships, or where the obtained relationships turn out to be curvilinear (or fluctuate as apparently unrelated events are modified), blame is typically placed on inadequate measures. The argument is made that analysis has not yet been reduced to an unconfounded level.

Whether psychology and other behavioral sciences (and organizational science in particular) *can* achieve perfect prediction remains in question. At least two assumptions must be satisfied for such prediction to occur: (1) that fixed relationships among organizational variables do, in fact, exist, and (2) that despite the complexity of the organizational setting it remains possible to determine, define, and measure the specific events or components that form the basis of the required invariable relationships. At present, we cannot be certain that organizational phenomena comply with these assumptions. We certainly have not reached a stage of analysis that even approaches perfect prediction. One may even question whether sufficient knowledge exists about which variables ought to be investigated.

In an attempt to overcome these problems, some disciplines have chosen a descriptive approach to the study of causal events. We can, for instance, learn a great deal about how people and events have shaped a particular organization, using a descriptive study technique. We may find some case studies that reflect surprisingly similar events and outcomes as do other case studies. However, yet other cases studies may show different event sequences and outcomes, and, in such cases, we can only guess why these differences occurred. With descriptive methodologies, quantification tends to be post hoc, if it is employed at all. Data analysis tends to be based on techniques that have their origin in correlational methodology—leading many a tough-minded scientist to turn away in dismay. That scientist is going to be persuaded only (and with at least some justification) where quantifiable predictions are possible. Descriptive approaches in-and-of-themselves cannot serve that purpose. Let us explore the potential of predictive mathematical and of descriptive approaches somewhat further.

Predictive Mathematical Approaches

The ancient Greeks considered mathematics to be the purest form of science, and current thought retains at least part of that belief. Many believe that quantification can solve complex problems, and that, in the final analysis, nothing can defy quantification. The fact that phenomena of physics typically adhere to relatively simple mathematical formulations may strengthen this perception. Clearly, using this logic, one should be able to discover a quantitative formula for organizational phenomena (for example, leadership) as well. But can one?

Mathematically based decision theory has probably gone further than other approaches in attempting to quantify organizational issues. Books, such as *Using Logical Techniques for Making Better Decisions* (Dickson, 1983), address the use of such techniques. However (as many decision theorists will readily admit), managers often fail to heed quantitative recommendations. And (as some would also admit) recommendations based on such techniques are often ineffective in organizational settings.

Mathematical prediction is essentially based on the (often undiscussed) view that a single optimal solution exists to any given problem, and that this solution can be captured via an equation. Yet, we all remember our math teachers telling us that two equations are required to solve for two unknowns. Clearly, even more are necessary to solve for larger numbers of unknowns. In addition, by using multiple equations, we are likely to obtain multiple possible solutions. Predictions of organizational events suffer from the same type of restrictive discourse. If we wish to solve for a single solution, we must overcome the large number of uncertainties that exist in the organizational world. Only by reducing uncertainty can accurate predictions concerning outcomes of contemplated actions be achieved. To do that, scientists develop parameters. Parameters reflect assumptions about relationships among variables, based on previously observed events. Thus, the more unknowns that exist in a situation, i.e., the greater the numbers of uncertainties that also exist, the greater the number of necessary parameter assumptions.

Clearly, mathematical prediction in organizational situations could be of value. Many organizational situations exist where unknowns are few, and where relationships among variables tend to be (at least partially) known. However, such situations are usually quite simple in concept. For example, calculating the probable acceptance of a new product on the basis of mathematical information concerning customer characteristics–interest, and supply–demand values, may be quite reasonable.

However, other forms of complex organizational decision making (for example, whether or not to purchase a new subsidiary) typically are much too complex to conform a strict mathematical prediction. In such complex situations, we often do not know whether we will ever have enough information about organizational variables and their interactions to calculate optimal solutions. In summary, at the present state of knowledge, we are not successful at capturing complex organizational processes with mathematical formulations. Few successes in predicting complex organizational outcomes using quantitative decision theory have been reported.

Further, mathematical predictions are generally based on defined (i.e., previously observed and therefore known) events or relationships. However, the world does not stand still. New events and relationships among events occur continuously. New objects and ideas are constructed. Relationships among variables tend to shift. Thus, increasingly greater complexities can emerge over time. Mathematical formulations however, are inherently stable—that is, they are unable to deal with shifting relationships without repeated modification. Where such modifications are descriptive (and most are, at least in early attempts), they are unable to contribute to causality-based prediction in science. Where, after experimentation or analysis of events, formulations are revised to capture changes, they must necessarily lag in time behind changing conditions. Such lag often produces inaccuracy. The necessary complexity of mathematical predictions and math models (often defying clear understanding by the organizational decision maker), as well as their lag-produced inaccuracy, lead many decision makers to reject their use (quite reasonably) in favor of making decisions on the basis of intuition or on some other (unknown) basis.[1]

From Description to Prediction

We have criticized the exclusive use of description in considering organizational processes. Yet, such a rejection may be a bit harsh when we think about the ways in which theories arise in science. Rarely does a predictive theory merely spring up in a scientist's head unless that individual has previously studied the relationships of variables under consideration. Some theorist, however, may not wish to admit that observation has preceded their theory—particularly if it was based on an "I wonder what would happen if" basis. Nonetheless, observations must precede theory. Where a resulting theory, once developed, permits testing of assumed relationships, and where that testing can lead to inferences of causality, a reasonable understanding of the phenomena of interest can develop.

[1]That this phenomenon is evident and widespread can be seen from the following passage, which is quoted from a 1984 Request for Proposals (RFP) for a Problem Solving and Decision Making Workshop for senior Department of Defense (DoD) officials:

> In the past, DSMC [the Defense Systems Management College at Fort Belvoir, Virginia] taught problem solving and decision making using various mathematical techniques such as statistics, utility theory, and decision trees. At one time an Analysis for Program Managers (APM) course existed at DSMC. However, this course was not fully successful because many students were unprepared for and uncomfortable with rigorous mathematical analyses. Also, students didn't grasp the relevance of mathematical techniques for some of the problems and decisions they faced in the program office environment.

> With the advent of the Program Manager's Workshop (PMW) targeted for the select group of designated service program managers, the requirement for a new problem solving and decision making workshop has emerged.

> The complexity of DoD program management demands that a program manager and his principal staff be capable of cutting through the complex issues to focus management attention on identifying problems, developing alternative solutions, evaluating the alternatives, and selecting the best course of action by utilizing sound decision-making practices.

> In June 1983, a one-week seminar in problem analysis was conducted for the DSMC faculty which stressed generic problem solving and decision making skills. The workshop was very well received and this type of generic, non-mathematical approach is being considered for the PMW for the problems and decisions program managers must face.

But what should we observe? Certainly an ethological approach, where *all* observed events are cataloged, will not produce rapid development of hypotheses, much less rapid development of theory. Observation of specific actions will probably not be extremely helpful either, because action content often varies greatly. An organization that is designed to provide services to the needy at no charge, for instance, may go about its business quite differently than will an organization that is established to design, manufacture, and sell automobiles for profit. The same holds for people that work in organizations: the specific content of their actions will likely vary considerably across individuals.

If we want efforts at description to provide a possible basis for subsequent quantification of organizational variables, then we must find phenomena that can be compared across individuals and/or across units within organizations. That is, we must focus on *structural* rather than on *content* variables. *What* a person thinks likely differs greatly from one individual to another. However, *how* a person thinks can be compared to *how* another person thinks, irrelevant of the content of those thoughts (see Streufert and Streufert, 1978). Similarly, what an organizational unit does provides for less comparability across units than *how* that unit deals with input and *how* it translates input into output. Thus, the way in which information is processed through an organization (from information input to action) can be compared across people (managers), across organizational subunits and across organizations, even if the organizations have divergent purposes and must deal with quite different kinds of information. This *how* approach focuses on organizational (and individual) information-processing *structures* and their effects on managerial actions and organizational outcomes.

Later in this book, we show that structural characteristics can be observed, quantified, measured, and used to develop a theory that is predictive of organizational success. Because our approach begins with assessments of excellence, it does not make pre hoc assumptions about the ingredients of success. It does not attempt to generate idealized mathematical formulations. It does not specifically define what managers and their organizations *should* do. Rather it studies the structured basis of what successful managers or organizations *do,* and what the effects of those actions are. Only *then* does it quantify the structural characteristics of successful persons or successful organizations.

Because this approach addresses *how* people and organizations process information, rather than the specific information content that is processed, it is minimally affected by shifts in informational or task content over time. Changes in content are processed by the organization (or the organizational decision makers) just as other variables and events are processed, generally requiring little or no modification of structural properties. Where some shifts in structural requirements are necessary, they are likely to occur quite slowly, often requiring years to complete. In other words, structural theory of organizational and managerial behavior is likely much more stable over time an task environments than content-based theory.

RATIONAL VERSUS IRRATIONAL
ORGANIZATIONAL DECISION MAKING

If we were to ask persons on the street whether organizations should make decisions on a rational or irrational basis, the majority consensus would undoubtedly favor rationality. Based on a dictionary definition of the term *rational,* we may well agree. Webster's Collegiate Dictionary defines rational as "(1) having reason or understanding, and (2) relating to, based on or agreeable to reason." Certainly decisions made without resort to reason would likely be absurd and probably would lead to failure. If decisions were made at random and were not meaningfully related to other events, we could not even hope to study the decision-making process.

Why, then, has it been argued that successful companies are often "irrational" in their decisions (i.e., Peters and Waterman, 1982)? Let us look at the dictionary definition again. A third definition of the term *rational* (that we have so far omitted) also exists. Webster adds that the term *rational* implies "relating to or resulting from the application of arithmetic operations to integers or to polynomials." Here, *rationality* refers to mathematical operations. Unfortunately, many organizational rationalists have embraced this narrow definition of rationality. Clearly, the mathematical view of rationality is attractive. It provides simple tools for analysis and prediction that was clear, precise, and unambiguous. Further, such a view implicitly supports the scientist's tendency to strive toward order.

We have already argued against overemphasis on a kind of rationality that takes the sole form of mathematical prediction. We are not alone. Peters and Waterman would certainly agree. Some writers make the point in much stronger language. For example, Wrapp (1980) considers the excessive use of the mathematical approach to be a "monster." Even writers who are concerned with the more hierarchical military organizations find that the prescriptive approaches of mathematical decision theorists often do not apply to real-world decision making. Wohl (1981), for instance, has argued as follows:

> Decision theorists have tended toward prescriptive definitions based on the concept of a decision as a selection from among given alternatives, while commanders and corporate executives have tended toward descriptive definitions involving such statements as "It seemed the best thing to do at the time" or

"We had to act immediately based on whatever information we had at the time" or "The final course of action became obvious after awhile." The qualitative difference between the two views is striking.

Nearly all classical decision theory, including its statistical . . . and sequential . . . branches assumes that options are given. Optimal choice usually has to do with the degrees of uncertainty in information input, the relative costs and gains in each of the possible choices . . . or the utility function of the decision maker. . . . The preponderance of work in decision theory has concentrated on techniques for option selection with little research on those portions of the process which are of greatest interest to military commanders, namely, the *creation, evaluation* and *refinement* of both hypotheses (i.e., what is the situation) and options (i.e., what can be done about it) [emphasis added].

Wohl has referred to Keen and Scott-Morton (1978), who suggest that system designers are often both emotionally and philosophically biased, and that they should study *how managers do, in fact, make decisions,* rather than focus on the logic of how they supposedly *should* do so.

In its narrow definition, the (mathematical) rational approach has several negative implications. It generally does not allow for contingency planning because mathematical solutions are required to be definite. It does not generally allow for experimentation and "testing the waters" because experiments may produce errors (even though such errors can provide valuable information). It is conservative, limits novel approaches (see Drucker, 1969), and restricts creativity. Finally, as stated earlier, it often fails when it is applied to complex problems with multiple uncertainties.

On the basis of similar considerations, Peters and Waterman (1982) have reached the conclusion that humans are *irrational* and that irrationally led organizations tend to perform better. These authors also argue that "if there is one striking feature of the excellent companies, it is (their) ability to manage ambiguity and paradox" (p. xxiv). They later state (in discussing various factors that should be considered by management); "Yes, quantification of these sorts of factors is difficult, probably not even useful. But the factors can certainly be considered sensibly, logically and fairly precisely in the face of modestly well documented past experience" (p. 32). [From J. J. Peters and R. H. Waterman, Jr. (1982) *In Search of Excellence.* Copyright 1982 by Harper and Row, Publishers, Inc.]

However, sensible, logical, and precise, consideration of phenomena or events hardly sounds like irrational behavior—at least in terms of the first two of the dictionary definitions of rational. What kind of rationality, if not mathematically described, are we dealing with? How does one manage paradox successfully, yet rationally? We would argue that rationality does underlie many, if not most, of the decisions made in organizations. These decisions, as required by the dictionary definition of rationality, are generally based on reason. The reasons may not always be adequate, yet they are reasons based on some—albeit possibly limited—rationality. They are not necessarily hierarchically organized, as *mathematical* rationality might require. For that matter, the reasoning underlying organizational decision making may often be flexibly multidimensional and, consequently, may escape mathematical description (especially, as long as the mathematical description posits a hierarchical derivation system).

It is our contention that creativity, experimentation, planning for the future, and similar organizational decision-making characteristics, which Peters and Waterman have advanced in arguments against the rational approach, can indeed be rational, although they reflect a different kind of rational approach, one that is evident in successful organizations and in successful managers. It is this kind of rationality that this book addresses.

THE RATIONALITY OF DIFFERENTIATON AND INTEGRATION

We have previously stated that complexity theory is concerned with differentiation and integration of dimensions. Thus, it views both organizations and managers from a perspective of potential multidimensionality, both as potential differentiators and integrators, and as potentially flexible and adaptive as they integrate various dimensions of information. Mathematical decision-making approaches, in contrast, tend to reflect either unidimensionality, or at best, an inflexible hierarchical system of multidimensional information processing where relationships among dimensions and their impacts are fixed. From a purely quantitative perspective, an executive who may perceive information or events on several dimensions (e.g., goodness, utility, employee satisfaction, pay-off for self and others, corporate profit) should weight those dimensions. From a quantitative perspective, the same logic holds for organizations. Information received by various departments (which might have diverse implications) must ultimately be weighted according to, for example, a single overriding principle, such as profit.

As you will see, this is *not* necessarily the way in which excellent organizations typically function. Neither is it necessarily the way an excellent corporate decision maker functions (if he or she did, we could and probably should replace him or her with a much faster computer). Rather, differentiation and integration in organizational functioning can, and in many cases should, be integrative and flexible. A variety of simultaneous inputs into the system (whether individual cognition or organizational system) in combination with current demands and opportunities may (or should) change weights or judgmental dimensions and may change the pattern with which relationships among dimensions (integrations) produce outcomes. These outcomes are likely based on observable events but, because they vary with situational and other demands, are not easily predictable in advance. While the information processing from which the outcomes emerge takes account of uncertainties, an observer (who is not aware of the many considerations as he/she tries to interpret the reasons for an outcome) may perceive irrationality or excessive effects of uncertainty. As a matter of fact, the observed behavior, because of its shifts over time and tasks, may appear uncontrolled or "wishy-washy." The apparent irrationality more likely reflects limited understanding by the observer (especially with regard to information integration) than lack of control or randomness of organizational or managerial activity. As long as the organizational behavior in question is both adaptive and (as the dictionary requires) "based on or agreeable to [multidimensional] reason"—that is, reasoned actions by the decision makers—it is necessarily rational.

Organizational science has typically neglected this form of rationality. To some degree, the neglect may be due to a failure to observe structural characteristics: We have focused so carefully on *what* organizations do rather than on *how* they do them. Another possibility is that we have simply not developed an adequate language to deal with the structural characteristics that underlie the behavior of managers and organizations. One may ask, is the linguistic terminology that is required to communicate or identify structural concepts relevant to managers and organizations available? Is it used in organizational science? Or, are such concepts as differentiation, integration, input, output, complexity, information, dimensionality, and decision making absent from the organizational literature? The answer to the latter question can hardly be "yes." Even a brief skimming of the organizational literature shows that such complexity theory terms are used over and over again.

A remaining issue then, is the extent to which these terms are used in interrelated fashion either in organizational theory or in the interpretations of organizational data, or both. Without adequate language and without organization of that language toward understanding the interrelationship of these terms, we cannot achieve the needed conceptualization of the structural underpinnings in organizational information processing. As Peters and Waterman (1982) have indicated, special forms of languages *are* required for specific orientations. In Chapter 3 of this book, we explore the extent to which the language of complexity theory is available to organizational science. In the next chapter, theory and research concerned with complexity approaches per se are reviewed.

2

Complexity: A Review of the Literature

STRUCTURE VERSUS CONTENT

Complexity theory had its origin in cognition. Early versions of various theoretical approaches to complexity were concerned with the styles persons employ when they process information. The first complexity theorists focused their interests primarily on the areas of perception, individual differences, and information processing. Invariably, the early orientation was concerned with individual human beings, specifically with the cognitive *structure* of those human beings. How did information flow through this structure? Where and when was information modified, distorted, used? How did this structure express itself in the behavior of a particular person under study? The possibility that information-processing structures of larger order (e.g., group structures or organizational structures) might be included within the predictions of complexity theory was not considered in early efforts.

The review of complexity theory and research that is presented in this chapter is historical in its approach, dealing first with earlier approaches to complexity theory and research. For readers who wish to become familiar with complexity theory as a general phenomenon, our review will be useful in its entirety. For those (more impatient) readers who want to know how complexity can address people in organizations (or the organizations them-selves) reading this chapter through to the next section may be useful, then skipping the "definitions" section and beginning again with the third section.

We have already touched on certain basic aspects of complexity theory in the first chapter of this book. Whether applied to individuals, to groups, or to organizations, the complexity theories are all concerned with the *how* of information processing. When viewed in a very limited and isolated fashion,[1] complexity-based approaches are not interested in *what* the information processed might be. The content of an attitude, for example, would not be of major interest. *How* an attitude, whatever its content might be, is developed, how contradictory information may modify that attitude, and how the attitude is used in contributing to information input–behavior-output chains *is* of interest. In other words, the focus is on the structure of information *processing*. The emphasis is on *how* information is processed.

In contrast, attitude content, specific attributions, even the content of a specific decision are not directly considered because they reflect the *content*, that is, the *what* of information processing. That is not to say that content is unimportant. Indeed, it is of considerable significance: Without knowing whether an attitude makes sense, whether an event is attributed to the appropriate causal agent, or whether a decision is meaningful in its environmental context, we have gained little information about some aspects of decision-making quality. But, an emphasis on content alone is equally insufficient. Nonetheless, behavioral content, decision-making content, and so forth has been and continues to be, studied extensively and—unfortunately—in isolation. Content alone is being investigated by behavioral scientists of many orientations, by economists, sociologists, and management scientists alike.

In most applied decision-making situations, there is minimal doubt that most actions taken by managers are appropriate in their content, especially if decisions are made by persons who are already in positions of influence. Executives have generally achieved their position by demonstrating that they are not likely to engage in actions (or decisions) that are irrelevant to current needs, i.e., of inappropriate content. Similarly, a good military leader is not likely to initiate an action that will result in immediate and unnecessary loss of life or equipment. Such individuals have been trained to optimize current outcomes, given current conditions. In other words, there exists

---

[1]Such an isolated view is mentioned for definitional purposes only. Content and structure should be considered simultaneously in terms of their joint effects on outcomes.

some basic assurance that well-trained and experienced personnel are not very likely to make major errors in decision content.

Complexity theorists suggest that we need to consider the effects of content where necessary—that is, where the possibility exists that decision content may not be handled appropriately in a task at hand. However, complexity theorists would argue that *structure*—that is, the *how* of information processing—is at least as important—and maybe more so. For example, though some specific decisions may be quite appropriate in content at a given point in time, it may be inappropriate on other occasions. Consider, for example, a situation in which a general commanding a force is facing enemy attack. An appropriate "content" response might be to engage the enemy, to hold a defensive line[2] at an optimal point in the terrain, and to possibly counterattack by increasing the number of forces at the location of the enemy attack. However, that action might draw substantial defensive forces away from other locations. If the enemy's attack was, in fact, intended to weaken the lines elsewhere, specifically at a location where the enemy intended to break through the lines in the near future, an appropriate response based on consideration of one dimension of content alone might have resulted in disaster. In such a situation, the military commander should (and certainly would) have asked such questions as

1. What is the purpose of the enemy's move?
2. What may their next action be?
3. What *strategy* is behind the action?
4. What is the best strategy in response?
5. How can we turn the enemy's strategy against them?
6. What are the long-range implications of the various potential outcomes of this battle?
7. What strategy and its likely outcome would be most successful in the long run, even if it does not necessarily appear so in the short run?

These questions reflect cognitive activity along a number of content dimensions. The simultaneous and interactive (integrative) application of several dimensions takes this form of information processing into the realm of structure. We are now concerned with the *how* of information processing by asking *how* the various and diverse answers to these questions are combined to arrive at action decision(s).

A similar example may be drawn from the private sector (see Streufert, 1983a). Consider two companies that manufacture a similar consumer product. Decision makers in one of the companies are informed that the competition has dropped their price by 25%. How should management deal

---

[2]At least in classical warfare.

with this situation? The reaction might be what complexity theorists term *respondent*: "We will drop our price by 25% also." Such a response may (or, in some cases may not) be content appropriate. But what about its long-run effect? Will it potentially result in bankruptcy? Will it result in a continuing price war that neither company can afford? What are the effects on development of new products for which research and development (R&D) investments are required? Again, management must deal with the interaction of several organizational dimensions—that is, with the *structure* of decision making.

For the moment, let us focus on the cognitive structure of the company's decision makers. How many factors are considered in their decisions? How do they evaluate the impact of a present decision on future decisions and on the overall goal? What contingency plans are made? To place these questions into the terminology used in complexity theory: How much dimensional differentiation and integration[3] is underlying each potential response? A cognitively complex (i.e., differentiated and integrated) decision (with variable and multiple appropriate content) might involve consideration of a variety of alternative actions as well as estimates of the consequences of each.

For example, the question "Should the price be dropped?" would certainly be asked. But by how much? The expected or estimated reaction of customers to each feasible level of price decrease might be considered. Should the company wait until the competition raises the price of the product (based on estimates of how long the competition might be able to maintain the price cut)? What are the problems encountered when one considers cost versus volume of production and sales? Is it possible—or useful—to try to persuade the customer that our company's product is of superior quality and has a greater longevity? Certainly the effects of sequential actions in a potential price war between the companies would be considered and included in the deliberations of various strategic options. The effect of each possible action on the various components of the company and their people would be taken into consideration. The final decision might combine several *interrelated* actions: for example, reduce price by 10%, advertise the product's quality and long life, plan for contingencies based on estimates of what the other company might do next, and try to make it less attractive for the competing company to maintain the 25% price cut.

These multiple, interrelated decision components involve considerable planning. Their development and interrelationships can be discovered, described and predicted by considering a *structural* approach to information processing, an approach that has been pioneered by the complexity theories.

---

[3]More-explicit definitions of complexity theory terms are provided later in this volume.

The terms *differentiation* and *integration* are used to describe those structural characteristics. While the use of these two terms has been similar across complexity theorists, other terms have varied somewhat in their definitions. Before continuing to discuss components of the complexity theoretic approach to information processing, it is appropriate to define the terms that will be used in this book.

DEFINITIONS

Dimension: A bipolar cognitive scale with two or more points of discrimination among stimuli. The scale represents the grouping or ordering of stimuli or cognitive concepts that have meaning in the space defined by the endpoints (or poles) of the scale. This definition may be aided by an example (similar to one used by Kelly, 1955). If an individual has in his or her cognitive space a dimension (scale) of short–tall, the endpoints of that dimension have meaning to the stimuli "man" or "building," but do not have meaning in relation to the stimulus "weather." Cognitive dimensions become institutionalized orientations in organizations. The "profit" and "productivity" dimensions provide good examples.

Discrimination: The process of dividing (or the degree to which division has been accomplished) a cognitive bipolar dimension into subsections for the placement of stimuli that have relevance to the endpoints of that dimension. Discrimination is meaningful only to the degree that sharp distinctions can be made—that is, to the degree that the distinctions can be labeled or can evoke differential outcomes in behavior. The minimum number of discriminations on any dimension is two (i.e., the endpoints). The maximum number of discriminations on any dimension is limited only by the capacity of the individual or organization to meaningfully subdivide the dimension.

Discrimination, defined as a unidimensional process, is nonetheless related to the processes of differentiation and integration. As in differentiation, it involves the division of cognitive–conceptual space (here, of one dimension only), and as in integration, it involves the assembling of various cognitive–conceptual points of meaning into a (here, unidimensional) conceptualization.

Differentiation: The process of dividing cognitive or conceptual[4] space (or the degree to which this division has been achieved relevant to specific

---

[4]The definitions apply to individuals, interacting groups, and organizations alike. The term, *cognitive space*, is likely more applicable at the lower—that is, individual—level. *Conceptual space* is typically more appropriate at the macroscopic (e.g., organizational) level of analysis. Similarly, the terms *system* and *subsystem* are more applicable at macroscopic levels. They

stimulus configurations) into two or more orthogonal or oblique (but near-orthogonal) bipolar dimensions, systems or subsystems—for example, the ordering and processing of stimuli in relatively intransitive fashion.

Integration: The process of relating a stimulus configuration of two or more orthogonal or oblique dimensions, systems, or subsystems in cognitive or conceptual space (or the degree to which this relating has been achieved), to produce an outcome that is determined by the *joint* (weighted or unweighted) demands of each dimension, system, or subsystem involved.

Hierarchical Integration: The fixed relationship among dimensions, systems, or subsystems with regard to stimulus configurations that produces a joint (weighted or unweighted, but stable) response to stimuli. In hierarchical integration, specific stimuli would always affect the same dimensions in the same way.

Flexible Integration: The varied, sometimes changing relationships among dimensions with regard to stimulus configurations, which produce diverse (over stimulus type, presence–absence, or frequency) weighted or unweighted responses to stimuli. Where *flexible* integration can be responsive to anticipated changes in the environment that would require reconceptualizations of event relationships, hierarchical integration cannot.

Content: The possible locations of specific stimulus objects at specific discriminated points on *one* cognitive or conceptual dimension (e.g., an attitude or an organizational policy). Cognitive content is concerned with the location of stimulus *objects* on a given dimension in relation to each other (as contrasted to structural relationships among dimensions). Content represents *what* persons think about a stimulus or what an institutionalized organizational response to a stimulus is, not *how* they think about it or respond to it. Content is also involved in specific organizational (cultural) belief systems, but not in *how* those systems function to affect the organizational process.

Structure: Represents the differentiative or integrative use of *dimensions* in cognitive or conceptual space with regard to specific stimulus objects or configurations. Structure is concerned with the number of dimensions and the number and pattern of relationships among them (i.e., the *organization* of dimensional space), rather than with the meaning of the specific dimensions involved. In other words, while content is, for example, concerned with what individuals think about a stimulus or what response an organization typically makes to it, structure is concerned with the processes underlying those thoughts or responses.

---

should not merely be understood in their sociological meaning. Rather, systems and subsystems imply components through which an organization (or task-oriented group) processes information.

Cognitive Complexity–Simplicity: Represents the degree to which a potentially multidimensional cognitive space is differentiated and integrated. A cognitively complex person would employ differentiation and integration as part of his or her information processing. In other words, that person's cognitive structure would likely function multidimensionally. A less complex person would respond to stimulus arrays on the basis of few or only one dimension—that is, would demonstrate less, little, or no dimensional differentiation and integration. At the extreme, such a person would function in unidimensional fashion in response to any or all stimuli.

Organizational Complexity–Simplicity: Represents the degree to which the conceptual space of an organization is differentiated and integrated. A conceptually complex (multidimensional) organization would function on the basis of a number of more or less independent (differentiated) organizational purposes, goals, means, and so forth and would generate outcomes on the basis of the (integrated) interactive weights of those conceptualizations. A conceptually less complex (more unidimensional) organization would likely function on the basis of few or single (e.g., profit) orientations.

Domains of Complexity: Represents the subdivision of cognitive or conceptual space into specific areas for which the degree of differentiation/integration may differ widely. For example, a person may process information multidimensionally in his–her dealings with nonsocial objects or ideas, but may be strictly unidimensional in perceptions of the *social* (e.g., family) environment. An organization may have an R&D department that operates in multidimensional fashion and an accounting department that functions in strictly unidimensional fashion. Domain-specific unidimensional functioning would likely provide conflict with domains that function multidimensionally whenever outcomes that are important for both domains are simultaneously considered or interrelated. Among the more important domains for both individuals and organizations are *perceptual-information-acquisition* functions versus *decision-making–executive* functions. In other words, the presence of perceptual differentiation or perceptual integration does not necessarily imply that differentiated and integrated decision-making activities will follow, and vice versa.

EFFECTS OF THE ENVIRONMENT AND OF TASK DEMANDS

Information processing is not static. The amount of stress, the workload, and task demands are, of course, factors in one's perception of the environment, and one's decision-making activity. The variable effects of environmental conditions hold as well for organizations as for individuals.

Earlier complexity theories did not consider the effects of environmental events. People were viewed as more or less static information processors: either they *did* or *did not* possess some specific degree of complexity (i.e., differentiation, integration, and so forth). Later theories suggested that optimal information processing, such as the employment of strategic planning occurs only when environmental conditions are appropriate for such efforts (e.g., Streufert, 1978).

Of course, one may ask questions about what *kind* of information processing, (i.e., what kind of structural activity) might be most appropriate for specific kinds of tasks and environmental demands. Such questions have not been generally considered in the past. They are, however, addressed in the present book.

In the remaining portion of this chapter we review previous complexity-theory efforts. We proceed historically, that is, from theories that were entirely cognitive and oriented only toward individual differences, to theories that encompass considerably greater ranges of behavior.

THEORETICAL POSITIONS IN THE DEVELOPMENT OF COMPLEXITY THEORY PRIOR TO 1977

The reader who is familiar with complexity theories may notice that some theory or another may appear modified from its original manuscript. These apparent changes are due to changes in terminology, not to changes in the content of the theories. By using the same terminology in reviewing all of the complexity theories, meaningful comparisons among the theoretical (and research) efforts are possible. In the following paragraphs, several of the theories published prior to 1977 are reviewed very briefly.

Kelly

Kelly (1955) proposed a psychology of personal constructs as a guide for psychotherapy and client–therapist interaction. His concept of personal constructs and its measurement via the Role Concept Repertoire (REP) Test, while not originally intended as a complexity approach, has nevertheless provided the basis for later complexity theories. Kelly's *construct* is a bipolar dimension that results from an individual's process of "construing or (cognitively) interpreting" events. Kelly considered dimensions in terms of similarity and contrast. According to his view, a dimension (construct) emerges when two events or objects are viewed as similar and a third is viewed as dissimilar. Dimensions are presumed to relate to each other in terms of ordinal hierarchical relationships, but these relationships may be limited to certain areas (*domains*). Location of objects or concepts within dimensions may or may not be fixed. The views of Kelly seems most closely related to our concept of differentiation (as defined previously), although the potential for some (minimal) discrimination and integration exists. Distinctions between content and structure are not made.

Bieri

The theories of Bieri (1961, 1966; Bieri et al., 1966) are based on the work of Kelly. As is the case with Kelly, Bieri's work has been concerned with the effect of an individual's cognitive orientation on the judgments he or she makes in response to environmental stimulation. Bieri views complexity as a structural characteristic describing the use of psychological dimensions. According to Bieri (1968), complexity is concerned only with social judgments and social versatility. The degree of cognitive complexity is related to the number of cognitive dimensions available to an individual. The more dimensions that are present, the greater the degree of individual cognitive complexity.

Bieri has discussed differentiation both in terms of an individual's cognitive structure (the number of dimensions available to that person), and in terms of the *social* stimulus environment (the number of dimensions possessed by the stimulus). Social perception, in this view, consists of an interaction between stimulus complexity and structural (person) complexity. Bieri also considered discrimination (termed articulation by that author)—that is, the process of making discriminations within dimensions, and a third judgmental process (there called discrimination), which involves making unique distinctions among stimuli.

Bieri's theory tends to emphasize analytic rather than the synthetic cognitions. The theory describes how stimuli are separated into meaningful categories, either on the basis of individual dimensions or on the basis of the stimuli themselves. It should be noted that Bieri's theory (in contrast to the early work of Kelly) is, however, clearly structural in its orientation even though it deals only with perceptual–social issues.

Zajonc

Zajonc's (1960) categorizing theory proposes that, given a set of stimuli and a set of responses made to those stimuli, a determinate correspondence between the elements of both sets can be derived. The value(s) of this correspondence are described as dimensions (called attributes) which may be inferred from a person's responses to a given stimulus set. The established stimulus-set to response-set relationship determines the value of any relevant new stimulus to which a person is exposed. Numbers of available dimensions reflect the degree of differentiation. Complexity reflects the degree to which classes of dimensions in a given cognitive structure can be subdivided. One of the major values of Zajonc's theory is that it provided the major impetus for the subsequent theoretical formulations of Scott (1969; Scott, Osgood, and Peterson, 1979) and associates.

Scott

Scott's (1969) early cognitive structure theory not only was based on the work of Zajonc (1960), but also combined that approach with earlier formulations suggested by Lewin (1936) and by Heider (1946). Previously proposed distinctions between personality content and structural characteristics were elaborated by Scott into an encompassing theory of structural characteristics which has considerable implications for social, personality, clinical, and to some extent, for organizational psychology. The definitions of content and structure advanced by Scott are quite similar to those employed here and in Streufert and Streufert (1978). Scott was one of the first theorists to emphasize that structural characteristics (e.g., differentiation) may be limited to specific cognitive domains. Scott described dimensions and discriminations on dimensions (called attributes) which are viewed as images (or concepts of objects). These images represent perceived combinations of object characteristics.

Scott's theory is extensive and complex. Again, the terminology does not match that of other theoretical orientations. A summary provided by Streufert and Streufert (1978) provides a useful overview of Scott's theory (pp. 25–26).

> Any perception by a person based on the phenomenological world results in an image which represents a point on one or more dimensions (attributes) of cognitive space. Where, on any dimension, the image falls depends on the number of segments of the dimension (degree of articulation of the attribute). The number of independent dimensions (attributes) into which a person sorts information reflects the degree to which he differentiates the specific cognitive domain into which he has placed the perceived stimuli.

> It should be noted that Scott views both dimensionality and discrimination (in his terms, attributes and articulation) as parts of the differentiation concept.[5] In this way he differs from other theorists (e.g., Driver & Streufert, 1966; Schroder, Driver & Streufert, 1967; Streufert, 1970) who view discrimination as a separate process.

[5]Scott's distinction between attributes and dimensions is not reported in this chapter. For some more detail, see the discussion of Scott's theoretical statements here and in the original sources.

Scott's view of "integration" also differs from that of other theorists who have been primarily concerned with that concept (e.g., Driver & Streufert, 1966; Harvey, Hunt, & Schroder, 1961; Schroder et al. 1967; Streufert, 1970). While all writers would agree that integration refers to the manner in which images are related, Scott includes a much greater number of cognitive operations in his "integration" concept. For example, if (to use one of his integrative processes) various attributes (dimensions) are highly correlated with "affective–evaluative consistency," then this form of association would be viewed by other theorists as the absence of complexity. Integration theorists would argue that integration must follow differentiation. The use of divergent verbal labels for what is otherwise known as the good–bad (evaluative) dimension would suggest to them that identity (unity) of these attributes has been learned, and that a differentiation process did not take place before the association was made. Alternatively, the structure which once was differentiated may have become resimplified through a process that may be called hierarchical (Streufert, 1970), as distinguished from what Schroder et al. (1967) called integration proper, and what Driver and Streufert (1966) and Streufert (1970) have discussed as flexible integration.

A final distinguishing characteristic of Scott's theory is his repeated emphasis (e.g., Peterson & Scott, 1974; Scott, 1963) on the limitations of complexity across cognitive domains (cf. also Cohen & Feldman, 1975). He questions the assumption of the existence of structural *types*, i.e., the description of a person as "simple," "complex," etc. He considers it to be probable that the number of persons who have consistent structural characteristics among many areas of their experience is quite small, and further suggests that such individuals may well be pathological. Scott states, however (personal communication, 1975), that the attempt to describe such types is of value if developed empirically, rather than on an *a priori* basis. Recent evidence (Peterson & Scott, 1974; Scott, 1974) suggests the existence of at least a limited typography: Some degree of generality of cognitive style across domains was obtained. Which style is utilized in a particular situation appears to be dependent upon an interaction between the structural characteristics of the person and the characteristics of the situation, [emphasis in original].

Impression Formation

Impression formation has been an interest of several complexity theorists (e.g., Bieri, 1955). Generally, theorists involved in impression formation suggest that persons who are cognitively complex (i.e., multidimensional) should form more veridical impressions (Bieri, 1955) or should include more information that may, on the surface, appear contradictory (Streufert and Driver, 1967), than will persons whose perceptual style reflects greater unidimensionality. In other words, complex persons should respond less to the primacy or recency orientation suggested by researchers associated with Asch (1946; Anderson and Barrios, 1961; Luchins, 1957,1958). Crockett (1965) and associates have carried out an extensive research program on impression formation. Their theoretical conceptions of complexity are based on the primacy–recency paradigm (see Asch, 1946). Crockett's work is derived from the developmental psychology of Werner (1957), where differentiation and discrimination (articulation) are viewed as developmental processes, resulting in "increased interdependence of elements" through integration into a *hierarchically* organized system. In this approach, complexity implies a cognitive system that contains a larger number of elements *and* the integration of those elements into a fixed hierarchical system of relationships. The relative number of constructs in a cognitive system defines the degree of cognitive differentiation.

Crockett's concept of differentiation has much in common with those of the aforementioned authors. It should be noted, however, that his definition of integration is hierarchical (i.e., nonflexible in the sense considered by the Harvey et al., the Schroder et al., and the Streufert and Streufert theories). Crockett's work is concerned with the generality of cognitive complexity; in other words, he does not assume that complexity is necessarily the same from one domain to another.

Harvey, Hunt, and Schroder (1961) proposed their systems theory as a developmental descriptive approach to behavior at four levels of cognition. The *System 1 person* was viewed as a "yea sayer," accepting demands, mores, folkways, and fads (of his or her source of training) without question. The *System 2 person*, in contrast, was viewed as a "nay sayer," rebelling against the imposition of authority (i.e., not accepting the simple good–bad orientation of established norms). At the developmental level of *System 3*, the *person* is able to view alternatives as acceptable, resulting in greater tolerance and displaying somewhat of a "nice guy" image. The *System 4 person* not only considers alternatives, but also relates them structurally to superordinate concepts, goals, et cetera. The authors suggest that persons may develop through stages defined by these systems and intermediate levels to reach System 4 or may become arrested at any one state or in a transition between stages. Development through the stages is seen as representing development toward greater differentiation and subsequently greater integration.

Harvey et al. use the term "concrete" to describe the developmental stage defined by System 1 and the term "abstract" to describe the System 4 person. Hunt (1966) added a "Sub 1 Stage" to the theory in order to describe the person who is less than unidimensional. Here, the good–bad dimension of the Stage 1 person is replaced by an inclusion–exclusion principle. With this addition, Hunt has added to the theoretical formulation by suggesting that discrimination does not exist in the Sub 1 Stage.

While the theory of Harvey et al. does include *some* structural characteristics, it is clearly confounded with content: for example, System 1 suggests authoritarianism along a right-versus-wrong evaluative dimension,

System 2 implies rebellion against that dimension, and System 3 often can represent an attitude of tolerance (rather than tolerance based on potential alternate dimensional interpretation). The theory places value on the level to which a person advances: that is, it is good to be at a System 4 level of cognitive functioning and bad to be at the Sub-1 level.

Interactive Complexity Theory

Early interactive complexity theory (Driver and Streufert, 1966; Schroder, 1971; Schroder, Driver, and Streufert, 1967; Streufert and Driver, 1967) and subsequent versions (e.g., Streufert, 1970) propose that effective cognitive complexity is not only a function of a person's structural dimensionality, but depends as well on environmental conditions. The theory proposes a family of inverted U-shaped curves (Figure 2.1) relating environmental complexity (e.g., information load) to differentiative and integrative performance.

Different persons, representing different degrees of cognitive complexity may reach diverse levels of differentiative–integrative performance as long as environmental conditions (e.g., stimulus load) are optimal. Lesser dif-

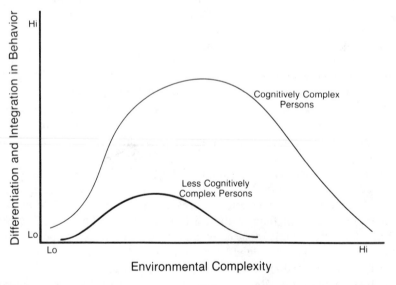

FIGURE 2.1.   Early interactive complexity theory interpretation of the relationship between cognitive complexity, environmental complexity, and differentiation–integration in task behavior.

ferences would be expected when the environment is greatly overloading (excessive environmental complexity) or when the environment deprives the individual of needed input. In other words, optimal functioning of individuals is viewed as an interactive effect of two variables, one concerned with individual differences, the other with environmental conditions.

A number of environmental variables are considered. The approach is entirely structural and deals with differentiation and integration separately. It is assumed (Streufert, 1978) that integration is probably best based on a moderate amount of differentiation. The interactive complexity theory, as its name suggests, is the only one of the earlier complexity theories that specifically deals with variations in environmental (stimulus) effects as equally important in relation to structural person variables. In addition, it moves away from the interpersonal domain and explores complexity effects in other (e.g., nonsocial, decision making) domains as well.

ADVANCES IN COMPLEXITY THEORY SINCE 1977

Two books are widely concerned with complexity theory. One is a volume by Scott, Osgood, and Peterson (1979), which expands on the earlier work of Scott. The other is a book by Streufert and Streufert (1978), which revises interactive complexity theory and adds a host of predictions about the effects of cognitive complexity and environmental complexity on a number of behaviors.

Streufert and Streufert.

Streufert and Streufert (1978) evolved their theoretical views from the earlier interactive theories of Schroder, Driver, and Streufert (1967) and the more than 50 research manuscripts published by that research group in the period between 1967 and 1977. In addition, the complexity theory advanced by Streufert and Streufert was extended to permit a more extensive focus on decision making (Streufert, 1978; Swezey, Streufert, Criswell, Unger, and Van Rijn, 1984) and environmental problems (Streufert, Nogami, and Streufert, 1980). The theory views dimensionality as a joint effect of individual or organizational differences in information-processing structure *and* of the characteristics of the current environment in which an individual or organization must function. A number of information-processing characteristics are proposed, as well as a series of associated measures. Differential predictions for differing environmental conditions and for individual (group or organizational) differences are advanced. For example, a family of inverted U-shaped curves relating environmental complexity to strategic

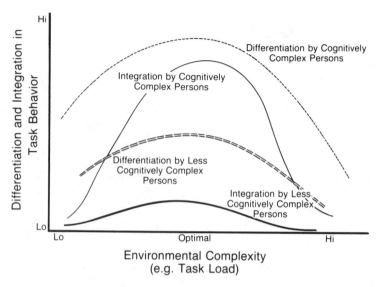

FIGURE 2.2.   Late interactive complexity theory interpretation of the relationships among cognitive complexity environmental complexity and differentiation–integration in task behavior.

decision-making performance is proposed. The different levels of those curves represent diverse differentiative–integrative capacity. The curves differ from those proposed by Schroder, Driver, and Streufert (1967) because they suggest a common optimal level on the environmental complexity (for example information load) dimension for both more and less complex persons (see Figure 2.2). The older theory had assumed that more complex persons would perform optimally at a higher level of environmental complexity.

A major advance of the Streufert and Streufert formulations is found in their examination of performance beyond the strategic (or planning) behaviors expected from more multidimensional decision makers. The theory also considers the appropriateness of specific levels of differentiative or integrative behavior (performance) with regard to particular task or environment demands and advances more than 100 predictions that relate cognitive structure to various fields within personality, social, and organizational psychology.[6]

---

[6]Because of the rather large number of hypotheses and propositions generated, a review of such detail would go far beyond the scope of this chapter. The interested reader is referred to the original source documents.

Scott

Scott and associates (Scott, Osgood, and Peterson, 1979) maintain an approach to complexity that has its basis in Zajonc's theory but refine and clarify their conceptualizations of cognitive structure and cognitive complexity. The authors continue Scott's earlier emphasis on cognitive domains and describe complexity in domain-specific terms. The description is based on a geometric model of multidimensional space founded on Euclidean geometry. In their view, objects (conceptual or perceptual) are defined by their projections into dimensions (called attributes). Objects that are projected onto identical discriminated segments of all dimensions to which they are assigned are indistinguishable, even if they have different names. Correspondingly, two dimensions that order or classify all objects in the same way are also indistinguishable and considered identical.

The geometric model measures the similarity (or the degree of distinctiveness) of cognitive domains. If, for example, a backward nation is described as having both untapped resources and as possessing great natural beauty; but a technologically advanced nation is described as a military threat and as a political democracy, then the two represent diverse domains. Following Zajonc (1960), the complexity of an object is viewed as the number of (different) ideas a person has about it. Viewed geometrically, complexity represents the number of different dimensions onto which an object is projected.

Angles among lines in the geometric model are determined by the experienced or imagined characteristics of objects in a domain. Together these lines constitute the multidimensional space in which objects are accommodated and to which any new object may be assigned. The dimensionality of this space is, geometrically, the number of dimensions of space required to accommodate all objects. Psychologically, it represents the independent considerations brought to bear by a person appraising a set of objects or cognitions.

The model (and its measurement) differs from others in that it makes a distinction between attributes that may be obliquely related and dimensions encompassing the attributes, which must be orthogonal. Some theorists would view such a distinction as artificial, obtained in the interest of mathematical neatness, but unfortunately, not representative of actual structural cognitions (e.g., Streufert and Streufert, 1978). Scott's approach differs from those efforts, however, by not considering systematic variation of the objects in potential perceptual space. In other words, such problems as stressors, originating through specific conditions of environmental complexity, are not considered.

RESEARCH RESULTS ON COMPLEXITY THEORY

A Summary of Research on Cognitive Complexity through Early 1977[7]

If consistency, as has been suggested, is indeed the "hobgoblin of little [i.e., undifferentiated] minds," then one might expect a negative relationship between consistency-seeking and complexity. It appears that the need for consistency is, in fact, negatively related to cognitive complexity, no matter how complexity is measured. Research data also suggest that cognitively complex persons form more complete and more balanced impressions of others when presented with some form of an impression formation task. Differences between complex and less complex individuals can, however, be decreased or eliminated by a number of environmental conditions or instructions, for example, stress, information overload, or a set to evaluate.

Earlier theories had suggested that complex individuals should be more open to information (of all kinds) than less complex (but in other aspects equal) counterparts. Careful experimental design has shown that information orientation interacts with stimulus conditions. Apparently less complex persons are more constrained by information obtained from the environment: they tend to search more (than complex persons) when they experience information deprivation, but they search less when already overloaded. Complex persons, conversely, tend to rely in some part on their own integrative effects, and consequently, are not as externally information bound. In addition, complex subjects seek more novel information and search across a greater number of information categories.

Research data on attitudes, attraction, and the potential for social influence have been obtained both in restricted (sensory deprivation) and in normal environments. Generally it has been found that attitudes of less complex persons tend to be stable and are not greatly affected by environmental changes. However, attitude change is more easily obtained for less complex persons where incongruent information is made highly salient. Interpersonal attraction among persons appears to be greatest where all involved are high in cognitive complexity. However, similar complexity characteristics (no matter at which level) can be useful in generating attraction. At lower complexity levels, similar cognitive content (e.g., similar attitudes) appears to be a precondition for lasting attraction.

---

[7]In the interest of brevity, research in this section will be summarized into rather short statements without references to the many authors whose data are considered. Researchers who desire greater detail as well as extensive lists of references are referred to Streufert and Streufert, 1978.

Several researchers have investigated whether complex persons, when compared to less complex counterparts, are more flexible and/or more creative. While data on this issue are not yet conclusive, they suggest that a tendency toward greater flexibility exists, permitting the kind of flexible behavior that is often associated with greater creativity.

Research on the role of complexity in problem solving and decision making has produced quite striking results. Complex subjects generally search for more different kinds of information when faced with a decision problem and are less certain after they have made a decision (especially if immediate correct–incorrect outcome information is not available). Complex subjects also are better able to plan and engage in more strategic actions than their less complex counterparts, yet this superior planning performance is much more evident at intermediate (optimal) environmental load levels. Higher levels of strategic (or planning) performance are a linear function of the proportion of cognitively complex persons in a decision-making group.

Training in differentiation and/or integration within a single domain and for relatively simple tasks has met with some success. General nonspecific instructions on how to perform tasks in a more complex fashion did, however, result in a decrease in already limited cognitively complex responding by less complex subjects.

Cognitive complexity relates to the ability of clinicians to interact successfully with patients. A match in complexity between clinician and patient and higher levels of clinician complexity were significant factors in reaching the patient. Preliminary research has also suggested that elevated galvanic skin response (GSR) measures were obtained in more complex subjects and that schizophrenics generally exhibit low complexity scores.

An interesting aspect of the various research efforts is the common predictive success for several of the complexity measures that, in and by themselves, fail to intercorrelate highly. It appears that complexity as a style may be an overall phenomenon and that the various earlier theories describe potentially diverse (summative or interactive oblique) parts of an overall complexity phenomenon.

Research since 1977 on Cognitive Complexity

This section of our review considers results of efforts that were not yet available when Streufert and Streufert (1978) prepared their review. Consequently the review is somewhat more extensive. References are provided.

COMMUNICATION

Hale (1980) has shown that complex persons are more effective at a communication-dependent task than are less complex individuals. Complexity has also been shown to be positively related to the frequency of interpersonal interaction (Zalot and Adams, 1977). Part of the greater success of complex persons may be due to their ability to be intimate with others (a finding that holds for integrators, but not for differentiators, see Neimeyer and Banikiotes, 1980). Finally, complex persons, as compared to their less complex counterparts, are more resistant to persuasive attacks if inoculated (Cronen and Lafleur, 1977), for example, if they have received information that provides them with counterarguments against the persuasion attempt.

ATTITUDES, ATTRIBUTIONS, AND ATTRACTION

Bhutani (1977) reported that attitude change occurs more easily in cognitively complex individuals than in their less complex counterparts. This result is probably due to greater consideration of additional (including novel and unexpected) information, resulting generally in a tendency toward more moderate attitudes (see Linville and Jones, 1980). Such moderation, incidentally, appears to apply more in familiar than in unfamiliar contexts. Similar data are also reported by O'Keefe and Brady (1980), who found that less complex subjects were much more likely to polarize (i.e., shift their views toward greater extremes on attitude scales) after thought about a subject matter.

Findings of this nature tend to make the concept of cognitive complexity interesting to applied researchers who study attitudes and intentions for specific purposes (e.g., marketing). Research has confirmed that complexity is related to product-relevant attitudes. For example, Durand (1980) obtained results indicating that complexity is related to effect and dispersion of affect ratings, both for brands of toothpaste and automobiles. Specifically, consumers with less differentiative ability tended to be more alienated (see Durand, 1979; Durand and Lambert, 1979). Further, less complex subjects formed more extreme (but potentially alienated) attitudes and tended to be more confident about those attitudes (Mizerski, 1978).

Moderation of attitude may impinge on an individual's interpersonal attractiveness. In line with previous findings (discussed earlier), possessing greater cognitive complexity may make a person more attractive to both complex and to less complex others. While previous research had shown that it is of advantage to counselors and clinicians to be complex (multidimensional) if they are to be attractive to clients, data (see Davis, Cook, Jennings, and Heck, 1977) report on the inverse direction of source and target of attractiveness: It was found that more complex patients were more attractive to both cognitively complex and less complex clinicians. The generality of the attractiveness findings in earlier research when combined with these data appears to suggest that the relationship between complexity and attractiveness to others is reliable and that it can probably be generalized to other situations, for example, supervisor–employee settings.

LEADERSHIP

Several theorists have suggested that cognitive complexity should show some relationship to leadership ability and/or leadership style. Streufert and associates (e.g., Streufert, Streufert, and Castore, 1968) compared cognitively complex and less complex persons on their leadership characteristics (see Stogdill, 1962). It was found that cognitively complex leaders emphasized different components of leadership than do their less complex counterparts.

Since that data was published, considerable discussion about a possible relationship between Fiedler's LPC (least preferred coworker) Scale and complexity has emerged in the literature. It was assumed (e.g., Mitchell, 1970) that the more moderate attitudes of the cognitively complex person should result in lesser rejection of the LPC. Early data relating LPC to cognitive complexity produced inconsistent results. More-recent data are quite similar: they either provide no support or only very limited support for the proposed relationship (e.g., Arnett, 1978; Schneier, 1978; Vecchio, 1979; Weiss and Adler, 1981). A closer look at data reported by several researchers may suggest that the proposed relationship between complexity and LPC might be moderated by interactions with one or more intervening variables.

INFORMATION ORIENTATION

Data support the early finding that complex persons are more information oriented, conditions permitting. Research also indicates that some variables, such as Machiavellianism and social intelligence can be partialed out without loss to the complexity effect on information orientation (e.g., Hussy, 1979). Complex persons (here managers) were found to be more effective in terms of information utilization (Hendrick, 1979).

PERCEPTION

How information is perceived has been of continued interest to complexity researchers. Part of that interest may stem from the social-perception focus of early complexity theories. Data obtained by a host of researchers suggest that cognitively complex perceivers take more information into account and form more well-rounded impressions than less complex perceivers. Such findings have led some researchers to view cognitively complex persons as "better" individuals than their less complex counterparts. Such a notion, however, has no basis in fact. Not all situations or tasks require or warrant the application of a cognitively complex style. In some settings such a style may even be counterproductive, limiting the effectiveness of those complex individuals who are unable to "turn off" their multidimensional approach as it becomes inappropriate.

Research supporting the greater breadth of perceptual information orientation for complex persons has been obtained from a range of settings and tasks. For example, complex persons spread perceptual cognitive categories more evenly across observed others, regardless of the role in which those others are perceived (O'Keefe and Delia, 1978). Perceiving others on multiple category content reflects potential differentiation and potentially some integration, leading to less rejection of apparent inconsistency in interpersonal information (Wojciszke, 1979) and more tolerance for inconsistent verbal messages (Domangue, 1978). As a result, attitude polarization following perception and thought is less likely for complex subjects (O'Keefe and Brady, 1980).

Yet, it is not only external cues that affect the perceptions of cognitively complex persons; these cues are integrated with the person's existing perceptual framework. As a result, complex persons appear to base part of their evaluation of others on the (perceived) internal motivational characteristics of these persons rather than on merely external characteristics. Consequently, the quality and quantity of hypotheses about reasons for the behavior of others as well as the number of questions raised about the underlying causes of another's behavior are both likely to be greater for complex persons (Holloway and Wolleat, 1980). Greater quality and diversity of hypotheses and a greater number of questions would serve to decrease the need for unidimensional evaluation as a sole determinant of perception (Wojciszke, 1979). Not surprisingly, when one considers gender-specific training, perceptual complexity in the interpersonal realm appears to be greater for females than for males (Zalot and Adams, 1977).

A number of researchers have focused on the impact of specific stimuli and their extent upon relationships to an individual perceiver, as a predictor of the degree to which a person may use an available level of cognitive complexity. It appears that close emotional involvement with another person is likely to reduce perceptual differentiation and integration of stimulus information about that person under some (but not all) conditions.

Generally, individuals whom one knows less, or with whom one is less involved, may be perceived on more differentiated and/or integrated dimensions (assuming the perceiver is able to employ a cognitively complex style). For example, Wojciszke (1979) found that little known, ambivalently, or even negatively valued persons are perceived in a more complex fashion than well known, positively valued persons. However, once neutral or negative valuation turns into dislike, complexity of perception appears to be reduced. Cioata (1977) reported that persons use more complex cognitive criteria in evaluating liked than disliked persons and similarly employ more complex criteria in evaluating themselves than others.

A somewhat inconsistent result was reported by Horike (1978) suggesting that a V-shaped relationship exists between complexity of perceptions and degree of acquaintance. Because this author manipulated acquaintance in the laboratory, it is not clear whether these data are comparable to those of other researchers. Finally, absence of information and absence of interest in others (here, political candidates) tends to reduce complexity of perception (Mihevc, 1978).

DEVELOPMENT AND PERSONALITY

A number of authors continue to research the relationship between cognitive complexity and individual cognitive growth and development (for example, in Piagetian terms). Generally, the findings suggest that cognitive complexity increases throughout the childhood years and may be realted to stages of development proposed by Piaget and others (e.g., Beagles-Roos and Greenfield, 1979; Chandler, Siegel and Boyes, 1980; Delia and Clark, 1977). Developmental differences among individuals appear to lead to behavioral characteristics that are, in part, associated with personality structure. For example, Bruch, Heisler, and Conroy (1981) have shown that complex persons develop greater content knowledge, possess greater delivery skills, and display more assertiveness when they are placed into difficult situations. Such differences between complex and less complex individuals were not obtained in simpler situations. Other findings suggest that persons who are cognitively complex score higher on ego identity.

It has been argued by several theorists that cognitively complex persons, in contrast to their less complex counterparts, should be more creative (but not necessarily on simple creativity tests) when creativity is measured in applied settings. Research by Quinn (1980) has supported these assumptions: a significant difference in cognitive complexity was obtained between creative writers and matched controls. However, no differences between writers with different *degrees* of demonstrated creativity was obtained (this result should be expected if one considers that the author selected a complexity test that measured only differentiation. Differences in degree of creativity would likely be due to differences in integrative capacity).

CLINICAL APPLICATIONS

In general, interrelations between measures of complexity and personality tests or measures of intelligence have been insignificant. However, personality measurement in clinical applications has shown some relationships to cognitive complexity. Complex persons who scored higher in ego development (Vetter, 1980), in both the U. S. and in Germany, also tended to feel less alienated (Durand and Lambert, 1979), and were more emotionally stable, but potentially more anxious (Cioata, 1977).[8]

The relationship between anxiety and complexity has, however, been contradicted by other research (Raphael, Moss, & Rosser, 1979). Part of the reason for the different findings may involve the degree of adaptation of a given person to his or her particular problem or situation. For example, experiencing an emotional handicap can in some cases increase cognitive complexity (Vace and Burt, 1980).[9]

PERFORMANCE

The previously discussed research topics have focused on perceptual phenomena, action tendencies, and personality outcome. We now turn to research as the relationship of individual differences in cognitive complexity to behavior, focusing on general performance. Research concerned with decision making are considered later as we review data that are relevant to organizations.

One would not expect that *all* kinds of performance in *all* environments would necessarily be affected by the cognitive complexity of the performing individual. Indeed, several studies have shown no such relationships. For example, Wolfe and Chacko (1980) found that although individual complexity did affect the perception of a business game environment, it did not produce changes in performance outcomes.

On the other hand, complexity has influenced performance measures in a variety of other task settings. Jones and Butler (1980), for instance, reported significant correlations between complexity and job performance among Navy personnel. Hendrick (1979) found that less-complex persons took approximately twice as long as complex persons to complete a problem-solving task. In that research, more-complex groups interacted faster and demonstrated better cue utilization. In other research, complexity predicted performance in a fault diagnostics task (Rouse and Rouse, 1979) and related to risk taking in traffic situations (VonEye and Hussy, 1979).

The conclusions reached by Hussy and Scheller (1977) are representative of a number of studies concerned with complexity and performance. These authors concluded that variables involved in cognitive complexity are highly

[8]An anxiety–complexity relationship has also been demonstrated in as-yet-unpublished research of Streufert and associates.

[9]Research completed after this chapter was written (Christan Kliger, 1984, August, personal communication) has shown that cognitively complex artists were least likely to have tendencies reflecting schizophrenia while cognitively less complex artists showed more schizophrenic tendencies. Nonartist controls distributed between those groups.

predictive of performance in *applied* problem-solving tasks. As is discussed later, the importance of cognitive complexity increases with the complexity and the degree of uncertainty of the task environment.

Following earlier demonstrations of environmental effects on performance and of their interaction with cognitive complexity, more-recent studies have explored the effects of stimulus or work overload (and related variables) on task performance. The data from these studies reliably suggest that excessive load is detrimental to evidence of cognitive complexity in performance across a number of diverse tasks. For example, Rotton, Olszewski, Charleton, and Soler (1978) report that overload (loud noise, loud speech) reduces both the ability to tolerate frustration and the ability to differentiate among roles occupied by persons in a problem-solving task.

White (1977) concluded that less-complex persons become overloaded and show effects of overload sooner than cognitively complex persons (these data appear to be in contradiction to the majority of findings that relate complexity, load, and performance). Most research results suggest no significant differences between more- and less-complex persons in the location of optimal environmental input levels. However, considerable differences in performance style between complex and less-complex individuals have typically been obtained, especially at optimal input levels.

However, most researchers who have varied load or other environmental input levels have selected independent variable ranges that compare optimal or near-optimal levels with one or more excessive (high) input levels. In a review of 75 publications relating environmental complexity (including load) to performance, Shalit (1977) concluded that effectiveness of coping (e.g., in problem-solving tasks) appears inversely related to the input level of the situation. Research by Streufert, Streufert, and Denson (1985), using a problem-solving task that permits some utilization of strategy, has indicated that strategic actions were typical of more-complex persons, particularly when load was optimal. Higher overall performance scores in favor of cognitively complex persons were also obtained. Finally, complex persons under overload conditions made fewer errors than did less-complex persons.

TRAINING

If complexity can develop, and if, as described, instructions in simple tasks may allow an otherwise less complex person to respond similarly to a cognitively complex person, then complexity *may* be trainable. Theoretical views on training vary, yet, in all probability, none of the complexity theorists would predict rapid and overall training potentials. Little research on training has been performed. Results of the few completed studies are equivocal. For example, Sauser and Pond (1981) were not able to demonstrate any changes in cognitive complexity with a combination of training procedures. On the other hand, Cronen and Lafleur (1977), using an inoculation–persuasion paradigm, obtained some increase in overall complexity with massive attacks on truisms. Whether these results are due to an actual increase in cognitive complexity or may be explained by learning of procedures and/or arguments cannot be determined without further research. Generally speaking, the area of complexity training is one of the least researched topics within the complexity framework.

One study (Stabell, 1978) investigated the relationship between training-oriented requirements and applications of cognitive complexity. Stabell suggested that it will be necessary to define task characteristics associated with cognitive decision making and their characteristic interactions with performance. Stabell found that volume and breadth of information source utilization in decision making are positively related to integrative complexity. Training procedures may have to focus on specific aspects of information processing (e.g., information utilization) as an initial step toward the development of cognitive complexity.[10]

THE APPLICATION OF COGNITIVE COMPLEXITY
TO DIFFERENT ENVIRONMENTAL AND TASK REQUIREMENTS

Theory (e.g., Streufert and Streufert, 1978) suggests that cognitive complexity may or may not be appropriate to any *particular* task environment. While some persons are able to adapt their degree of differentiation and integration to task demands to obtain optimal outcomes, others may not be as flexible. Application of a differentiative and integrative style to very simple unidimensionally based task demands may be as inappropriate as the application of a unidimensional approach to some complex planning problem that requires the application of strategy. Unfortunately, no research has addressed the underlying basis of an individual's stylistic flexibility.

Theory and Research Relevant to Organizations

Complexity theory as applied to organizations focuses on two levels of analysis —that is, the information processing of organizational personnel and the information-processing characteristics of the organization itself.

---

[10]Cognitive complexity is most often viewed as a style—suggesting some potential for training that would change stylistic thought processes. However, some authors (e.g., Streufert and Streufert, 1978) have suggested that cognitive complexity may be viewed (partly or entirely) as a preference or an ability. To the extent to which complexity is an ability, and to the extent that this ability has physiological underpinnings (as we show in Chapter 8, there certainly are clear relationships between physiological responsivity and cognitive complexity), effective training may be restricted.

Previous work (both theory and research) that addresses the second of these levels is minimal. In Chapter 5, we consider this issue from a theoretical perspective. However, some research on cognitive complexity and its effects on functioning of personnel in organizations has been reported. Some of these studies have investigated the performance of organizational personnel in research settings that remained outside of the organization itself (e.g., via simulation techniques and related methodologies). In other cases, laboratory studies were designed with potential application to organizations in mind. Some data was collected within organizational settings. The following pages summarize four of these research programs. Additional research by the present authors is reported in Chapter 7.

Pioneering efforts involving simulation techniques that compared the performance of persons (here, college students) who differed in cognitive complexity were conducted by Michael Driver (1962). These studies employed Guetzkow's (1959) internation simulation (INS) technique, a *free simulation* (see Fromkin and Streufert, 1983) where decisions made by participants affect the complex and subsequent environment that participants experience over time. Driver established that the decision-making and interaction characteristics of cognitively complex (simulated) organizational decision makers differed from decision making by less complex decision makers. For example, more cognitively complex decision makers (assembled into structurally homogeneous groups) employed considerably more strategy and engaged in more extensive planning.

Streufert and associates (e.g., Pogash, Streufert, Denson, and Streufert, 1984; Streufert, Clardy, Driver, Karlins, Schroder, and Suedfeld, 1965; Streufert, Kliger, Castore, and Driver, 1967) developed a series of experimental and quasi-experimental simulations (again, see Fromkin and Streufert, 1983) in which participants *believe* that they affect future simulation outcomes, although events are, in fact, experimentally controlled (permitting the application of independent variable manipulations over time). In an extensive research program, participants were drawn from student populations, professional organizations, midcareer personnel of national government departments, military organizations, and corporations. Participants varied in job level from beginners to experienced executives. Decision-making groups were formed. Simulation content was, in some scenarios, quite similar to typical work environments of simulation participants. In other cases, the scenarios generated realistic work environments that differed from those which participants had experienced in the past.

Data obtained by Streufert and associates clearly demonstrated that cognitively complex executives are excellent planners, employ considerable strategy and perform well at tasks where planning and strategy has some importance. Less complex executives did not perform as well. Apparently the degree of familiarity with the simulated task environments had little effect: in some cases the unfamiliar task environment was an even better predictor of decision-making excellence. Wherever possible, Streufert obtained information about performance of executives who participated in the simulation in their normal work environment: those who employed more strategy in the simulation (as measured by indices of differentiation and integration) also were known as better planners at their jobs and were considered superior performers at executive tasks (peer and supervisor ratings).

Schroder and associates (e.g., Schroder, 1982) have measured the performance of executives in leadership management simulations, in-basket techniques, fact-finding exercises, and leaderless group exercises (with or without assigned roles) to assess differences in performance levels that are contributed by the executives' level of cognitive complexity. The data clearly indicated that the more cognitively complex executives exceeded their less complex counterparts in analytic skills, in the capacity to make and carry out plans and in some aspects of decision making.

A series of research efforts by Suedfeld and his associates (e.g., Levi and Tetlock, 1980; Porter and Suedfeld, 1981; Suedfeld and Tetlock, 1977) have investigated the effects of cognitive complexity on decisions and careers of political leaders. Suedfeld's efforts have been of considerable interest to scientists from other disciplines and have generated similar research efforts, for example, by political scientists (e.g., Raphael, 1982). The latter work has supported Suedfeld's findings.

Suedfeld and associates studied the public statements and writings of revolutionary leaders from George Washington to Che Guevara, the pronouncements of Middle East leaders at the United Nations and the deliberations of the Japanese leadership prior to Pearl Harbor, among others. They found that more cognitively complex (more multidimensional) information processing was required for dealing successfully with the complex governmental, organizational, and societal problems that these leaders encountered. For example, the political survival of revolutionaries as subsequent leaders of their nations required greater cognitive complexity once the revolutionary period had ended. Further, they reported that lessened complexity in statements of Middle East diplomats foreshadowed war in the region. Lessened complexity also occurred in discussions of the Japanese leadership prior to their entry into the Second World War. Similar findings of reduced dimensionality immediately preceding the First World War has been observed by historical analysis and has been replicated in INS simulations.

It is apparent that reduced complexity may generate or (at least) reflect conflict, can reduce performance quality, and may lead to failure. It is important to note that reduced dimensionality *may* lead to detrimental outcomes, not that it always will. As stated, there certainly are situations where a decision maker's potentially high levels of cognitive complexity, or an organization's conceptual differentiative and integrative structure, if inappropriately employed, might be harmful. Inappropriate application of differentiation or integration in organizational decision making could occur, where a simple unidimensional information stimulus is optimally dealt with by a fixed established response.

In other words, performance in complex environments requires more than the *capacity* to differentiate and integrate. It is equally important to know when that capacity should be used and when a simple, undifferentiated (and unintegrated) *respondent* decision would be more appropriate. Unfortunately, as stated earlier, research data on that kind of choice behavior are not presently available.

Further, research is currently missing on the *direct* application of complexity theory to organizations as information-processing systems. This book will set the theoretical stage for such research efforts. Indeed, there is much *indirect* evidence for the applicability of complexity theory to (successful) organizational functioning. That evidence is discussed as our theory is presented in Chapter 5.

3

The Place of Complexity
in Organizational Science

In the previous chapter, we reviewed previous theory and research on complexity. We have shown that considerable theory as well as a large amount of data on the *cognitive* complexity of individuals has been published. Somewhat less work has addressed the effect of individual or group differences on managerial decision making and organizational outcomes. Theory and data focusing directly on the complexity (e.g., differentiation and integration) of organizations is entirely absent. This book provides the theoretical framework for such an approach (Chapter 5). To develop that framework, however, it is necessary to consider the possible impact of both ideas and concepts of complexity theory on organizational science as it exists to date. In other words, we need to answer the questions we posed in Chapter 1:

1. Why has complexity theory not been applied to organizations?
2. Is the failure to apply the theory due to an absence of an adequate language (terminology) that would aid scientists and observers in the identification and communication of concepts inherent in the theory?
3. If such a language (terminology) does exist, is it applicable to organizational science?
4. If an applicable language (terminology) is available, do organizational

scientists view relevant terms as unrelated to each other or as interrelated?

This chapter primarily deals with these questions, with a methodology that was developed to answer them, and with conclusions that may be drawn on the basis of the obtained answers. Generally speaking, the answers we are seeking should provide us with useful information about the potential value of complexity-based approaches to the extent organizational literature and, to some extent, to organizations. More specifically, we wish to determine whether complexity theory can be interrelated with other scientific approaches to organizations or whether it must stand by itself. A possible long-range benefit of interrelating specific theoretical or data-based approaches with a more encompassing complexity theory may be the opportunity to locate a considerable number of overtly divergent views of managerial and organizational behavior within a single theoretic framework.

In this chapter, we are reporting on a quantitative treatment of the existing organizational and systems-theoretic literature that was developed, in part, to answer the questions we have raised.

CHOICE OF METHODOLOGY

Taxonomy

Swezey, Streufert, and Mietus (1983) developed a taxonomic technique for classifying organizations and their behavior. The intent of that analysis was different from previous classifications by other writers: We wished to address *functional* organizational phenomena. Most previous organizational taxonomic studies have considered organizations either from a structural[1] (i.e., bureaucratic, vertical, hierarchical, etc.) or from an output (i.e., high technology, steel, aerospace, consumer goods, etc.) perspective. Such approaches are not necessarily helpful in answering concerns about the functioning of organizations. Our immediate purpose was to determine how the functioning of organizations might be classified (based on previous efforts in organizational and systems theoretic science). Our secondary purpose was to determine whether complexity-theory-based terminology (and

---

[1]The word *structural* is here employed in the sense prevalent in the organizational literature—that is, as, for example, derived from organizational sociology. Such an organizational structure may or may not overlap widely with the organization's information-processing structure in the use of the term by complexity theory (Chapter 2).

complexity theory concepts) do or do not play a prominent role in organizational theory and research and, if they do play a major role, whether
these terms or concepts are meaningfully interrelated in that literature. Because we desired to have as wide a representation of the organizational literature as possible, we decided to apply our taxonomic technique to both
the management organizational psychology and to the systems theoretic literatures.

Procedure

One reviewer of organizational classifications (Warriner, 1980) has suggested that organizational taxonomic efforts have been founded on three
perspectives. Warriner views these taxonomies as frequently based on so
called commonsense principles or on theoretically based perspectives. A
major problem with both of these approaches is that they are necessarily
bound by the theoretical or commonsense limitations (or biases) that are
introduced. In other words, such classifications are, at least in part, matters
of opinion.

A third classification technique (which is generally termed *empirical*) does
not suffer from bias problems to the same degree because it is based on
statistical treatment of a selected class of variables. Statistical taxonomic
techniques tend to be multivariate and typically involve cluster analysis,
factor analysis, or the numerical taxonomic techniques developed in the
field of biology by Sokal and Sneath (1963).

In considering the purposes of our taxonomic effort, we concluded that
a multidimensional statistical approach was required. First, organizations are
themselves complex multidimensional entities. That complexity demands
an approach that is potentially capable of reflecting inherent multidimensionality. Second, a large number of potential variables could
possibly contribute to various taxonomic *classes*. In other words, a multidimensional technique that is able to reduce the number of taxonomic
categories appeared appropriate. Third, we felt that our selected technique
should be compatible with the systems theory perspective, one of the literature areas that was to be addressed.[2] Based on these considerations, we
selected a factor analytic methodology for our efforts. The specific methodology employed in this procedure has been described in considerable detail elsewhere (Swezey, Streufert, and Mietus, 1983; Swezey and Unger,
1982). Only an overview of the technique is provided here.

A group of over 1000 articles was selected from the literature of orga-

---

[2]It has been argued that multivariate approaches are themselves adapted from a general
systems perspective (Sells, 1964).

nizational psychology and systems theory on the basis of currency, representativeness, and completeness. The survey of manuscripts covered more than 100 primary sources (journals, proceedings, books, technical reports, etc.) and included publications covering more than 80 aspects of organizational behavior, organizational effectiveness, training, systems theory, and more.

To develop a method for assessing the contents of these publications, organizational psychology and general systems theory textbooks were reviewed, and a preliminary list of terms that appeared to exhaustively address the attributes or concepts within these fields was identified. This effort produced a list of some 350 terms. Next, a review team was organized to consolidate the list according to a consensus approach. Synonymous or redundant terms were combined. Others were eliminated according to agreed-upon criteria. Using this procedure, the number of terms was reduced to 84. Third, a checklist-based rating procedure was developed for reviewing the journal articles, reports, and books selected earlier. A score on each term was assigned to each publication. Values represented the degree of emphasis that each publication placed on the concepts reflected by the 84 terms. Scores varied from 0 (not mentioned) to 3 (emphasized). Fourth, a pilot study determined the extent to which trained document raters could produce similar ratings. This study resulted in interrater reliability indices ranging from +.85 to +.94, enabling us to conclude that the raters were, in fact, consistently able to make the same kinds of judgments about manuscript content.

Finally, a second pilot effort determined whether a factor analytic approach was, in fact, appropriate to develop an empirical classification system of the organizational and systems theoretic literatures. That study (reported in detail by Swezey, Streufert, and Mietus, 1983) led to the conclusion[3] that maximally seven meaningful factors might be extracted from the data base. Consequently, subsequent efforts to factor analytically develop a statistically based taxonomy of the literature was terminated at the seven-factor level. For more optimal data interpretation, solutions for the major analysis of the data base were specified at the seven-, six-, and five-factor levels. On the basis of the amount of variance explained by the factors and by the overall analysis, a six-factor solution was ultimately selected. When we compared the variables and item loadings of the six-factor solution with solutions obtained in pilot factor analyses, a surprising degree of overlap, indicating a very reliable factor structure, was evident.

---

[3]This conclusion was reached on the basis of stepwise procedures employed in extracting factors.

RESULTS AND INTERPRETATION

Table 3.1 shows the selected six-factor solution and the terms loading highly on each factor. The factors were names as follows:

Factor 1—Multidimensional Information Processing

The first, and most important, factor that emerged from the analysis is concerned with terms–concepts from complexity theory. Variables that loaded meaningfully on this factor appear to reflect the individual, group, and/or organizational functions associated with acquiring, processing, and disseminating information (including decision making) as components in a complex, multidimensional environment. The implications of this factor are discussed in detail later. The remaining factors are less relevant to complexity-based approaches to organizations. Readers who desire more detail and interpretations than can be found in the next paragraphs are referred to Swezey, Streufert, and Mietus (1983) and to Swezey, Davis, Budhuin, Streufert, and Evans (1983).

Factor 2—Organizational Systems Dynamics

The second factor concerned the adaptation and flexibility of an organization, as well as how the organization utilizes its resources for planned growth. The variables included in this factor are systems theory variables that address such concepts as open versus closed systems, adaptation, and growth.

Factor 3—Organizational Change Technology

In order to adapt, an organization must have the capability and resources for change. The large amount of literature on organizational change and development reflects the importance of this attribute among organizational theorists and researchers. The variables that loaded on Factor 3 focus on techniques typically associated with the organizational development (OD) and organizational effectiveness (OE) domains of interest, and reflect concern for growth and development in an individual's interface with his or her job and with the work process. This factor addresses human resource technologies associated with enhancing individual perceptions regarding job development and/or modification.

TABLE 3.1
Six-Factor Solution Variable Loading Matrix[a]

Factor	Loading/Variable	Eigenvalue	Cumulative % Factor Variance
I	.71 Input		
	.69 Integration		
	.66 Complexity		
	.65 Output		
	.62 Information		
	.58 Differentiation		
	.56 Sensing		
	.55 Decision Making		
	.54 Environment	5.193	22.88
II	.55 Subsystem		
	.54 Equilibrium		
	.51 Open System		
	.49 Direction		
	.44 Growth		
	.47 Adaptability		
	.46 Closed System		
	.42 Rigidity	3.867	39.91
III	.66 Change Agent		
	.53 Feedback		
	.49 Intervention		
	.47 Job Enrichment/Enlargement		
	.45 Organization		
	.42 Process		
	.41 Training	3.662	56.04
IV	.57 Influence		
	.52 Power		
	.42 Conflict		
	.48 Hierarchy		
	.41 Interaction		
	.57 Authority		
	.41 Role	3.503	71.48
V	.67 Independence		
	.61 Centralization		
	.64 Size		
	.55 Decentralization		
	.51 Interdependence		
	.45 Authority	3.366	86.31
VI	.61 Goal Setting		
	.56 Goals		
	.52 Goal Succession		
	.52 Goal Attainment		
	.44 Goal Displacement	3.108	100.00

[a]From Swezey, Streufert, and Mietus, 1983.

Factor 4—Management Authority–Compliance Characteristics

The variables included in this factor are associated with the dimensions of influence and power as components in the superior-subordinate organizational scheme where compliance is necessary. These variables address attributes normally associated with management control. Power and related characteristics, such as authority and influence, appear to be necessary components of effective organizational systems. Use of power (and its associated components) may lead to noncompliance and/or to conflict within an organization. Management then requires techniques to manage the conflict before it becomes deleterious.

Factor 5—Organizational Coordination and Control

The variables that loaded on this factor reflect the structural[4] characteristics of organizations, as well as concerns leading to organizational control. Coordination and control, in conjunction with planning and motivating activities, are basic components of the managerial processes. The literature reflected in Factor 5 deals with (1) effects of the environment, (2) organizational structure, and (3) interdependence on control processes at various levels within an organization.

Factor 6—Goal Orientation

This factor reflects activities in which organizations and managers engage to determine desired organizational outcomes. The variables included in this factor focus on goal-oriented activites required to determine priorities, achieve objectives, and modify or replace objectives as a function of changing organizational requirements. Goals and goal orientations can be approached from several perspectives including long-range views, short-run real-world approaches, and management by objectives (MBO) type approaches, among others.

If one considers the fields of organizational psychology and systems theory as two intersecting domains, the obtained factors can be viewed as describing certain bounded areas within that intersection. Each of the six factors appears to represent a more or less[5] independent aspect of the organizational systems literatures. Of particular interest for present purposes

---

[4]Again, the word *structure* is here meant in the sociological, not necessarily in the information-processing sense.

[5]Independence is generated by varimax rotation of the data base, and consequently, cannot necessarily be considered as an exclusively accurate representation.

is the finding that the lead factor in our analysis concerns multidimensional information-processing aspects—that is, the tenets of complexity theory. We now look at the terms included in that factor in somewhat greater detail.

Multidimensional Information Processing

The fact

1. that complexity theory terminology and/or concepts are evidently widely used in the organizational and sytems theoretic literatures (albeit generally without reference to that theory)
2. that complexity terms relevant to multidimensional information processing (integration, complexity, differentiation, sensing[6]), their antecedents (input, information, environment) and their sequels and consequences (output, decision making) load on one common factor, and
3. that this factor accounted for the largest single amou of common variance in the literature analysis, demonstrates the importance that the common impact of complexity-oriented terms or concepts have on scientists' views of the organization.

With these findings, we have answered all but one of the questions raised earlier. We now return to that question: the concern with the previous lack of application of complexity theory to organizational science.

If complexity theory is applied to organizational science, will it merely represent yet another view of the organization, based on an already existing terminology? We do not think so. Rather, it appears that the theory would help to integrate a variety of approaches that have been employed by other researchers. Some examples may be useful. Our examples are drawn from the two most central concepts in complexity-based views of organizations: differentiation and integration.

In Chapter 2, we defined *differentiation* (with reference to organizational processes) as "the process of dividing conceptual space (or the degree to which this division has been achieved) into two or more orthogonal or oblique dimensions, systems, or subsystems—for example, the ordering and processing of stimuli in relatively intransitive fashion." The definition is concerned with the components of organizational information processing. Certainly, it may involve the number and kinds of organizational units or subunits that are involved in relating an organization's input to its output.

---

[6]*Sensing* is, as used in the organizational literature, quite similar to the terms *perception* or, where applicable, *perceptual complexity* as used in the literature based on complexity theory.

But, organizational differentiation can go beyond such a simple and primarily "sociological" structuring. For that matter, quite similar information processing may well occur across unit boundaries. In contrast, quite diverse information processing may be evident among the various managers within an organizational subunit. Conceptions of the organization's functioning, its typical information flow, its purposes, and its needs may certainly be differentiated apart from its formal structure.

The organizational and systems-theoretic literature reflects some of these diverse forms of differentiation. Huse and Bowditch (1977), for example, consider differentiation in organizations as "the difference in cognitive and emotional orientation among managers in different functioning departments." These authors distinguished between formality of structure, interpersonal orientation, time orientation, and goal orientation as signs of differentiation.

In contrast, Lawrence and Lorsch (1967b) take a view that is more bound to the formal structure of an organization. In their opinion, differentiation is seen as the segmentation of an organizational system into subsystems, each of which tend to develop particular attributes in relation to requirements posed by the external environment. A similar view was presented by Porter, Lawler, Hackman (1975). These authors suggested that because not everyone in an organization does the same thing, the environment and goals of an organization require that some degree of differentiation must necessarily take place. Porter et al. further suggested that differentiation within an organization can be horizontal (e.g., division of labor) or vertical (e.g., hierarchical, having differing amounts of authority and power and decreasing amounts of responsibility from higher to lower positions).

Diverse concepts of differentiation in organizational functioning cease to be incompatible when viewed on the basis of complexity-theory definitions of that concept. But, a focus on differentiation per se is not enough. Important in conceptualizations of differentiated organizational functioning is that each component performs a unique information-processing function, similar in concept to various cognitive dimensions of an individual. However, an organization does not typically process incoming information (e.g., an order for a particular service) within a single subsystem (e.g., in the billing department) to the exclusion of other important subsystems (e.g., the shipping department). In other words, some minimal degree of intraorganizational *integration* is needed for successful functioning in complex situations.

Of course, the degree of both differentiation and integration evident in organizational information processing would vary with

1. the complexity of an organization and of its task environment

2. the degree that informational multidimensionality is potentially present in that task environment
3. the formal and/or informal structure of the organization
4. input to output demands
5. the characteristic cognitive complexity of organizational managers

and more. We provide a theoretical overview of the antecedents and consequences of organizational complexity levels in Chapter 5.

We have considered the relationship of *differentiation* in the organizational literature to *differentiation* in complexity theory. Let us do the same for *integration*. We defined integration, with relevance to organizations, as "the process of relating a stimulus, concept, or idea impinging on the organization to two or more orthogonal or oblique dimensions wihtin the organizational system (or the degree to which this relating has been achieved) to produce an outcome that is determined by the joint (weighted or unweighted) demands of each dimension." Stimuli, concepts or ideas, for this purpose, may originate outside or inside the organization and may include such external stimuli as orders for products or threats of takeover and such internal stimuli as developments of new products or personnel turnover. Dimensions within the organization may be reflected in organizational units or subunits, in the conceptualization of organizational processes by managers, and more (dimensionality was defined in the preceding definition of differentiation above). Again, our emphasis is on the processing of information from input as some point(s) in the organization toward potential output.

Clearly, the complexity-theory-based view of integration is more encompassing than other views from the organizational literature. For example, some authors have considered integration as relating organizational structure to individual attitudes and behavior (James and Jones, 1976). Others, (see Lawrence and Lorsch, 1967a; Lorsch and Lawrence, 1969) have been more concerned with the interaction of organizational subsystems. Integrative activites have also been viewed as important in strategy development. Here, integration has, at times, been considered an interaction of strategies. Such strategies can then be progressively linked together toward oganizational action (e.g., Vancil, 1976). Complexity theory would encompass all of these only apparently diverse views of integration within a single information-processing framework. All of these integrative processes involve the flow of information, communication among various components of an organization, and interactive modification of the information through action and interaction of the components.

We have attempted to show via some examples that organizational theory could well be improved by the imposition of a more parsimonious complexity-theory framework on the existing intercorrelated terminology. Our conclusion must inevitably return us to the question that we have not yet answered: Why has there been no previous extensive application of complexity theory to organizational science? After all, the terminology relevant to that theory is well known and frequently employed. Moreover, the terms, when used in the literature, are used together. Certainly the understanding that these terms refer to some common or interrelated phenomena must exist among organizational researchers and theorists.

An examination of titles of the published literature indicates that complexity terms (with the exception of antecedents such as environment and outcomes such as decision making) are rarely used in book and article headings. The key concepts of complexity theory (i.e., differentiation and integration) are especially rarely found in these titles, yet they are quite common in the text of manuscripts. When they appear, they are used with some frequency *and* they are used together. However, when used, they are typically related to a variety of diverse theoretical orientations that remain independent of each other and consider only parts of what we would call organizational information processing. One might say that the theoretical integration of these concepts simply has not yet occurred.

A relevant and encompassing theory has not yet been proposed—or at least has not yet been applied to the organizational context. In other words, the time appears ripe for the presentation of an organizational complexity theory. It is our task to generate at least part of the necessary theoretical orientation (Chapter 5). Because complexity theory applied to organizations is, at least in part, an extension and modification of complexity theory applied to individuals and to managers, we initialy proceed with a presentation of *cognitive* complexity theory as it applies to individuals (Chapter 4). Following that presentation, we focus our theory on the structure of information processing in organizations.

4

Complexity Theory: The Cognitive Structure of Individuals in the Organization

In the preceding three chapters, we introduced and reviewed a complexity-oriented approach to managers and organizations. We have placed that approach within the context of organizational science. It is now time to present complexity theory in its current form. We discuss our theoretical views on various topics at some length, typically followed by short summary propositions (printed in italics). Each proposition is numbered by chapter and sequence. For example, the first proposition in this chapter will be numbered 4-1; a third proposition in Chapter 5 would be designated 5-3. We may introduce the various propositions as "hypotheses," "postulates," "statements," "suggestions," and so forth. The use of these various terms has no implication about the importance or expected validity of the propositions. Rather, different words are chosen to avoid repetition.

Nonetheless, we do not want to deny that there are degrees of established validity for the status of our various propositions. Many of them have been subjected to extensive testing in our own research efforts and/or the efforts of other scientists. Others, especially those concerned with training and with organizational functioning, have been less extensively tested. Yet others are based only on observation. Chapter 7 presents relevant data we have collected. In each case, reported research results will reference the proposition that is the basis of the data collection effort. Chapter 9, the final chapter of the book, considers the degree of support for various groups of propositions, as well as applications that can be justified at the present time. Nonetheless, the reader will recognize that a number of hypotheses have not yet been tested or tested extensively. We hope that readers in search of research projects will find a fertile field among the propositions that are yet in need of research support. The majority of that work has investigated theoretical predictions in perceptual contexts. Complexity theory as applied to individual perception has been extensively reviewed elsewhere (e.g., Streufert and Streufert, 1978, and, to a lesser extent, in Chapter 2 of this book). To avoid unnecessary duplication, this chapter does not discuss perceptual matters extensively.

We do, however, devote considerable space to a discussion of complexity-theory-based predictions for individual *executive* functioning, especially in complex decision-making situations, because only a few complexity researchers have focused on this topic (see Streufert, 1978). Because decision making in complex organizational settings is vital to appropriate organizational functioning, we believe that the study of executive complexity in individuals is particularly important.

In the next chapter (Chapter 5), we discuss the direct application of complexity theory to organizations. The concern with cognitive complexity of individual members of organizations provides a useful foundation for the later discussion of complexity theory as applied to organizational systems.

Peters and Waterman (1982) have suggested that the old organizational theories have been attractive because of their straightforward approaches, lacking in paradox. They add: "The world is not like that." Indeed, they are correct. Scientists are often biased toward simplification and regress (even if it might take a touch of distortion). Theoretical predictions that are multivariate and/or curvilinear are often viewed as suspect. Interactive variables have been frequently controlled and their effects ignored in the name of eliminating confounds. True, organizational scientists have been somewhat less guilty of streamlining their science than their more behavioristically experimentally oriented colleagues. The emergence of contingency theories that demand multiple predictions reflects the willingness of some organizational researchers and theorists to accept more than single variables as causal of organizational phenomena. Nonetheless, degrees of simplification have reigned and have hindered some organizational insights as well.

To develop an organizational theory that is not guilty of oversimplification, we should again begin with people. As stated earlier, organizations are people and their plans, interactions, responses, communications, and products. In turn, organizations function best when they can be *understood* by their people—that is, when there is some degree of match between the cognitive information-processing characteristics of the individuals who control an organization and the characteristics of an organizational structure. While we are *not* necessarily arguing for a system theoretic approach (e.g., Miller, 1978), we are suggesting that people have certain abilities, limitations, and styles of information processing. A person whose style does not match the culture or management style of an organization is likely not a good match for that organization. Unless such a person is capable of changing the organiztion, his or her contrasting style will probably result in rejection by the organization. On the other hand, where the abilities, limitations, and styles of an individual match an organization's characteristics and needs, the liaison between person and organization will more likely be happy and productive.

A match of organizational structure and/or information flow with individual information-processing characteristics is particulary important as a manager reaches greater and more encompassing levels of responsibility. Where disparity exists between the two, the manager is probably less effective. Peters and Waterman have discussed the missing perspective of many managers. Others have called for an understanding of the gestalt of an organization. Managers who emphasize only one component within the organizational structure and fail to understand or recognize the importance of the interplay of organizational components (e.g., managers concerned only with net profit) are likely to mismanage rather than to manage. They are conceptually similar to an army general who knows every detail of helicopter design but little if anything, about infantry warfare. In peacetime, such a general may perform adequately; however, in wartime his or her ignorance might spell disaster. Fortunately, generals tend to get a wide range of experience as they advance through the ranks. Unfortunately, not all managers of private sector organizations do.

In this book, we do not discuss specific kinds of knowledge about various parts of organizations. Understanding of these functions reflects knowledge of organizational *content*. We do, however, assume that most managers either have such specific knowledge or can acquire it via training and/or experience. After all, career managers, vice-presidents, and CEOs may well work for a detergent manufacturer yesteryear, a computer company today, and a service organization in the future. Specific new content knowledge needs to be acquired with each such change. In this book we are not concerned with content: we are focusing on structure. In this chapter, the emphasis is on the information-processing structure of individuals. We are concerned with the differentiative and integrative processes that managers employ to deal (1) with interrelationships among organizational components and their needs and (2) with flow of information through the organization.

We do recognize that a sufficient understanding of content, including the capabilities, limitations, and specific functions of organizational components (and people) is necessary for competent managerial performance. Yet, we will leave concerns with the adequacy of content performance and with the training and acquisition of content knowledge to other theoretical and research orientations. It is our view that *most* cases of mismanagement are not due to insufficient knowledge and experience with organizational content. Rather, we believe that the majority of mismanaged organizations suffer from an inadequate understanding and/or utilization of the differentiated and integrated organizational system by its managers *or* that they suffer from the fact that the organization is itself either insufficiently or excessively differentiated and integrated for a given task.

COMPLEXITY THEORY APPLIED
TO THE INDIVIDUAL

Early complexity theorists, such as Harvey, Hunt, and Schroder (1961); Schroder, Driver, and Streufert (1967) distinguished between structure and content in information processing. At first, that distinction was not sufficiently focused (as in Harvey et al., 1961) and certain content characteristics tended to infiltrate structural definitions. Within a short time, however, the distinction between the two approaches was clarified, both in differentiative (e.g., Bieri, 1966, 1968) and in differentiative–integrative approaches to the definition of cognitive structure.

Most theory within the behavioral sciences has been *content* rather than structure oriented. The frequent focus on content has been for good reason. It is of great importance to understand *what* people think. It is equally important to recognize what they do and do not understand. It is, for instance, of considerable value to be able to estimate the extent to which an individual is likely to make correct decisions in a specific situation. Knowledge of content can indeed be of considerable importance, as long as behavior is or must be determined by a single information input and as long as it is irrelevent to other information, strategies, plans, or goals. Clearly, that is not always (or, for that matter, often) the case. As a good example, consider the attempt to use attitudes to predict a variety of behavior. As Fishbein and associates (e.g., Fishbein, 1963, 1967a, 1967b; Fishbein and Ajzen, 1972) have shown, it requires at least two dimensions of cognition (e.g., attitudes and intent) to approach a meaningful prediction of behavioral outcomes.

With the identification of two dimensions we have already moved toward a structural approach to cognition and information processing. For example, where the two dimensions are employed separately, resulting in two diverse and independent ways of viewing information, events, et cetera, a differentiative approach to structural information processing is evident (see Bieri, 1966, 1968). Where an outcome—whether a perception, cognition, or an overt behavior—is variably dependent on the placement of a stimulus on more than one dimension (i.e., where the dimensions interact to produce the outcome), we need to focus on a theoretical orientation that includes both differentiation and integration as cognitive processes. Such a view was presented in some detail by Streufert and Streufert (1978). With considerable data supporting that theory, it can be considered generally valid in, at least, its basic propositions. The remainder of this theory chapter closely follows the views of Streufert and Streufert but will provide some extensions of that theory.

In contrast to pure theories of personality structure (e.g., Bieri, 1966; Harvey et al., 1961) Streufert and Streufert describe their approach as well as the theory presented by Schroder et al. (1967) as an *interactive complexity theory*. It is *interactive* because it considers both the effects of cognitive style and the effects of the environment on the application of that style. As suggested earlier, the approach is structural. By itself, it is not concerned with the content of thought or behavior patterns, including questions about the correctness or appropriateness of cognitions or behaviors. This limitation needs to be recognized: Where behavior is measured (or predicted) on tasks where an individual is inexperienced, or where response correctness is based on a single dimension, the content of that dimension must be of primary concern. However, where environment and behavioral outcomes are interactive, where multiple behaviors may be variably appropriate, where uncertainty continues across time and where personnel are relatively well trained and/or experienced, structural approaches become increasingly important. In other words, there are many situations where content should not be, and cannot be, ignored. The reader might wish to consider when and where content best fits into the structural theory we are presenting in this chapter and in Chapter 5.

SOURCES OF COMPLEXITY

Physiological Differences

More and more evidence about physiological differences among persons who are described as cognitively complex and persons who are not has accumulated. We can only speculate whether these differences involve some aspect of a genetic predisposition for specific individuals or whether physiological changes follow behaviorally acquired styles. Work by Driver and associates and more-recent data collected by Streufert and associates (e.g., Streufert, Streufert, and Denson, 1983) demonstrating significant differences in cardiovascular functioning of individuals varying in cognitive complexity could be explained as secondary effects of a learned style, similar to the changes that appear to be generated by components of Type A behavior (see Dembroski, MacDougall, Williams, Haney, and Blumenthal, 1985).

However, EEG patterns appear to differ in cognitively complex versus less complex persons as well. Unfortunately, we know too little at this point to determine whether such patterns are genetically determined or can be explained as a function of experience and learning. Clearly, learning and experience play a significant role in the development of individual (cognitive) complexity. Whether or not a physiological basis exists which allows some persons to acquire complexity but hinders others has yet to be clarified.

Training

Let us, for the purposes of this discussion, assume that there are no innate differences with which we need be concerned—or, if there are such differences, that we are only concerned with persons who *do* have the capacity to develop a cognitively complex style. How are differentiative and integrative styles developed? What kind of potential experiences are required? How can—and should—training to increase complexity in an adult proceed?

To date there is relatively little knowledge about the development of complexity. Most conclusions have been based on observation rather than on controlled experimentation. It appears that cognitive complexity in parental behavior and communication can be helpful in generating differentiative and integrative cognitions in their children. Where parents are willing to expose a child to various ways of looking at a problem, rudimentary differentiation may emerge. Encouraging a child to take another person's point of view may also be helpful. Suggesting to a child that he or she should try to imagine why another person might think the way he/she does, and what led him or her to a particular thought process may be useful.

Similarly, one may train the capacity to differentiate and integrate by asking questions about goals and strategies (i.e., How do we achieve a desired end? What means can be used? Can we use more than one? What are the joint and long-term effects of the means we consider using, etc.). Of particular importance may be training in the suspension of (unidimensional) moral or other good–bad-oriented thought processes (temporarily) to permit the development of other dimensions. In the process of integration, the moral–attitudinal dimension may then be reconsidered and play its appropriate part in the development of judgments and plans for subsequent behavior.

Training a child to a low or a high level of cognitive complexity is often unintentional. As Streufert and Streufert (1978) have reported, different subpopulations tend to have diverse levels (frequencies) of cognitive complexity, determined, in good part, by specific kinds and levels of exposure in childhood and adolescence. An overprotected child, even if he or she is the offspring of cognitively complex parents, may demonstrate lesser complexity. Similarly, a child that is exposed early to the overwhelming overload of ghetto life may develop more unidimensional approaches to the world. The greatest frequency of complex thought processes that we have found among teens appear to exist in middle-class neighborhoods where both parents work, yet where love and protection of the child exist. Under these conditions the child is on his/her own part of the time, and is able to explore, to try different experiences, and to deal with different views. Yet, the child is not overwhelmed by these experiences. Novel ways of thinking can be absorbed in the absence of stimulus overload. The result can be the acceptance of a view that alternate ways of thinking may be legitimate and potentially useful (differentiation) and that they may be employed, together with others, in interpreting and acting upon the world (integration). To summarize, the following hypothesis is offered:

4.1   *Given that a physiological potential exists, complexity can develop in a person if he/she is frequently presented with clear and directed evidence about the existence of multiple dimensions, assuming that the person is not generally overloaded or underloaded by events in the environment.*

Training across Domains

Of course, levels of cognitive complexity within a person may be quite specific to particular cognitive domains. Scott and his associates (Scott, 1969, 1974; Scott, Osgood, and Peterson, 1979) have presented extensive discussions of these cognitive domains (see also Chapter 2). Clearly, complexity within any domain is likely to develop only where experience or communication has generated multidimensional differentiative or integrative thought processes. Other cognitive areas may remain relatively untouched. Initial probing into these latter domains may generate strictly unidimensional responses. For example, where executive X might be willing to consider alternate interpersonal liaisons among his or her close associates to resolve some organizational problem, he or she may not be so flexible in tolerating changes in personal relationships. Multidimensional thought processes may well exist within the work domain that would not even be considered within the personal–social realm.

In earlier work, Driver and Streufert (1969) argued that at least four overall cognitive areas (represented by a 2 × 2 matrix, in Figure 4.1) should be considered in assessing a person's cognitive complexity. These authors distinguished between social–nonsocial complexity and perceptual–executive complexity. Other early work in complexity theory (especially by Bieri and associates) tended to focus specifically on differentiation in the perceptual–social cell of this matrix. Later efforts, for example by Streufert and associates (Streufert, 1970, 1978, Streufert and Fromkin, 1972, Streufert and Streufert, 1978), by Driver and his coworkers (Driver and Mock, 1974), and by Schroder (Schroder, 1971) have expanded the application of the theoretical structure to the other cells as well. A later section of this chapter is, for example, concerned specifically with executive (both social and nonsocial) complexity.

Without question, the division of cognitive functions into the four cells seen in Figure 4.1 is overly restrictive. Undoubtedly, many more domains exist. Cognitive interrelationships among domains may or may not exist. Some domains are likely further removed (and consequently less accessible) from each other than others. One might, for example, argue that training for complexity in a domain that can be classified within the perceptual–social cell of the matrix should be easier, if some other domain within the perceptual–social cell already contains cognitively complex cognitions; that transfer of complexity to, for example, a domain in the perceptual–

	PERCEPTUAL	EXECUTIVE
SOCIAL	Perceptual – Social Area Domains	Executive – Social Area Domains
NONSOCIAL	Perceptual – Nonsocial Area Domains	Executive – Nonsocial Area Domains

FIGURE 4.1. Example of four cognitive areas containing domains of cognitive complexity. Many additional domains may exist in an individual's cognitive structure.

nonsocial cell of the matrix would be more difficult, and that transfer to a domain within the executive–nonsocial cell could be even more problematic and time consuming. For example, a person who has achieved the ability to differentiate and integrate information about the political views of various candidates (the political domain within the perceptual–social matrix cell) is likely more easily trained to understand potentially differentiated and integrated views of executives than to make differentiated and integrated decisions about the distribution of goods and services to a specific population (i.e., the nonsocial–executive cell).

With our discussion of domains we arrive at the issue of intentional training within and across domain boundaries. In many cases such training may be useful. Before considering training and training methods, however, we need to raise the question whether some complexity does already exist within the cognitive domain on which the training will focus. We would argue that:

4.2 *Training for complexity in a previously noncomplex cognitive domain is more difficult to accomplish when no previous complexity exists in any cognitive domain.*

Where training across domains is needed and where previous complexity *does* exist in one or more other cognitive domains, training will be more effective if similar aspects of the two domains are emphasized during the training procedure. For example, if a person's perception of the behavior of various political figures is essentially multidimensional, then using that domain as an example for explaining multidimensionality in actions by executives would likely be facilitative:

4.3 *Training for increased complexity within a cognitive domain where complexity currently does not exist should emphasize components from a related domain where complexity does exist.*

Unfortunately, we still know relatively little about the speed and effectiveness of complexity training across domains. Research in this and in related areas is in progress. If we desire to improve executive performance, we need to be concerned with some secondary effects of training for greater cognitive complexity, in particular physiological and health effects (see Streufert, 1983b). We discuss problems of that nature in Chapter 8.

Discovery of Dimensions

Up to this point, we have considered the effects of external influences on the development of cognitive complexity. Certainly, at least a portion of the initial impetus for multidimensionality is learned from other persons, either directly or indirectly. Where, for example, a person discovers that people from another country or culture use different basic (e.g., moral) dimensions than do people from the observer's own country or culture, rudimentary differentiation can occur (i.e., the realization that several potentially legitimate ways of thinking about some issue exist). Often, of course, the observer will simply reject the alternate perspective as wrong, thereby maintaining a unidimensional point of view.

Once *some* multidimensionality exists (i.e., the acceptance that there are various ways to look at things), a person may become more open to alternate conceptualizations. Such openness requires, among other things, a degree of flexibility. With more extensive experience, flexible complexity (described subsequently) may emerge—that is, an approach to multidimensional information processing where external cues are no longer needed to generate additional ways of viewing issues, concepts, and their interrelationships.

We may now propose that:

4.4 *Development of cognitive complexity in domains were complexity does not presently exist can be aided by discovery of multidimensionality in the environment, as long as (1) the person involved is open to the potential existence of additional dimensions, and (2) sufficient flexibility to permit reorganization of relevant cognitive concepts is present.*

HIERARCHICAL VERSUS FLEXIBLE COMPLEXITY

The concept of flexibility is of considerable importance in interactive complexity theory. Training in complexity may lead *either* to hierarchical *or* flexible organizations of a person's cognitive system. Where training procedures emphasize dimensions and their relationships but communicate these relationships as invariant, or where entire systems of relationships are transferred to the trainee as one single and fixed set (particularly if variants of the systems are rejected) *hierarchical complexity* will likely develop within that particular domain.

In contrast, training for *flexible complexity* would not emphasize system characteristics so much as the building of insights about dimensional relationships. Rather than training emphasis on a specific relationship, a trainee may be encouraged to recognize apparently obvious multidimensional patterns, *but* he or she might also be encouraged to explore whether other interrelationships might (potentially) exist as well. In other words, training for flexible complexity would emphasize the *exploration* rather than the *memorization* of conceptual relationships. With these thoughts in mind, we offer the following postulates:

4.5   Both the number of dimensional concepts (differentiation) and their relationships (integration) can be either fixed and hierachically organized, or can be flexible and open to modification with additional informational input.

4.6   Hierarchical complexity is emphasized and likely generated when an entire system of dimensions and relationships is presented to an individual at one time, and/or when the system is presented as invariable.

4.7   Flexible complexity is emphasized and likely generated by encouraging an exploration of the components and relationships existing within a system, by permitting developmental explorations, and by de-emphasizing memorization for the system.

Clearly there are advantages both to flexible and to hierarchically complex cognitive systems within specific domains. Novelty, change, and input that includes unexpected components are most compatible with flexible complexity. Fixed input with given meanings that can be quantified in advance are best accommodated by hierarchically complex styles.

Up to a certain level of complexity, the hierarchical system may be compatible with sophisticated (e.g., artificial-intelligence based) computer systems. At the present state of the art, however, computer-based systems and/or programs that deal with input akin to flexible complexity do not exist.

DEGREES OF COMPLEXITY

As children first learn to understand their world, they tend to employ an exclusion–inclusion principle. Things of one kind are lumped into a single category, and everything that does not belong is lumped into a second. For some adults, this phenomenon continues to be a typical mode of thought, even though different inclusion–exclusion principles may be relevant to diverse stimulus groupings. For example, all people of a certain characteristic (some group, nation, color, religion, or whatever) may be viewed as good guys and everyone who does not belong to that group is automatically suspect. In effect, the person has lumped people into an in-group and an out-group. Prejudiced attitudes, whether toward people or toward innovative ideas, can with some frequency be expected from persons whose cognitive processes are basically exclusion–inclusion oriented.

With movement toward greater perpetual complexity, discrimination (sometimes described as shades of gray) between the included and the completely excluded stimuli is established. A person may, for instance, determine that a few others who were previously considered as members of the out-group have certain acceptable features while still others who may have previously been favorably considered are now not totally acceptable. The former may now be viewed as exceptions to the rule (but some of my best friends are) while persons included in the latter category may belong to a similar—but still not *quite* the right group, nation, religion, et cetera.

In any case, no matter how many shades of gray are established, the resulting cognitive conceptualization is still *unidimensional*—that is, the relevant stimuli (e.g., persons in this example) are still categorized within a single specific cognitive delineation.[1] Such shades of gray existing on a single cognitive dimension are termed dimensional discrimination by complexity theorists and may, of course, occur in varying degrees.

At this point, it may be worthwhile to temporarily change our focus to discuss a common misconception. The reader will probably have concluded, at this point, that he or she is not cognitively unidimensional. That may or may not be true. Let us consider an example. Imagine a football player. Clearly we may wish to invoke a number of dimensions to describe the player's characteristics. For ease of communication, let us use dimensions from the semantic differential (Osgood, Suci, and Tannenbaum, 1957). A football player might be good or bad. He might be weak or strong. He might be active or passive. He might be fast or slow, and so forth. All suggest different dimensions, and we might score a football player on any or all of these dimensions. If we do, can we conclude that we have at least a four-dimensional view of football players? Not quite yet. To test whether we do, let us try the following: imagine a good, weak, passive, slow football player. If we conclude that this is an impossible combination, our views of football players may not be as multidimensional as we thought. If, in fact, good also by necessity means strong, active and fast—that is, if the other dimensions we have employed are highly correlated with the evaluative dimension and its good description, then we have used a number of verbal descriptions, all of which collapse into the same unidimensional conceptualization.

We have intentionally chosen the example of a football player. Football as a spectator sport is enjoyed by many people, but few of us are multidimensional about football. Coaches must be. Some sports commentators are. Spectators need not be, particularly if their favorite team wins a lot. However, even if an individual does not employ multidimensional styles as far as football is concerned, he or she may well be multidimensional in other domains.

---

[1]Note that we continue to discuss unidimensionality in a specific *domain* to which the stimulus input is relevant. Multidimensionality may or may not exist in *other* domains.

Let us return to our discussion of degrees of complexity. The next level of cognitive structure takes our individual toward differentiation. Here, stimuli are considered on more than one dimension. The diverse dimensions may function as alternatives. Sometimes a given dimension is employed, sometimes another. Which dimension is called forth may depend on the time, place, situation, or some other salient cue in the environment. Often, an individual is unaware (at low levels of differentiation) that he or she is actually employing different dimensions across diverse situations. Consider, for instance, a pawnshop operator in a ghetto area who overcharges the local population for items sold: After all, they cannot get credit elsewhere. Yet the same shopowner may make substantial contributions to help people in the ghetto when asked by a religious organization. The inconsistency of these two behaviors may not even be recognized.

At a somewhat higher level of differentiation, a person may be aware of his or her discrepant views of a person, object, idea, or situation. These discrepancies may be so great that, if they were explained to a unidimensional person, he or she could view them as inconsistent and consequently as wrong, inappropriate, et cetera. To the true differentiator, however, such presumed inconsistencies may be entirely reasonable. He or she may, for example, explain these diverse conceptualizations with some external cue. For example, in describing a co-worker our differentiator may say, "He is a terrific worker and easy to get along with at the office, but his personality changes completely when he gets home. It is no wonder that his wife and kids hate him."

Differentiation, like unidimensional discrimination, can occur at a number of different levels. At its extreme (excessive differentiation), a person may consider so many alternative interpretations of the same set of stimuli or events that it becomes nearly impossible to decide which interpretation to apply at a particular time. In this case, decisions may be made by toss of a coin or by blindly stumbling into some action. Excessive differentiation is a substantial hindrance in the development of a more sophisticated form of information processing: *integration.*

Integration without differentiation is impossible. Without the existence of more or less independent dimensions, there is no way of relating those dimensions. For an example, let us return to the differentiator who considered another person to be a good guy at work, but a bad guy at home. If our differentiator learns to integrate, he or she may begin a search for some overriding principle that can be used to reconcile the observed differences. Why does George act differently at home when he is such a pleasure to work with? Where is the motivational basis? Are there diverse influences at the workplace and at home that create the discrepancies? He may find that George, who is competent at the office and therefore socially and financially rewarded, must deal with a situation at home that is punishing. Because George is unable to deal with punishment effectively, a good (integrated) reason for his not at all inconsistent behavior does exist. His behavior is controlled by a less obvious but superordinate personality characteristic. The application of that superordinate explanation reflects an integrative process.

Integration, where diverse dimensions that may, on the surface, have appeared to be inconsistent are related in terms of *one* superordinate concept, is termed *low-level integration*. The word *low* is appropriate because only one integrative level exists to interconnect and govern diverse dimensions. In contrast, it is possible to employ several low-level integrations, each of them based on two or more (possibly partly overlapping) dimensions. These sets of low-level integrations, in turn, may be related to each other in terms of higher integrative levels.

Thus far, our examples have all been derived from social–perceptual domains. Because we do not want to create the impression that complexity is related only to perceptual–social domains, let us consider another kind of example, taken from a nonsocial–decision-making domain.

Consider a decision maker who works for the XYZ Corporation, which has a major competitor, the ABQ Corporation. Both manufacture a product of about equal quality at about the same price. Their respective market shares are roughly 60% for XYZ and 38% for ABQ (with 2% distributed among other small and weak companies). Assume that our executive decision maker received information that the Vice President for Sales at ABQ appears to be in trouble with their CEO. Other information arrives that ABQ has just dropped the price of their product by 20%. Our executive must make a recommendation on how XYZ should respond.

Several options are available. XYZ could hold its original price and wait until ABQ stops the price war. Another option is to reduce the price by 20% as well. A third might be for XYZ to drop the price by only 10% and advertise the high quality and longevity of the XYZ product. Naturally, other options exist as well. A less cognitively complex (e.g., unidimensional) decision maker might initiate a search for the correct option (possibly on the basis of a computer model). And a differentiator may consider alternative interpretations of ABQ's action and capacity and would select a course of action dictated by either one of these alternatives. However, an integrator would probably consider (if sufficient time is available) various alternative reasons for ABQ's action. An interpretation of these reasons would be followed by a strategic response that maximizes responsiveness to an overall view of the reasons for the opponent's actions—that is, one that will be strategically best in terms of a number of possibilities. A high-level integrator may, in addition, use available information and respond simultaneously to advance the future strategic position of XYZ.

For example, such a decision maker may consider whether the difficulties of the Sales VP at ABQ have anything to do with the price drop. Is that person doing something desperate to hold onto the position or to defend other actions? If so, clear implications about the expected length of the price war may be derived. If the two points are independent, can the weakness of that executive be used to influence policy of ABQ? What was the overall profit of ABQ during the last 2 years? How long can they stand to lose money? How much are they losing? What is the likely effect on customers? Is there such a thing as brand loyalty among consumers of this product? How much of a price discrepancy is required for that loyalty to disappear? How much would XYZ stand to lose at each of the various potential price cuts? How long can the XYZ company maintain reduced price levels? What methods of advertising and product modification can be used to sell the XYZ product to the consumer *despite* the competitor's price cut?

Answers to some of those questions will be easy. Answers to others will be more difficult and may be less certain. Let us assume that our decision maker concludes that the ABQ VP is in difficulty because he had been expected to garner 45% of the market but did not succeed. He must have persuaded the corporate staff that only a price cut would result in a loyalty switch by consumers—a strategy that was put into effect. This action temporarily places ABQ in an advantageous position as far as sales volume is concerned.

Brand loyalty, however, is another matter. Because the product involved is a relatively expensive item, a price cut of 20% will mean a lot. Some customers are going to switch brands and buy from the competition unless their price cut is countered. However, XYZ cannot afford a price cut for very long without compromising quality. A drop in quality, however, would presumably cause customer dissatisfaction—resulting in reduced sales. It appears that ABQ is in a similar position. From this perspective, both ABQ and XYZ are likely to experience potential losses.

The fact that the ABQ Sales VP is under fire may be helpful. If he cannot get a greater share of the market he may lose his job and ABQ's corporate policy might be reversed; after all, the corporate ABQ staff is not known as a patient group of people. That, then, puts ABQ in a poor position, *if* XYZ can maintain or increase its market share in the immediate future.

Expanding our hypothetical example, assume that recently a national consumer group has criticized the ABQ product because it contained an unsafe part. The part was immediately replaced with a safer component but the consumer perception of ABQ's unsafe product may have stuck. The XYZ executive considers that event as well. If consumer perceptions of ABQ have been indeed affected, and if those perceptions can be (indirectly) exploited, then XYZ may be in a better position to hold, or even to increase its market share. The more rapidly that increase occurs, the sooner ABQ would presumably stop the price war.

Conceptualizations such as these are, at the surface, partially inconsistent with each other. Some place XYZ in a favorable position; others do not. At a low level of integration, they may be combined into a policy recommendation: To obtain a quick shift in ABQ's policy, XYZ needs to get ABQ's VP into additional trouble—that is, to ensure that his actions will not be successful. XYZ needs to increase or hold its market share without much of a financial loss, if possible. Clearly, XYZ needs to cut the product's price as well. Maybe 10% or a little more will be enough, *if* XYZ simultaneously emphasizes product quality (implying lesser quality by ABQ—after all, they *were* criticized). Such actions need to be taken immediately to avoid a consumer surge toward ABQ.

Low-level integrations of this kind might be used by a high-level integrator *as a part* of an overall goal-directed metastrategy. The decision maker, in this case, does not want to push ABQ out of the market entirely—an action which migh result in an antitrust investigation by the government. Yet, he/she may want his/her company to gain something like an 80% share of the market. (These conclusions may have been reached on the basis of *other* low-level integrations.)

Those views (also obtained via a low-level integration), the suggestion to drop the XYZ price by 10%, and the plan to advertise quality must now become part of a general future-oriented (highly integrated) strategy. Say, the products that are manufactured by both companies fall into A, B, C, and D subcategories, all of about the same price. Of these, the D category represents about 20% of the market. If it were possible to eliminate ABQ from all but the D market, that would be satisfactory. Possibly, XYZ's D line products are the most expensive to produce, given the current manufacturing process. More profit per unit can be made from A, B and C line products. One might then consider a differential price drop together with quality advertising, with D line products held at the existing price, but with the popular A line products dropped even below 20%. Increased quantity of A line products, as long as the sale price remains barely above cost, might make up for losses engendered from other line products that are sold at reduced prices.

In addition, some direct influence on the executives of ABQ may be possible. Some rumors about forthcoming actions of XYZ corporation could be initiated. XYZ might let it be known that they are probably less able to compete with quite another product which is made by both companies (where no market shares are actually lost in the long run), in order to entice ABQ to concentrate on manufacturing and marketing that product and, otherwise, restrict its production to the D line. The important decision-making process in this example *integrates* diverse purposes and relevant strategies in terms of an overall goal. Note, that this higher-level integration is *not* bound by the involved content, nor is it bound by specific (unidimensional) value systems (such as, for example, morality). Unidimensional concepts are not necessarily rejected in such complex integrations; rather they are used as part of an overall structure in which they may play some strategic role. The extent of their influence (of lack thereof) depends on the interrelationships among the involved dimensions.

High-level integrators are often admired for their leadership in strategy development. A number of researchers and theorists in organizational psychology have described such individuals in terms that are closely related to integrative complexity. For example, Mintzberg (1976) talks about cognitive processes in managers who draw out the vaguest information and use the least articulated of mental processes that are more relational and holistic than ordered and sequential, more intuitive than intellectual. Peters and Waterman also talk about intuitive reasoning. Simon (1979) describes the true professional manager as having a rich vocabulary of patterns. Barnard (1968) probably comes closest to our terminology in his description of "few men of executive genius" who, he states, are "comprehensively sensitive and well integrated."

Up to this point, we have viewed our cognitively complex executive decision maker as a flexible thinker making decisions on the run, decisions that are based on (and revised because of) up-to-date information. If such a person makes a decision today, it might be somewhat (but not likely entirely) revised tomorrow,[2] because new information inputs have arrived and are available for modified integrated strategies and goals. Changes in decision strategies are, however, typically partial and different from changes in decisions made by less-complex individuals who are more likely either to stick to their initial decision or to flip-flop from one kind of decision to another.

Clearly, the high-level integrator we have described is flexible. As stated earlier, however, flexibility does not apply to all integrators. Some persons process multidimensional concepts in a fixed hierarchical fashion. Let us

---

[2]Of course, in many situations a decision, once made, or an action, once it is taken, is no longer subject to revision. Where such situations exist, the highly integrated decision maker would likely use novel information to employ supplementary strategies to optimize the earlier (final) decision.

take another look at the differences between flexible and hierarchical integrators. Hierarchical integrators place information input on a number of dimensions (differentiation) and relate these dimensions into overall conceptual integrations. However, placement of any single stimulus on a given dimension is constant each time the stimulus occurs. That is, the placement will have precisely the same dimensional meaning as it did on previous occasions. The same holds for relationships among dimensions (i.e., integration). Each time specific dimensions are involved, they will be related to each other in precisely the same way. At some point, that decision maker has probably learned the specific meanings of stimuli and how the responses to these stimuli are used in determining a perceptual or decision-based outcome. As a result, hierarchical integration is inflexible: The hierarchical integrator cannot adapt to changes in the meaning of either stimuli or dimensions unless the changes are specifically cued.

Nonetheless, such a person—even though he or she may be quite uncomfortable about it—*can* learn to process information in new ways, if some aspect of the situation has drastically changed. Such a shift in information processing would likely result in major rearrangements of the components of the person's cognitive conceptual organization of dimensions and stimulus locations on dimensions. These adjustments will be required (just as they would be in a fixed mathematical system) to bring relationships back into equilibrium.

Considerably fewer changes in the same situation would probably be required for flexible integrators because part of the adjustment may be made by such persons via partial reconceptualizations of cognitive dimensions and their relationships. In contrast, hierarchical integrators are much less able to reconceptualize structural components. They may well represent the executives whom Simon (1979) had in mind when he discussed chess masters with highly developed long-term memories that are remembered as subconscious patterns—that is, old friends from previous experience. To the degee to which the friendship of these patterns is unchanging, such an individual may be able to deal with complex and challenging environments, only as long as they are familiar. Any major modification of the challenging environment, however, would likely result in either distortion or inability to perform.

As long as the world in which a hierarchical integrator operates is constant, however, he or she is likely to be just as (or even more) effective as the flexible integrator. We would propose that:

4.8   *Early experience typically involves cognitive conceptualizations that employ inclusion–exclusion principles.*

4.9   *Subsequent experience and/or training can lead to the development of unidimensional conceptualizations that include discrimination. These conceptualizations are typically fixed with regard to specific sets of stimuli.*

4.10   *Experience with alternate conceptualizations of stimulus sets may lead to development of alternate dimensions of judgment (differentiation), which may be employed independently, cued by specific stimulus or cognitive conditions.*

4.11   *Excessive use of dimensionality (excessive differentiation) may generate confusion concerning which dimensions to apply to specific stimuli or cognitive events and may prevent development toward integration.*

4.12   *Experience or training with possible relationships among differentiated conceptualizations of stimuli may lead to low levels of integration where diverse cognitions are related and combined into an overall view (e.g., a strategy).*

4.13   *Experience or training with interrelationships among various integrated conceptualizations or strategies may lead to higher levels of integration where several (low-level) integrated conceptualizations are combined into metaconcepts, long-term goals, and so forth.*

4.14   *Where differentiation and integration are hierarchical (organized without flexibility in response to subsequent information, see 4-5, 4-6, and 4-7), a person will function appropriately only in a steady-state environment.*

Just as an excessive differentiator is potentially unable to settle on an appropriate dimension to be employed in response to some specific set of stimuli, there are also some integrators who are unable to "close" even on a temporary conceptualization to use as the basis for an action. The higher the level of integration and the more flexible the integrative style, the more likely an inability to close for decision making may emerge.

This is not to say that there is necessarily a strong association between high-level flexible integration and problems with closure. Many successful decision makers in organizations are quite able to close and act—only to reconsider (and, if necessary, adjust) the decision at a later time.[3] An observed association of inability to close with higher levels of flexible integration is, in part, due to measurement error: The more interpretation and decision options and the more relationships among options exist, the more

---

[3]Note that the tendency to reconsider decisions may be made for present adjustments or for future reference, and may be made without commitment to reconsideration, particularly where a decision maker must appear decisive to others, or where changes—once a commitment to a particular decision has been made—are not feasible.

difficult it will be for the continually open person to make a temporary decision—that is, the more likely the resulting vacillations will be observed. In other words, any (low order) correlation between cognitive complexity and inability to close is probably due to the fact that vacillations cannot occur as easily in individuals who cannot differentiate or integrate because incoming stimuli tend to be associated with fixed responses. In other words,

4.15 *Decision makers who employ high levels of integration are likely to be effective only if they are able to close on decisions when required, despite remaining uncertainty. Effective integrators are likely to reopen their cognitive considerations after a decision has been made (where a previous decision may yet be modified) and can (where useful) make adjustments or other modifications to the previous decision.*

The likely developmental sequence for degrees of cognitive complexity is presented in Figure 4.2. The figure considers two cognitive characteristics: flexibility and complexity. While it is true that an increase in cognitive complexity is often associated with an increase in flexibility, many exceptions to that rule do exist. Where it occurs, simultaneous growth of complexity and flexibility is often associated with experiential learning across considerable time. In contrast, growth in cognitive complexity without growth in

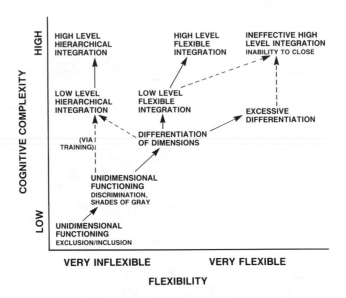

FIGURE 4.2.   Development of cognitive complexity in individuals from less to more cognitively complex functioning.

flexibility, attaining a hierarchical and fixed approach toward differentiative and integrative processes, is often generated by specific training procedures that include little trial and error experience. For example, training for hierarchical forms of cognitive complexity may provide precise instructions on how to view and interrelate concepts.

Figure 4.2 provides solid arrows where growth is more likely to occur and broken arrows where growth is possible but not likely. "Via training" describes the connection between unidimensional functioning and low-level hierarchical integration. The inclusion of that term does not imply that growth along other arrows cannot be based on training procedures. Rather, it is suggested that growth from unidimensional functioning toward low levels of hierarchical integration will only be achieved via training procedures.

WHY WOULD ANYBODY WANT TO BE COGNITIVELY COMPLEX?

Some complexity researchers and theorists have made it sound very desirable to be classified as a differentiator and integrator. Others have expressed doubt about the generality of assumptions that the capacity to behave in a cognitively complex fashion (and particularly the tendency to consistently behave in such a fashion) is of value in all situations and at all times. To consider the appropriateness of cognitively complex functioning, we should ask what, in fact, is achieved by cognitively complex performance.

Unquestionably, the capacity to differentiate and integrate allows an organizational decision maker the option to consider a wider variety of implications of environmental events, to develop more complex performance strategies, and to develop more inclusive long-range goals. A cognitively complex executive is likely to be a superior planner who is able to actively consider a larger number of contingencies and their implications. Is such a person consequently a better executive? The answer in not necessarily "yes." Under some conditions, "overplanning" can be just as detrimental as underplanning. In some cases, a simple, straightforward decision might be preferable to a well-considered strategic decision.

Again, an example might be useful. In a stimulated competition among various investment corporations, decision makers in a research project were provided with stock market information via a number of indicators. The decision makers were unaware that only one indicator contained useful information, modified somewhat by random variability. All other indicators provided only random data. Both less cognitively complex and differentiating or integrating, that is, cognitively complex, participants soon recognized which of the indicators provided the most useful information and began to invest accordingly. However, integrators among the participants soon began to experiment with other indicators to determine whether or not they could be used to add useful information to the data provided by the reliable indicator. The less cognitively complex persons, on the other hand, stayed religiously with the indicator that had been shown to have predictive validity. The outcome of the simulation was not surprising. Most of the integrators lost their investments. The less complex investors took home the spoils.

In fact, most organizational decision-making situations are not as simple—that is, they are not based on a single valid information source. Where complex interrelationships need to be considered, an integrating decision maker, particularly a person who is flexible and is able to reach closure (temporarily) for decisions, will be much more effective. Nonetheless, complicated decision settings where decisions are best made in response to a single informative dimension (including computer-generated probability functions, e.g., of market characteristics and consumer demand probabilities) do exist. In situations of that kind, unidimensional decision making may, at times, be appropriate.

Can we sharply distinguish between cognitively less complex and cognitively complex (integrating or differentiating) decision makers? Do cognitively less complex decision makers ever integrate? Can complex integrators base decisions on single dimensions? The likelihood of obtaining differentiated and especially integrated behavior from less complex persons is not very high (unless we are dealing with a person who functions unidimensionally in one relevant domain but multidimensionally in other domains, *and* some cue is available to translate other-domain multidimensionality into the relevant domain area).

Whether or not a cognitively complex (differentiating or integrating) person can and will operate at a lower dimensional level when useful or necessary is quite another matter, however. There are integrators who can and do function well in a unidimensional fashion if they perceive that the environment demands such action. Unidimensional functioning here has some aspects of strategic action: It may be viewed as the appropriate way, for example, to communicate with a less complex person. Similarly, speeches by many effective cognitively complex politicians are often phrased in unidimensional language. Many an average voter would consider multidimensional statements by a politician as too complicated, too wishy-washy or filled with too much uncertainty. When it comes to actions, however, the same politician may employ a multidimensional strategy, at times disappointing and annoying less cognitively complex voters who presume that the politician is not keeping promises.

On the other hand, some cognitively complex decision makers, particularly integrators, may never have learned to select unidimensional modes of action when such an approach appears to be appropriate or required. The reasons why some persons are, and others are not, able to switch complexity levels at will (based on appropriateness of the task) are known. To some degree, the capacity to shift from one information-processing mode to another may be related to issues concerning the ultimate source of cognitive complexity. It has been argued that complexity might be a style, a genetically based characteristic of the CNS, a preferred method of dealing with the environment, or some interaction of these (see Streufert and Streufert, 1978). To the extent to which the capacity to differentiate and integrate is learned (even if based on differential levels of a physiological foundation), both that capacity and the capacity to shift toward unidimensionality, as required, can probably be generated via training, at least, in some individuals. To the extent to which complexity is a genetically determined, or purely a preferred style of responding, the basis of the capability to shift complexity levels would be more difficult to establish. Research conducted at the Pennsylvania State University College of Medicine is, in part, investigating such issues. It is still too early to advance clear propositions about such phenomena.

COMPLEXITY AND RELATED STYLES AND ABILITIES

Differentiation and/or integration should also affect other behaviors that are products of cognitive structure. We cannot possibly discuss all classes of behaviors that could be included; nor can we provide explicit detail on those that are included. In the present context, we discuss creativity, use of strategy, and leadership. Much elaboration and synthesis will, however, be left to the reader.

Creativity

In the mid-1960s, psychologists spent considerable effort in attempts to come to grips with the meaning and foundations of creativity. Mednick (1963), for instance, considered remote responses to be reflective of creativity. Jackson and Messick (1965) have devoted considerable effort to evaluating the various views of creativity and to their relationships to societal and intrinsic values (see Maddi, 1965). Jackson and Messick have argued that creativity is more than just unusual or remote associate responding: it also involves transformation. Streufert and Streufert (1978) presented the view that this transformation is a structural characteristic, reflecting some (probably initially low) level of integrative activity. Where Jackson and Messick applied the term *condensation* to highly creative productivity, Streufert and Streufert have replaced that term with *flexible high-level integration*. The emphasis on flexibility is of considerable importance: A hierarchical integrator would be most uncreative.

Creativity in an organizational setting also implies more than merely the unusual use of some technique or resource. It implies generating a product that can be patented, a service that is innovative, an organizational procedure that has considerable benefits. It implies the ability to view interrelationships among components—whether organizational or product–service oriented—in a fluid pattern that has not previously been seen (or accepted). When provided adequate opportunity, a high-level integrator should, at least, have the potential for creative thought and action. Whether or not such an opportunity is present does, however, depend on the organizational environment. We discuss questions of organizational support for creative efforts in Chapter 5. We suggest that:

4.16   *Creativity in an organizational setting depends, in part, on a person's ability to generate novel (unusual) and potentially remote views and actions within an organizational setting that can be integrated with organizational structures and needs of the organization and are supported by the organization's structure.*

The Use of Strategy and Planning

We have previously used the word *strategy* in discussing high-level integrations. Let us now consider strategic decision-making a bit more closely. Strategy involves planning, usually across a number of steps, each with potentially uncertain outcomes—that is, planning toward one or more alternative or additive goals. Strategy involves dealing with uncertainty by employing contingent planning. The use of strategy requires flexibility and often novelty in approaching problems (somewhat akin to creativity) as well as openness (on a continuing basis) to new information.

Use of strategy, where environmental (e.g., load) conditions are not detrimental, involves flexible integrative information-processing and decision-making efforts. It implies considering many possible, reasonable and meaningful interpretations of events and their likely consequences. It implies considering various potential actions (or lack of actions) that may be invoked in response to those events, effects of these potential actions on these events and other probable short-term and long-term outcomes. It implies plans to deal with the potential consequences of one's own actions as well as with other's reactions in an overall approach. Most of all, it implies considering a sequence of potential actions that are to lead to a desirable set of goals.

With uncertainty given, with unknowns and unknowables, with insufficient information about interrelationships among series of uncertain events, a pragmatic approach to integration must be employed. Development of strategy is a continuous process, requiring consideration and reconsideration of events, decisions and, in some cases goals, as events unfold. The development of strategy is not an emotional or irrational process. It is rational, but not in the terms of narrow mathematical definitions. Mathematical models, so popular in decision theory, reflect a hierarchical integrative approach—an approach that has difficulty dealing with change and is incapable of dealing with unforeseen events. Yet, unforeseen events must be dealt with frequently by organizations and managers as the task environment changes more and more rapidly with time.

One might say that the utilization of strategy, particularly at highly integrated levels, is a form of creativity. It may be used to forge novel and desirable outcomes that had not been anticipated. Certainly Kissinger in his Middle East negotiation efforts (Rubin, 1981; Streufert, 1984) employed a creative integrative and flexible strategy that was designed to (and at least in part did) lead to an overall set of goals. As we discuss later (see the chapter on research related to complexity theory), the use of cognitively complex strategies may also be beneficial in avoiding conflict.

Strategies involve planning. Further, people differ in the ability to apply differentiation and integration (and with it strategy) in complex task settings. Additionally, our theory differs considerably from another that makes some similar and some quite different predictions.

Elliott Jaques (1968, 1977, 1984; Jaques, Gibson, and Isaac, 1978) has advanced a stratified systems theory, whose purpose it is, among other things, to assess the current and future capacity of persons who function at a variety of cognitive levels. Among other predictions, the theory is concerned with the capacity of executives to carry out various levels of responsible tasks in organizational settings. Jaques employs a temporal scale to describe cognitive processes and cognitive power of individuals who are located on discontinuous (multimodal) indicators of cognitive (and organizational) functioning. *Cognitive power* is viewed as the degree of complexity of a person's cognitive processes. The amount of available cognitive power is represented by the size or scale of the world that an individual is able to pattern and construct, live with and work in. Cognitive complexity in this theory represents the number and range of variables that individuals are able to use in the construction of their world.

Jaques considers external demands on the individual as well as the individual's response and degree of comfort with those demands. An individual's current level of work is externally determined and reflects the time span of tasks assigned to that person. To measure time span, Jaques and associates ask an individual's superior about the longest time span (to completion) of any tasks assigned to that individual. The individual, in turn, is considered in terms of his or her *time frame*, indicating that person's capability of dealing with tasks that require specific time lengths to completion. Where time frame and time span match, the level of work is appropriate, and the individual should be satisfied with the assigned job level. Pay level is expected to match that work level. If it does not, dissatisfaction would result.

Jaques views a number of discrete time spans as representative of discrete levels of tasks and responsibility.[4] Major steps occur between time spans of 3 months, and 1, 2, 5, 10, and 20 years. Persons are apparently genetically predetermined to reach a certain level as they mature. They move through lower levels along maturation bands, maturing at predictable rates, irrelevant of the content and cultural characteristics of their experience. Deprivation may diminish their performance in general but not their maturation along those bands toward greater cognitive power. Training, in other words, is useful only to aid a person toward full use of inherent cognitive power. Persons cannot be shifted from one maturation band to another.

A person's capability to perform work is determined by his or her cognitive power in coordination with other psychological tools and orientations, such as knowledge, skills, emotional make-up, experience, and values. Those characteristics and specific circumstances determine the effective level of work performed by an individual.

Jaques presents considerable evidence for his time-span concept. However, his supporting arguments for individual differences in time frame appear, at best, circumstantial. He asks (Jaques, 1984) why time span increases with greater felt weight of responsibility and with higher levels of executive systems. In response, he argues that he has been able to construct only one hypothesis that represents a reasonable interpretation of these findings— that is, that maximum time span with which a specific person is able to work measures that person's level of cognitive power (remember, cognitive power is, in turn, related to cognitive complexity).

If higher job levels in organizations and increased responsibility are to

---

[4]His theory of cognitive quintaves views cognitive–organizational functioning along a number of partly similar steps. The interested reader is referred to the original papers.

be the measure of cognitive power, we may, unfortunately, have entered a state of partial circularity. We have not answered the question why some persons are and why others are not able to reach higher levels of performance and/or job status. Clearly, an exact measure of cognitive power is needed. Aside from an attempt by Stamp (1981), Jaques and associates have not attempted to generate such forms of measurement.

Jaques has described a number of stratums of performance (Stages 1 through 7) that, in some cases, show some similarity to cognitive functions proposed by complexity theory (Streufert and Streufert, 1978). In referencing Streufert and associates, however, Jaques suggest that complexity theory conceives of discontinuity (e.g., among stratums) in a fashion that is similar to his own view. That conclusion appears, at least partially, inaccurate: Streufert and Streufert have permitted development through various cognitive functions described in complexity theory. For that matter, Streufert's developmental views would not necessarily match the development along maturation bands that Jaques has suggested.

Clearly, there are some similarities and some major differences between complexity theory and the theoretical approach of Jaques. Both approaches speak about differences in personnel that are predictive of task performance. However, Jaques does not deal extensively with effects of organizational environments on performance (e.g., decision making) or with the matching of organizational systems and individual cognitive structures. Jaques has some difficulty in identifying underlying processes that may explain individual or organizational performance discrepancies. Measurement of these processes, aside from assessing time length of assignments, is not extensively attempted. In contrast, complexity-theory-based approaches have developed a number of techniques to measure differences in cognition, information processing, and performance.

The major discrepancy between the two views, however, is based on Jaques's concept of time span of responsibility. Without question , meaningful measurement of time span (but not time frame) is possible. It appears to us that Jaques is arguing that assigned time span implies relevant cognitive power that, in turn, is expressed in the cognitive complexity necessary to function within a specific time frame. We would agree, that one may obtain a correlation between the level of (in our terms) integrative strategic functioning and time responsibility (capabilities) assigned to executives. However, the present authors would not postulate a *causal* relationship between these variables. We would say that the more accomplished manager is likely a better stategist and probably a better *stepwise* planner. He or she will employ a number of tentatively conceived decision steps as plans for potential future actions are developed. Where planning occurs in a relatively stable environment without the necessity for sequential decision making in rapid steps, a strong correlation between executive job level and time span of planning may emerge. However, when sequential actions and plans call for sequential decisions in rapid succession, or when long-range plans would be inappropriate because of multiple uncertainty and rapid changes in task environments, a correlation would not be obtained. If the high-level manager, as described by Jaques, would plan years into the future under conditions of rapid change and considerable uncertainty, he or she would be overplanning (see Peters and Waterman, 1982).

Our research on strategic planning (see Chapter 7) has shown that sequential planning steps in a time-compressed simulation are highly descriptive of excellent managers. Simulations last only a few hours; Jaques's time-range perspectives last over years—yet the managerial actions in such diverse environments are equivalent in the number of steps and in the quality of strategic decision making. Both in long-range planning and in compressed simulated time, Jaques's proposition that "alternatives are generated in an open context and apparently unrelated material is linked" applies. In fact, this proposition of Jaques's describes low levels of integration. Higher levels of integration may well fit into the as-yet-undescribed highest stages of functioning in Jaques's theory.

In other words, we suggest that time span is not a primary component of executive planning styles. Further, persons who are capable of integrated strategic actions should excel, not only in terms of the potential steps in planning per se, but also in terms of (1) the number of factors they consider, (2) the interrelationships among these factors (e.g., actions and reactions) that they understand and generate, (3) the outcomes, sequential reactions and subsequent outcomes that they predict, and more. Such persons should be capable of working toward distant goals that are several steps and several strategies away from realization.

A Vice President for Planning (categorized by Jaques and his associates as a person involved in a 10-year time span) may be quite capable of developing 10-year or longer planning sequences. These sequences may reflect high-level integrations. By necessity (considering the uncertainty of the future), however, such a plan can only take gross points in the development of an organization into account, if long-term planning is to be useful at all.

For that matter, Peters and Waterman have suggested that excellent companies are not typically long-term thinkers.[5] They have pointed out that many successful companies do not even have 5-year plans. In a rapidly

---

[5]Long-term planning based on integrative activity in rapidly changing and uncertain task environments would suggest that a hierarchical integrator is at work. Such a person would not be able to adapt planning to fluid environments and changes in events from the expected. This person would, indeed, be overplanning.

changing environment, such plans may become rigid structures that would mislead rather than lead future decision makers. As events flow more and more rapidly, as strategies must shift from long-term toward more immediate goal structures, and as organizations must adapt their strategies to frequent unforeseen events, decision makers cannot typically plan far into the future. However, their capacity to generate sequential, stepwise, highly integrated strategies toward an overall, now not so distant, goal can be of considerable value. We would expect the highly integrated and flexible decision makers (who, as Jaques states, redefine rules, generate alternatives, and link apparently unrelated material) to excel in developing complex sequential strategies toward often less distant and realistically achievable goals. We propose that:

4.17 *Strategy development reflects stepwise, flexible, integrative processing of information. Sequential actions are considered in terms of their potential outcomes and of the anticipated and varying consequences of those outcomes. Strategy development involves the selection of decision sequences toward one or more desired goals and the modification of these sequences, where possible, as task environments change or unexpected outcomes are produced.*

Leadership

A number of theorists have considered leadership behavior and leadership effectiveness (e.g., Fiedler, 1964, 1965; Stogdill, 1948, 1962). Often, leadership is considered to be a phenomenon with multiple component parts (e.g., Stogdill, 1962). Leadership, quoting from Burns (1978) and from Selznick (1957), is many things.

> It is patient, usually boring coalition building. It is the purposeful seeding of cabals that one hopes will result in the appropriate ferment in the bowels of the organization. It is meticulously shifting the attention of the institution through the mundane language of management systems. It is altering agendas so that new priorities get enough attention. It is being visible when things are going awry, and invisible when they are working well. It's building a loyal team at the top that speaks more or less with one voice. It's listening carefully much of the time, frequently speaking with encouragement, and reinforcing words with believable action. It's being tough when necessary, and it's the occasional naked use of power—or the "subtle accumulation of nuances, a hundred things done a little better," as Henry Kissinger once put it. Most of these actions are what the political scientist James MacGregor Burns in his book Leadership calls "transactional leadership." They are the necessary activities of the leader that take up most of his or her day.

A similarly large number of leadership characteristics are referenced by Peters and Waterman (1982) when they discuss James Brian Quinn's (1980) concern with leaders who are strategy builders:

> Leadership tasks required toward that end are amplifying understanding, building awareness, changing symbols, legitimizing new viewpoints, making tactical shifts and testing partial solutions, broadening political support, overcoming opposition, inducing and structuring flexibility, launching trial balloons and engaging in systematic waiting, creating pockets of commitment, crystallizing focus, managing coalitions and formalizing commitment.

Clearly, leadership tasks consist of a variety of components. An excellent leader does not view these components as separate but rather as interactive in their effects on performance. In other words, the successful leader dealing with complex and fluid organizational environments functions best if he or she is an integrator. On the other hand, he or she must be a person who can shift to a unidimensional style when task requirements favor unidimensional actions— for example, when the occasional use of naked power is required. Yet, that unidimensional approach would emphasize different (i.e., differentiated) leadership components at different times—depending on current requirements of the organization and its people (see Stogdill, 1962). All in all, we might agree with the political scientist James MacGregor Burns that leadership should be transactional. The transactional leader, however, is most likely a high-level integrator. We propose that:

4.18   *A highly integrated flexible leader is more likely effective because he or she is engaged in a wide variety of component actions that are characteristic of leadership. He or she would likely spread these leadership activities more evenly across those characteristics.*

COMPLEXITY AND THE ENVIRONMENT

So far, we have only dealt with individual differences. However, every individual behaves quite differently in diverse tasks, under diverse stressor impact, and so forth. It is time to emphasize that differentiation and integration, where they are potentially present in an individual, are, in part, increased or decreased in frequency or degree by concurrent environmental conditions.[6] Where a task requires and where environments are optimal,

[6]Other phenomena may affect concurrently observed individual differences as well. For example, a person's present physiological status (e.g., as produced by drugs and disease) may generate changes in structural variables. We are currently engaged in research on that concern.

differentiators are likely to differentiate and integrators are likely to integrate. *Optimal,* in this case, means that excessive stress is not present in the environment. However, as an individual is stressed, either by excessive or noxious stimulation or by stimulus deprivation, his or her capacity to differentiate and integrate may be diminished. As the integrative and/or differentiative cognitions and behaviors drop off, differences between cognitively complex individuals and less complex individuals become less pronounced.

Load: An Environmental Stressor

Certainly, many stressors exist in the organizational environment. Considerable previous research has focused both on single and on multiple stressors and their effects on task performance. Because we cannot deal with the wide variety of potential stress experiences that exist within organizational environments in this book, we focus on information load as a representative environmental stressor. *Information load* is useful as an example of stressor impact in organizational settings, because (1) it is ubiquitous, and (2) its characteristic effects appear to be similar to the effects of several other stressors.

Organizations and their personnel typically receive and process large quantities of information. One approach to the study of information quantity (i.e., load effects) focuses on the H statistic (uncertainty reduction, e.g., Attneave, 1959) of information theory. If we employ that statistic, we might be concerned with the degree to which information can reduce uncertainty by some specified quantity (e.g., by one-half). However, such an orientation is often not appropriate in complex organizational settings. Although a specific item of information may decrease uncertainty on *one* relevant dimension, it may simultaneously *increase* uncertainty on one or more other dimensions. Information theory is useful (and applicable) in simpler (i.e., unidimensional) task settings. It is less applicable to the multidimensional environments and processes of organizations that function in fluid and uncertain environments.

Information is received in large quantities by organizational systems. The specific quantity of that information received within a specified period of time is often measured and defined as information load (see Streufert, 1970). Sources for an organization's information load may vary. Some load is generated within the organization. Other information is generated as an outcome of an organization's present and past activity. Information may also be produced through the actions of other (e.g., competitive) organizations. Yet other information provides feedback to information search in the task environment. In addition, considerable irrelevant information is typically received which is (or, at least should be) of little use to an organization.

As sources of information vary, so do topics. However, all information, no matter what topic, represents quantifiable load. From the standpoint of the present theory, we measure the value of information in terms of its total surface quantity. A simple subject–predicate–object statement does, on the surface, provide a simple source of information when placed on a single cognitive dimension. For example, the statement, "The XYZ corporation has raised its product price," reflects a single quantity of load. This is not to say that such a sentence cannot have multiple meanings where it is cognitively processed on *several* dimensions. It may, for instance, have quite different meanings for those involved in pricing, manufacturing, planning, and marketing. It may, for a responsible executive in another company, have additional implications in terms of the policy of XYZ.

If the sentence had read: "The XYZ corporation raised its product price because they believe that it will sell equally well at its new price level," there would be more than one item of information contained within that communication. For purposes of controlled research, complexity researchers generally have taken great care to limit information to simple subject–predicate–object statements, representing a single load item per communication because multiple statements are difficult to classify in terms of their load value.

What about irrelevant information? If the executive in our example is not interested in market factors and if the sale price of this product has no implications (e.g., inflation) for that executive, does the statement about the increase in the price of our product still produce one unit of information load? We believe that it is wiser to make two separate distinctions than to potentially confound two variables. Let us talk about load values within the classes of relevant and irrelevant information. Our research experience suggests that people are not always able to distinguish between information relevance and irrelevance and that irrelevant items of information may, under certain environmental conditions, be treated as relevant.

Complexity theory argues that stressor (e.g., load) effects in the task environment interact with the cognitive information-processing characteristics (differentiative and/or integrative style) of individuals to produce specific levels of information-processing performance. That prediction holds as long as individuals are motivated to perform. A person who is primarily working on a crossword puzzle and not on a required or assigned task may not show any differentiative or integrative performance in that assigned task. Similarly, a person who cares little about a task or is bored by it will likely perform that task in more or less unidimensional fashion. In other words, where lack of interest, boredom or, in general, low motivation prevail, we cannot expect to obtain the differences in differentiative and integrative cognitions proposed by our theory.

Interactive complexity theory suggests that maximum differentiative and integrative information processing will occur at intermediate information load levels. This prediction holds as long as tasks are sufficiently complex to allow for the processing of information on multiple dimensions and as long as the information content is relevant. As discussed later in this book, this proposition has been widely tested across people, cultures, and group sizes. On the basis of these data, predictions may now be made for specific load levels:

4.19 *Maximum levels of differentiative and integrative cognitive activity should be observed at intermediate (i.e., optimal) information load levels, as long as tasks are sufficiently complex to allow multidimensional information processing and as long as information content is relevant.*

4.20 *Given the conditions stated in proposition 4.19, maximum levels of differentiated and integrated activity should be observed when information load levels are set at approximately one load item[7] of information per 3-minute period (optimal information load).*

4.21 *Given the conditions stated in proposition 4.20, the fall-off in differentiative information processing with increasing (above optimal) and with decreasing (below optimal) load should be less than the fall-off in integrative information processing.*

The greater effect of suboptimal and superoptimal load levels on integrative processes suggests that higher levels of cognitive functioning (i.e., integration) are more severely affected by load changes than are lower levels of functioning. In terms of individual differences, the least amount of change in differentiative and/or integrative functioning with changes in load (absolute but not proportional terms) would be expected for less cognitively complex individuals (see Figure 4.3). If we carry these predictions to higher levels of integrative information processing, we should expect the greatest decreases in integrative information processing as optimal load levels are exceeded.

The former assumption appears quite reasonable: excess load, particularly where it must be responded to without delay, can seriously interfere with higher levels of integrated information processing. Moderate underload, however, need not be as problematic. Particularly high-level integrators are quite resourceful and, at least for some time, tend to generate plans

---

[7]As previously defined: subject–predicate–object statement of single meaning on any one content dimension.

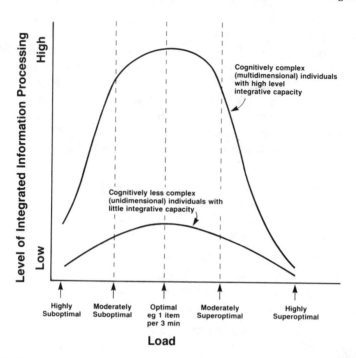

FIGURE 4.3.   Effects of load (an environmental stressor) and cognitive complexity on integrative information processing.

and environmental probes that are to provide the basis for future strategic (planned) actions. In other words, more moderate decreases in integrative activity are expected with moderate underload.

4.22   *High levels of integrative information processing will diminish rapidly with moderate increases of information load beyond the optimal level, and will decrease less rapidly with decreases of information load below the optimal load level.*

Multidimensional information processing, of course, represents only one kind of cognition in response to environmental stressor (e.g., load) impact. There are other cognitive processes that can be generally classified as structural activities as well. Complexity theory predicts stressor impact on these cognitions and their behavioral sequels as well. We have already mentioned that responses to information input that produce output in a direct one-to-one fashion are termed *respondent* or, in case of hostile interaction, *retaliatory.* We propose that:

4.23 As information load increases from low to high levels, respondent behavior should first increase slowly, then quite rapidly after an optimal level of load has been exceeded, reaching a level where information input and respondent output are approximately equivalent. As load increases even further toward very high superoptimal levels, respondent behavior should begin to level off as the individual's maximum response capacity is approached.

Another form of structurally determined behavior tends to be unrelated to the content of information received, but not unrelated to information load levels. It reflects sometimes task-relevant, at other times task-irrelevant cognitions that are not integrated into planned or completed strategy. In other words, these cognitions and their action sequels are not a reflection of differentiative or integrative task-relevant activity. Complexity theorists have termed this behavior *general unintegrated activity.* This form of behavior is expected to be at its lowest level as information load approaches optimality.

4.24 As information load increases from low to high levels, general unintegrated activity will decrease until optimal load levels have been reached and will then increase as load levels rise beyond the optimum.

Another characteristic that appears to have some structurally determined characteristics is risk taking. We propose that:

4.25 Risk taking will increase as information load exceeds optimal load levels.

Risk taking, however, is in part a function of familiarity with a task and of time spent on the task performance. As persons become more familiar with their environment, they are less likely to depend on the environment for cues that affect cognition and performance. That effect is especially prominent in cognitively complex individuals. Where taking risks appears to be a reasonable strategy, the tendency to take risks will be increased. An absence of previous negative reinforcement for risk taking in such a task may play a part as well. We propose that:

4.26 Long-term exposure to a given task environment can increase risk taking. Where risk taking represents a potential strategy, this effect should be particularly prominent in cognitively complex individuals.

As load increases beyond a level where persons involved in a given task would normally function in a multidimensional fashion (i.e., where differentiation is restricted due to excessive overload), one would expect that risk-taking behavior would become excessive and would be focused on fewer aspects of the task. Where, on the other hand, additional dimensions are externally imposed (as may occur, for example, in combat pilots who are about to end their tour of duty and are thinking about going home or in law enforcement officers who are about to retire), risk taking may be sharply reduced:

4.27 *As load increases far beyond the optimal level, risk taking will (especially with time) increase sharply and will tend to become restricted to a single operational mode. However, such risky behaviors may be sharply diminished by the external imposition of another relevant cognitive dimension (see Streufert and Streufert, 1970).*

We have already mentioned the distinction between relevant and irrelevant information. Under normal circumstances, irrelevant information should be ignored in decision making. Unfortunately, however, it is, at times, not ignored. Particulary when information load levels are low, many individuals tend to scan irrelevant information for potential (often remote and highly inappropriate) relevant content:

4.28 *As information load decreases below optimal load levels, increasing amounts of irrelevant information will be processed as partially or entirely relevant, producing potentially inappropriate actions.*

We have stated earlier that less cognitively complex persons are more likely to engage in respondent behavior; they are more cue dependent. We have also stated that cognitively complex persons, particularly those who integrate, tend to be self-sufficient in generating their own cues for differentiation and integration, particularly at low load levels. Taken together, these propositions suggest an increased dependence on irrelevant information by less cognitively complex persons when such information is available or provided. This would be especially the case where irrelevant items represent a large proportion of all information items and/or when information load is relatively high (above optimal). The more self-reliant integrators, however are more likely to incorrectly use irrelevant information under conditions of information deprivation. We propose that:

4.29 *Irrelevant information may be perceived as relevant, particularly by integrators, when information load is suboptimal. Irrelevant information may be perceived as relevant, particularly by less cognitively complex individuals when information load is superoptimal.*

It goes, of course, without saying that optimal (particularly optimally appropriate differentiation and integration activity) information processing would most likely occur when information irrelevance is minimal.

We have previously suggested that differentiated and integrated information processing and their behavioral sequels are not always appropriate. Let us reemphasize that point with regard to the concept of information load. Where load conditions are low and where both task and task environment contain considerable uncertainty and complexity, some initial differentiation–integration is certainly valuable. Probes designed to provide information that could be useful to develop potential long-range strategies can be initiated. Contingent plans can be developed. A time comes, however, when one cannot reasonably proceed in a multidimensional fashion unless meaningful relevant information exists. Integration without adequate information is likely to lead to misconceptions and faulty outcomes. Excellent multidimensional decision makers may have to search and/or wait until sufficient information is available. On the other hand, where rapid responding is necessary, a decision maker may be forced to respond on the basis of limited information or even in unidimensional fashion.

The same holds for conditions of overload. Where large quantities of relevant information are received and cannot be partially ignored, and where decisions must be made quickly, there may not be sufficient time available for differentiation and/or integration to occur. Immediate, even unidimensional, responses may therefore have to take precedence. Integrative processing in situations where those integrations would omit information input that requires responses is—despite its strategy value—often doomed to failure. In other words, the excellent decision maker who is potentially able to differentiate and integrate must be sensitive to the demands of the current environment.

4.30 *The excellent decision maker uses differentiative and integrative processes in cognition and its sequels only when information underload, excessive information overload, or task requirements for instant responding, are not demanding more unidimensional (e.g., respondent) activity.*

Information Orientation, Search, and Utilization

We have already suggested that less cognitively complex individuals are likely more dependent on current information. They tend to cognate and respond more on cue than based on self-generated processes. This dependence is, of course, more or less general across cognitive domains. For example, one might expect a less cognitively complex executive to experience difficulty if he or she is placed in a complex and fluid task situation that contains relatively little information input. Such a person would probably maintain relatively constant or even rigid orientations toward that environment (together with unchanging attitudes and attributions), which may turn out to be inappropriate if the task (even at low information load levels) is nonetheless fluid. One might expect a less cognitively complex executive to deal in such a situation in either or both of two ways: (1) wait for the next item of information to arrive, and/or (2) search quite actively (both directly and via delegation, if possible) for additional information.

Actions of cognitively complex executives in the same situation would be more self-reliant, resulting in some search, but also in the generation of strategic plans. With load increasing toward an optimal level, search activities would decrease for both groups. As highly superoptimal levels of information load are reached, less cognitively complex individuals would have more than enough cues to which they may respond. While they may delegate search, they would typically initiate little, if any, search of their own. Differentiators and integrators, on the other hand, would find that some additional information is needed to develop specific integrated strategic plans (despite information overload). The lack of specific information would result in some—even less frequent—search activity. We propose that:

4.31   *Self-initiated information search should decrease with increasing information load. At low suboptimal load levels, search activity of less cognitively complex persons would exceed search activities by cognitively complex persons. At superoptimal load levels, however, search activity by cognitively complex persons would exceed such activity by less complex persons.*

Information obtained from search activities may, of course, be used in the same fashion as any other information, except that it often represents part of an already initiated strategic sequence. Particularly for cognitively complex individuals, information search efforts are likely to lead to a continuation of strategic actions. It must be noted, however, that information search often adds quantities of information to any existing load level. As a result, excessive search may lead to information overload. This in turn, can diminish differentiative and integrative information processing. That problem is especially significant because the search for information is often considered to be a desirable activity. It is supposedly advantageous to obtain as much information as possible. Unfortunately, the belief in the value of obtaining large quantities of information is often counterproductive. At times, search activities may delay decision making activities beyond a reasonable point or may even be employed as an excuse for avoiding decision commitments. Training personnel toward a more optimal management of information and of information search strategies is, however, possible.

4.32   *Information search may be partly counterproductive, especially if it is likely to lead to considerable information overload. Training for optimal information management, including training for seeking optimal information levels can be highly useful.*

BEHAVIORAL AND COGNITIVE CONTENT

So far we have dealt strictly with structural phenomena—that is, with *how* people think and behave—as opposed to *what* they think. Although we maintain that focus throughout, a slight digression is appropriate here. Structural characteristics of information processing can affect content more or less directly. In general, multidimensionality tends to have moderating effects on cognitive content. Where content (e.g., attitudes) is affected by only one structural dimension, any change in placement of stimuli on that dimension will have a direct effect on any measured outcome. For example, a negatively evaluated person would be treated quite differently from a positively evaluated person where the evaluative dimension is the only dimension governing behavior.

Let us, however, employ a two-dimensional example. Say, an executive negotiates with a business associate. Because he is a moralist, he views that associate, who has been known to have defrauded others, as a morally bad person. However, in his interaction with the associate, he may be able to make a considerable profit in a legitimate transaction. In those terms, he views the associate as good (i.e., useful) in a business sense.[8] Were he a purely unidimensional moralist, he would not likely have dealt with the associate in the first place. As a differentiator he could refer his two views of the associate to respective and separate contexts and could unashamedly maintain his moral convictions of the associate's moral turpitude. As an integrator, however, he could no longer do so. Asked to give an opinion of the associate he would have to combine (in some fashion) his apparently discrepant views, resulting in a less severe condemnation (if any). In other words, a specific content judgment that may appear unidimensional to a person who questioned our executive about his views of the associate would, at least, seem to be less severe.

Similar predictions could certainly be made for just about any content judgment. For example, we might expect that attributions (of causality and responsibility) by a less cognitively complex individual would potentially be severe and cue dependent. Perceptions of and actions toward an out-group

---

[8]Our executive has, in effect, invoked two quite different dimensions: (1) evaluation, i.e., goodness vs. badness, and utility, i.e., usefulness vs. uselessness.

would presumably hinge on salient aspects of the group or on its direct perceived effect. Similar examples may come to the reader's mind.

COMPLEXITY AND PRACTICAL INTELLIGENCE

Work by Sternberg (1984) and others has attempted to go beyond intelligence, as generally conceived and measured, to predict adaptation and interaction with the environment. It is well known that standard measures of (academic) intelligence predict only about 20% of the variance for success in the organizational world, with experience contributing about another 20%. The search for more than half the variance in the prediction of success via some ability, style, or other capacity is certainly legitimate. Sternberg's triarchic theory, for example, considers contextual intelligence, componential intelligence, and a combined contextual–componential aspect of intellectual functioning. The first intelligence component is concerned with adaptation and shaping of the external world, the second with the individual's internal (cognitive) world, and the third with the interaction of both.

Popular publications (e.g., the *New York Times,* July 31, 1984) have discussed the complexity approach of Streufert and associates as though it is identical to Sternberg's practical intelligence. At least at present, the two views need to be considered separately. Indeed, both views attempt to predict complex behavior within the environment as independent of (or in addition to) the effects of standard intelligence. However, at their present levels of development the approaches differ sharply. Sternberg (and a number of others) are hoping to find an overall definition of intelligence that predicts a wide range of intellectual functioning.

In contrast, Streufert and associates have limited their approach to cognitive styles (which may, in the long-run, turn out to play a considerable part in so-called practical intelligence). The more restricted approach of Streufert and associates has, so far, been more productive than the practical intelligence approach. This difference is not surprising for two reasons. First, the work on practical intelligence is relatively new, and second, a more limited approach is likely to bear fruit more quickly. Nonetheless, it should be quite interesting to follow the development of the practical intelligence views over the next few decades. We hope that the multiple, popular biases that have been attached to the word *intelligence,* especially with the prefix *practical*, are not going to hinder those researchers who have chosen to explore that realm of human functioning in a more extensive and certainly worthy fashion.

5

Complexity Theory: The Structure
of Information Processing in Organizations

COMPLEXITY AND ORGANIZATIONS[1]

In Chapter 3, we examined interrelationships among the terms and concepts of the organizational sciences. The largest factor in our analysis reflected the structural concepts of information processing inherent in complexity theory—that is, input, integration, complexity, output, differentiation, information, sensing, decision making, and environment. We have already shown how all of these terms interact in their application to individuals. The terms are equally applicable to complexity-theory-based approaches toward information processing in organizations. They again describe the structural process of translating input into output. At the organizational level, they apply to the cognitions of managers, to the interactions of organizational personnel (e.g., in task groups) and to information flow through organizational structures.

As in the chapter on cognitive complexity in individuals, our emphasis in this chapter is again on the key concepts of complexity theory—that is,

---

[1] A manuscript by Isenberg (1984) was not available to us when this chapter was written. A reading of that paper reveals striking similarities between the observational data of Isenberg and the theory advanced in this chapter. The interested reader is referred to that paper.

differentiation and integration, their antecedents, correlates, and multiple effects. We consider these structural processes as they apply to individual managers who sense, perceive, conceive, and act for the organization, as they have an impact on the interactive efforts of organizational personnel and as they relate to formal or informal relationships among the structural segments of an organization. We consider environmental impacts on organizational information processing (e.g., load) that are generated within an organization and/or impinge on the organization from the outside. Finally, we discuss the effects of various phenomena on an organization's output into the surrounding environment.

A closer look at the terms that loaded highly on Factor 1 in our analysis reveals that they represent a set of antecedents of information processing on one side and a set of terms describing information processing and its sequels on the other. Antecedents are described by the terms environment, input, information, and (where employed as a characteristic of environmental conditions) complexity. The other group of terms refers to processes within the organization: sensing, differentiation, integration, decision making, output and (where employed in the sense of structural information processing characteristics) complexity. A further distinction may be made among the latter set of terms. The concepts *differentiation* and *integration* reflect characteristic information-processing tendencies that may vary from low to high levels. Sensing, decision making, and output are affected by (if not in kind and degree determined by) the characteristic differentiation and integration levels of a manager's or an organization's structure. An understanding of organizational information processing must then proceed from an analysis of differentiation and integration characteristics to their effects on sensing and decision making and so forth. It must also consider how environmental characteristics affect the degree of differentiation and integration, and with it, in turn, decision making and output.

In this chapter, we initially consider the impact that differentiation and integration have on organizational performance—at individual, task group, and organizational levels. Subsequently, we focus on the degree to which environmental impact—either generated from within the organization or generated by external characteristics—can affect organizational differentiation and integration. Further, we consider a number of other phenomena that are affected by structure (e.g., decision making). We also consider the degree to which differentiation–integration levels in organizations are favorable or unfavorable to organizational functions, such as strategic planning, leadership, and creativity.

Some readers may be surprised by the number of divergent phenomena to which we apply complexity theory. Why should one accept that, for example, integration as a structural process can predict such widely disparate organizational functions as decision making, leadership, strategic planning, and creativity? The answer, in our view, resides in the fact that these functions differ primarily in content, but contain considerable similarities in the underlying structure of managerial information-processing activity. For example, where decision making is based on dimensional judgements, complexity theory views it as multidimensional, irrelevant of decision content. Where leadership as a construct concerns several dimensional phenomena, it is also multidimensional, even though the content of the employed dimensions may be different from those used in such other activities as decision making, strategic planning, and creativity. For all of these organizational functions, complexity theory suggests that differentiation and integration are processes that underlie and determine their effectiveness, at least in good part. In other words, differentiation and integration at the organizational level are considered applicable to a wide range of organizational functions. *What* information (i.e., content) is actually processed through organizational structures may vary widely from task to task, setting to setting, time to time, and organization to organization. *How* information is processed, however, describes a common thread along which a majority of organizational activities can be measured and predicted.

PEOPLE

Differentiative and integrative functioning in organizations occurs at least at three levels: (1) at the level of organizational structure per se, whether formal or informal, (2) at the level of interaction among organizational personnel (e.g., in a committee, task group, or informal exchange of thoughts), and (3) at the cognitive level of individuals within an organization. Before delving into organizational structure, let us first take another look at the cognitive complexity of the organizational personnel.

Japanese successes in management have been widely admired by Americans, although detractors have argued that Japanese management methods are merely borrowed from earlier American views, or that successes are only a function of current Japanese culture and cannot last. Whether or not these criticisms are, at least, partly valid remains to be seen. More important, however, is the realization that the Japanese management style, even when it is transferred to the United States, tends to focus on people. The organization is often designed to match its people, and people are trained and even indoctrinated to be compatible with the needs and structure of the organization. The result, in many cases, is a shared organizational culture and *symbiosis* of structure and—often—a symbiosis in level of complexity. The consequences of these practices are evident in the excellent organizational performance of many Japanese industries and frequently in the enhanced levels of job satisfaction among employees.

In contrast, American corporate management often views employees merely as another resource, even (considering labor unions) as a sometimes bothersome resource. In such a situation, a symbiosis between the structural demands of a corporation and the beliefs and information-processing structures of individuals cannot emerge easily. A successful organization, where the components of the production process are integrated, must consider the characteristics and needs of its human resources, at least as comprehensively as its financial or other resources: It is, after all, their interactions (in a wider sense) that determine the overall organizational performance.

Structural matching between organizations and employees should, however, work in both directions. It is not enough to merely train or select employees to match the structural needs of any organization. No two individual employees are the same, and no candidate for a vacant position will have quite the same characteristics as the individual who formerly held that position. Possibly an assembly line worker who engages in a single, simple operation might be replaced with a different worker without serious regard for structural information-processing characteristics. However, even that change in personnel may generate social, motivational, or other imbalances in an existing work team.

When an employee in a responsible decision-making position is replaced, however, one cannot necessarily expect equivalent attitudes, abilities, and cognitive information-processing characteristics. A newly hired manager may, for instance, not adapt easily to the ways of doing things that the predecessor had introduced and used. The new manager may seek different information or have different sets of job priorities. In other words, he or she will function differently.

If it is true (as most research appears to suggest) that individual structural characteristics are quite slow to change, then it may be necessary, at least in some cases and to some extent, to match organizational components to changes in personnel whenever possible. An organization that consists of people must retain a primary focus on people, even, and especially, as individuals within the organization change. The organization that can create an adequate match between organizational and individual information-processing structures should be more successful in today's competitive marketplace.

We suggest:

5.1 *Optimal organizational functioning is most likely to occur when organizational structure and information-flow characteristics are well matched with the structural information-processing characteristics of responsible organizational personnel. This match can be achieved through either selection and/or training of personnel and/or through adaptive changes in organizational characteristics.*

Individual members of organizations may or may not understand, support, or initiate adaptive changes in an organization. In many cases, a long-term manager will insist that the organization's culture requires that things be done in a certain way. This rigidity across time can have detrimental downsteam effects. Ideally, the interrelationship between organization and manager should consist of give and take or, in our terminology, reintegration. Where managers carry what Weick (1979) has called "mechanical pictures of organizations" in their heads, they will not likely be able to adapt to necessary change. In the terminology of complexity theory, these mechanical pictures imply (at simpler levels) a unidimensional organizational perspective, or (at more complex levels) an excessively differentiated or hierarchically integrated view of the organization and its functioning. The result can retard badly neded structural and information flow chnages for a given organizational system.

Unfortunately, mechanical views of organizational functioning are often shared among responsible managers whose way of doing things may, in previous situations, have been quite successful. Where the majority of the management or the entire management of an organization shares views that are neither flexible not integrated, inertia tends to develop (see Pettigrew, 1973). As we discuss, such inertia can generate maladaptive organizational performance, absence of strategy or faulty strategy and, in the long-run, failure.

5.2 *Where organizations must function adaptively in fluid task environments, lack of flexible integrative functioning by managers may lead to rigid organizational processes (inertia) and to potential failure.*

We have emphasized that people differ. Some are able to integrate; others have considerable difficulty in perceiving and using more than a single dimension. Some are flexible, others tend to be rigid. Most moderate to large size organizations can find niches for a variety of people. Different jobs require diverse individual characteristics. Particularly where a person's potential contributions are rare but useful to an organization, that person's skills can and should be used. For example, the organization should use the services of high-level flexible integrators at appropriate places in the organization where their talents are especially useful.

There are a number of additional characteristics that are related to flexible integrative complexity and likely equally important. Take, for example, creativity[2]. Most organizations have much to gain from the potential ideas that may be generated within the organization—ideas that emerge from individuals or small groups of people. It is well known that the majority of such ideas do not pan out. It is well known that the development of ideas may require considerable time and resources. Some managers would argue that the majority of creative efforts simply represent losses of effort, resources, and personnel. Yet, the small minority of creative efforts that can generate vastly profitable products or services may be well worth an overall organizational investment in all kinds of creative activities. Unfortunately, the manager with a mechanical view, the management with inertia who cannot differentiate or integrate (or does so excessively or hierarchically) may not realize the potential of these development efforts.

To state it differently, people are not only a resource for effort, they are also a resource for a variety of other actions that may be of considerable long-range benefit to an organization—if the organization knows how to use these resources. One way of using creativity in organizations that function in less than flexible integrative fashion is the champion concept that Peters and Waterman have discussed in some detail. Other methods employ a more open and less precisely structured and controlled organizational system. Whichever method is used, a person with a particular characteristic that may be of value to an organization should (and usually can) be protected from unidimensional demands for measurable output.

We have talked about the indoctrination of personnel by Japanese companies. Indeed, even in American companies, new employees must adapt to the existing culture of an organization. Yet, that indoctrination may be viewed as occupational socialization or as acculturation to the organization. In other words, it may be less overtly intentional and may not necessarily be understood to conflict with Western and especially American views of individual freedom. Nonetheless, even on the basis of an American point of view, much can be done to motivate employees toward absorbing organizational culture and adapting to unique organizational structure and information flow. Happy and satisfied employees are considered desirable and, in fact, may, in some cases, be more likely to contribute to their organizations. (Recall the example of Delta Airlines employees buying their company a new plane.)[3] However, to be happy, employees must be treated not as a resource of labor but as partners within the organization.

---

[2]The concept of creativity and its relationship to organizational complexity are discussed in greater detail later in this chapter.

[3]Note, however, that research generally has not substantiated a simple positive relationship between satisfaction and performance.

A number of psychological concepts come to mind that have been shown to predict not only behavior, but even health (see Pomerleau and Brady, 1979; Prokop and Bradley, 1981; Simons and Pardes, 1981; Weiss, Herd, and Fox, 1981). Take, for example, control. A person who feels that control over his or her life resides outside of the self is often both unhappy and likely to experience illness—resulting in more frequent absenteeism and less effective job performance.

A person who is reinforced for good performance, however, (with primarily nonreinforcement for less than adequate performance) is much more likely to perform well than is a person who is punished or continuously reminded that he or she has not reached a prescribed goal.

A person who is mismatched in belief content and/or information-processing structure with organizational task demands is less likely to perform adequately than a person who has found a match between his or her information-processing structure and the characteristics of the task environment. Clearly, it would take volumes to discuss the various people characteristics that may be of importance in organizational job settings. Our purpose is merely an emphasis on people as a dimension to be considered and integrated with other concerns when organizational planning and decision making occurs.

5.3   *People, their respective abilities and needs, should be considered and used as unique resources during organizational planning and decision making. An integrated view of people as partners in an organization is more likely to lead to organizational success than a view of people as basic resources that are otherwise unrelated to organizational outcomes.*

WHAT IS ORGANIZATIONAL COMPLEXITY?

Some Necessary Limits on the Present Discussion

Without question, organizational researchers or consultants who focus on a particular organization will need to consider other organizational components beyond those covered in our structural approach. Volumes of research and theory have covered various relevant content approaches (see the handbooks of Dunnette, 1976, 1983, and Lorsch, in press). We recognize that superior organizational performance does not depend on structure alone: it is, for example, affected by resources, skills, and knowledge of organizational members, by motivations of personnel, organizational culture, and leadership, to mention a few topics. It depends on belief systems, attitudes, and tendencies to attribute responsibility and causality. Some antecedents of performance are strictly content based; others are determined by both content and structure; and some are generally structural. We will not deal with all antecedents of oranizational success; however, we will provide examples of organizational functioning where structure represents the major source of organizational outcomes and where it is a major force in its interactions with organizational content variables.

In this chapter, we are considering the structural characteristics of individual managers, of groups within the organization and the structural functioning of the organization as a whole. This three-fold approach has considerable value: as stated previously, individuals are the basic units of any organization. Their structural characteristics, therefore, have a broad influence on information processing in their organization. In addition, there are numerous similarities in characteristic structural information processing by individuals, groups, and organizations. We do not wish to mislead the reader: It is not our contention that organizational, group, and individual information-processing structures are one-and-the-same, occurring merely at macro and micro levels. Instead, there are likely to be major differences as well as similarities.

For example, the cognitive domains encountered in individuals may be considered to be similar (but by no means identical) to organizational units such as departments and divisions. Unfortunately there are, at present, no data that delineate structural similarities with some precision. In the absence of such data, we suggest the use of a similar template for considering information-processing characteristics of individuals, of groups, and of organizations. In the event that future data should indicate considerable dissimilarities, some of the views derived from our similar but not identical conceptualization may require rethinking.

When we speak about information processing, we do not intend to suggest, as some research has done, that organizational input is directly, and without additional or secondary effects, translated into organizational output structure variables. Clearly the processes involved are more complicated. Organizations are continuing systems, consisting of individuals, groups, departments and so forth that scan information, process it, and generate output. Organizations may translate output back into scanning or direct information search. They are capable of modifying internal processing by changes in scanning behavior, by restructuring information flow, and by achieved output levels. Processing and output may be, at various times, partly independent yet interacting phenomena. Even without concurrent input, organizational processing and output may continue. In other words, we view the organizational input–processing–output relationships as interactive rather than necessarily sequential and as potentially changing with both time and organizational experience.

In much of this chapter, we consider organizational information processing (i.e., structural phenomena within the organizational setting) in some detail. However, we focus on only a few organizational output characteristics, primarily those that are closely related to and determined by structural characteristics (i.e., decision making, strategy formation and creativity). We also attempt to clarify the meaning of intuition in managerial behavior.

An even more severe restriction must be placed on our treatment of input variables. In the previous chapter we limited our discussion of input to individuals to the load variable. That restriction was justified with two arguments: First, a wider discussion of a variety of input conditions would expand this book beyond the present scope. Second, existing data suggest that (at least at the individual level) many other input variables are quite similar to the load variable (in effects on performance) or may be reduced to load effects. Equivalent data that would suggest a potential primacy of the load variable in organizational settings are not available. Nonetheless, in the absence of helpful information, we again select information load as our primary example. Information load is ubiquitous for both individuals and organizations.

Adequate Organizational Information Processing: From Input to Output

From an organizational perspective, let us define *load* as information that enters the organizational structure. The information may have been generated by scanning (see Pfeffer and Salancik, 1978) or some other form of information search, or it may be part of the normal information flow into the organization. Information may be verbal or it may be in the form of a product of service translated into verbal representation. The sensed information must be processed, distributed (appropriately), and acted on. These processes can be complicated because an organization functions both at an individual and at a collective level. It continues to function even though individual members of the organization come and go and even when organizational units (departments, divisions, and so forth) are added or eliminated. One might say that in receiving and dealing with information, the organization understands its task environment in some fashion. That understanding is concurrent as long as the filtering process does not eliminate information that is erroneously considered unimportant or is mismatched with organizational culture or assumptions. To the degree to which relevant, undistorted, and sufficiently complete information is distributed within an organization, the potential for flexible integration of that information exists.

Adequate integration at the organizational level requires that organizational segments to which information is relevant do, in fact, receive relatively accurate information. It further requires that additional relevant information can be sought and obtained where the current understanding of a situation is inadequate. It requires that organizational segments employ personnel who are capable of obtaining, sensing, and perceiving relevant information, understanding the content of the information, and are able to view the information in terms of its potential implications for the organizational segment's purpose, goals, resources, capacities, and more. These individuals should be able to employ, where needed, sufficient cognitive differentiation and integration to understand and, where possible, predict the short-range and long-range implications of the information. Adequate processing requires that levels of uncertainty generated by the receipt of information be decreased when possible, but that remaining uncertainty levels be accepted as given and used in tentative or contingent planning.

Adequate integrative processes at the organizational level further imply that organizational segments not only are open to information that arrives from outside of the organization, but also must remain (at least for periods of time) open to input from other organizational segments. In other words, organizational boundaries and segment boundaries must be sufficiently permeable. This openness involves both receptivity to and search for information across organizational segments as well as the ability to interpret information generated by other segments in terms of the conceptualization by that segment (at the individual level we might have talked about empathy rather than sympathy). Unfortunately, that kind of organizational empathy is not always achieved. Frequently, of course, information received from another segment or from some outside source is distorted. Such distortions are based on preconceptualizations of the supposed interests, intents, or error-proneness of the information source, no matter whether that source is located inside or outside of the organization. Distortions can feed the mechanical views and organizational inertia mentioned previously. They can be exceedingly detrimental to a meaningful integration process across organizational segments.

At a higher level of management, organizational integration implies an overall interpretation of events, of their effects on organizational segments, as well as a consideration of their interactive consequences for the organization today and in the future. It further implies development of an (at least partially) shared understanding of current events, of their meaning and implications for organizational functioning, and for organizational goals across time.

Adequate integrative processes in an organization require the development of goal-based plans of action(s) and the implementation of plans without losing sight of the effects that these actions might have on all aspects of organizational functioning. However, sufficient alternate options to allow for changes in strategies or even plans, if and when present actions are not as appropriate as (in the presence of some uncertainty) they might have appeared, must also exist.

In other words, adequate integrative organizational information processing requires that integration of current information with other organizational phenomena occur at appropriate levels throughout the organization, and that decisions made at the highest appropriate levels within the organization be based on multiple integrations at lower levels.

Integrated organizational functioning, particularly if it has existed for some time and has proven to be successful, may become reflected in the formal or informal organizational structure (via characteristic interactions among organizational segments such as departments, departmental subunits, and people). Information flow through an organization will often follow these structural channels, generally improving but potentially also rigidifying (in terms of a hierarchical integrative pattern) communication among the various segments of an organization. The extent that information flow follows a differentiated and integrated pattern that matches the informal or formal organizational structure, information processing may become more effective. In addition, where the structure of an organization and the information flow through that structure matches the cognitive structure of relevant individuals in the organization (e.g., where managers understand and empathize with integrations that take place at various locations in an organization), the organization should become increasingly adaptable to both external demands and to internal changes.[4]

In summary: to study organizational complexity, we need to foucs on the physical structure of the organization, the information-processing characteristics of its personnel, both as individuals and in groups, on information acquisition techniques, the flow of information through the organization and the relevance of organizational outputs (e.g., decisions) for the entire organization, its people, and its products. Most of all, we need to determine whether integrated information processing, where appropriate, is indeed used across the various levels of an organization and across the organizational processes we have described.

Organizational Differentiation versus Integration

Discrepancies in the degree of differentiation and integration can, of course, occur across and within various organizational levels. On first thought, one might express the hope that differentiation and integration

---

[4]Adaptation as (in part) a function of informational complexity has been extensively discussed by Lawrence and Dyer, 1983.

would occur equally (and appropriately) across all levels. Can such even distributions of organizational complexity be expected?

At the individual level, one might have wished for a relatively even distribution of differentiative and integrative capacity across cognitive domains. But, are such even distributions actually needed? An individual may never encounter stimuli from remote domains that require integrative cognitive activity. Worse, integrative processes might, in some cases, be counterproductive, paticularly where an individual's culture or job environment is incompatible with multidimensional functioning. Similar arguments may be advanced for segments of organizations. There probably are sections where internal procedures are best carried out in a more or less unidimensional or, at least, in a hierarchically complex fashion. We may, for example, not want all procedures used by an accounting group to become flexibly integrated. In other words, differentiation and integration can be highly useful in an organizational setting, but can, for some organizational segments and under some task conditions, be misapplied or inappropriate. In some cases, unidimensional functioning may be optimal for certain employees of an organizational segment, while multidimensional functioning would be preferred for the segment's manager as he or she interacts with (and needs to empathize with) managers of other parts of the same organization.

Serious mismatches in complexity among organizational segments (especially their managers) can be quite problematic. Consider, for instance, an organization where incoming information is scanned, analyzed, and distributed in an integrative fashion in line with known organizational requirements. This way of treating information may be used to generate strategic options with both short- and long-run implications. Imagine, however, a situation where the unidimensional senior managers of the organization ignore this valuable information to focus on only a single dimension: for example, current profit. Ignoring the integrative efforts that occurred at lower levels in the organization not only would represent a potential waste of time, energy, and capacity, but also would likely lead to considerable frustration among organizational personnel.

We propose that:

5.4 *Integrative information processing at the organizational level requires: (a) that all organizational segments to which specific information is relevant receive that information in sufficient detail and without serious distortion, (b) that additional information be sought and appropriately distributed where understanding of a current or future task environment is inadequate, (c) that organizational segments employ individuals who are able to comprehend the meaning and content of received information and are able to integrate that information, as appropriate, in terms of the purposes, goals, and capacities of the relevant organizational subunit,*

(d) that levels of uncertainty be reduced, where possible, and that remaining uncertainty be channeled toward the adoption of alternate strategies and contingent planning in case of unexpected negative outcomes,

(e) openness to available information both from outside the organization and from other organizational segments without distortion of information to fit existing beliefs and assumptions,

(f) strategic interpretations of events, of organizational responses to the events, and of potential effects of such events both on various organizational segments and on the organization as a whole,

(g) development of a method for an (at least partially) shared understanding of the meaning of events and their implications for current and future organizational functioning, for organizational goals and their implications for various organizational segments,

(h) developing and implementing strategic plans designed to optimize productivity and goal orientation, without losing sight of the effects that these plans might have on all aspects of organizational functioning.

Without question, these processes describe differentiative and integrative activity, however,

5.5   The degree of differentiated and integrated activity within organizational segments should be appropriate to, and should potentially be restricted with regard to specific task requirements.

Finally, we suggest that:

5.6   Mismatch in structural characteristics, particularly in integrative information processing among diverse organizational segments is likely detrimental to organizational functioning.

SOURCES OF ORGANIZATIONAL COMPLEXITY

Let us be more specific about the impact of organizational complexity variables. One way to consider the issue is to follow a hypothetical organization through its growth process. How does organizational personnel in such a situation translate their own individual information-processing characteristics into organizational structure and organizational information flow? How can the cognitive complexity characteristics of managers be translated into and be matched with organizational information-processing systems? Will the capacity to differentiate and integrate, will the creativity that may be evident in the strategies and goals of young and small companies find their way into equivalent processes within the evolving and growing (see March, 1980; Weick, 1979) organization?

In tracing the development of complexity in organizations, let us eliminate from consideration those companies that are formed on the basis of some recognized demand (e.g., companies where an inventor is able to produce a product that others cannot easily duplicate). Such a company may do well until the patent runs out or someone else invents an even better product for the same purpose. Rather, we consider more typical organizations that are based on less insular ideas, organizations that may expect competitors and changes in the environment. Let us view the latter kind of organization in its early beginnings.

Often a single person, or possibly a few managers, may try their skills on a new product in an environment that may or may not be receptive to the efforts of their organization. To be successful, these managers may have to be flexible, innovative, and even creative. They may have to experiment, to adapt, to modify, to reconsider and to realign. Initially, their organization may be quite simple. One or a few persons often perform most tasks, regardless of their diversity. Although outside consultant(s) or worker(s) may be brought in, such individuals typically have little effect on the structural characteristics of the new organization. Trial and error or experimentation may be a necessary ethic. At this level, the organizational structure may look unidimensional: In such situations, the differentiative and integrative handling of information flow from initial sensing to final output is often handled only and specifically by the few managing people who define the organization. Few, if any, differentiations exist among organizational functions.

As the new organization becomes successful, it may grow. Individuals now begin to specialize in diverse tasks. Departments and other organizational units may emerge. Power differentials among employees may become evident. The structure of the organization is beginning to become differentiated. Information is now directed toward some relevant person or group for processing and potential decision making. With a differentiated structure, a differentiation of organizational views and conceptualizations on various relevant topics may also emerge. Unique ways of viewing and of dealing with the environment and even with aspects of the organization itself may develop. For some time, this novel division of effort may work quite well.

Yet, likely pitfalls can exist in differentiation. Where division of labor becomes excessive and where communications among differentiated subunits of an organization decrease, information flow can be hindered and decision making may become fractionated. Even if individual managers with separate responsibilities effectively employ cognitively complex strategies (e.g., differentiative and integrative to *their* specific departments or sub-units), the overall effect on the organization might be very small. Without integrative effort across their areas of responsibility, resulting decisions and/or strategies may well be mismatched or at cross-purposes.

A frequent problem in newly differentiated (and, unfortunately, also in some older, but insufficiently, integrated) organizations occurs when manager A makes a decision that may be ideal for A's department but could have disastrous consequences for the department headed by manager B. A number of effects may occur. Manager B may object. If so, manager B may be calling for a rudimentary form of integration or convergence, which Weick (1979) has characterized as an "act of organizing." Another possibility is that B may not notice, may not care, or may be so unidimensionally focused on the internal workings of his or her organizational segment that he or she does not recognize what A is doing until it is too late. A third possiblity is that manager B may accept some unidimensional policy (for example: "the only concern we have this year is profit," which the CEO of the company has recently formulated), a policy that is compatible with the decision of manager A but detrimental to the department headed by B. If B heads R&D operations, he may, under these conditions, have to cut back drastically on product development. If the unidimensional policy followed by the CEO and by manager A remains in place—and is accepted (or at least submitted to) by B, their company may, over the long-run, succumb to the more research-oriented competition as older products fail to sell and newer ones are not available.

Different points of view by different managers of departments or entire departments are similar in concept to different and partially incompatible dimensional views of an individual. Within an individual, diverse dimensionality (and its perceptual and behavioral outcomes) may remain dormant because the cognitive domains across which the diversity exists might remain unrelated. For organizations, however, this is less often the case. Organizational subunits, at least in small and midsize companies, are designed to cooperate and coordinate their activities. Where they operate at cross-purposes, problems usually become evident after some minimal amount of time. Diverse points of view and incompatible policies or actions demand resolution. One kind of resolution is to follow a single unidimensional fixed orientation, often imposed from above. Another, based solely on differentiation, is to follow one view at a time, or for a particular kind of organizational problem. Today, manager A may get his or her way. Some other time, manager B may be more lucky. This year profit may be emphasized. However, as profit drops sharply because there is less of a market for the old standby product, an influx of funds to R&D may occur. Such a differentiated approach may be (but is not necessarily) preferable to a unidimensional emphasis on a single overriding approach to management.

Unidimensional (where the dimension used is appropriate) or differentiated decision making may work well when the organizational environment is simple and easily understood, or where the organization is producing a product or service that is in demand and cannot be duplicated. In other words, such approaches may work well during a time period where the external environment eagerly accepts the organization's output. Temporary successful implementation of such processes, however, may also lead to rigidity in an organization's structure and to inflexibility of associated information processing. The result can be a structurally inadequate organizational system that cannot adapt easily (or has to go through major upheavals when it tries to adapt) when external demands or marketplace characteristics change.

Let us assume, however, that our two managers, with their diverse views and purposes, ultimately resolve their differences. Their process of reaching convergence and its outcome (Weick, 1979) may, however, differ widely. At a simple level, the two managers might compromise. Each of them gets something. In such a situation, the organization is experiencing a minimally multidimensional approach to management. Although this approval is primitive, in part because the two managers may not understand (and may not care about) the reasons for each other's views, compromise is, at least, a starting point. Once managers begin to discuss their intents and decisions, the opportunity for low-level flexible integration has a chance to develop. In fact, the sometimes aggravated question "Why should I bother with you and your ideas" (whether actually stated or not) may provide the very basis for integration as an established organizational process. One manager's explanation of why he or she cannot go along with a proposed policy may actually engender some understanding of the requirements of the disagreeing organizational unit. That, in turn, can lead toward the development of a more mutually acceptable form of decision making, and with it mutually acceptable strategy development.

Where an individual manager frequently disagrees with existing policy or standard procedures, his or her views may be disregarded, based on unidimensional rejection of divergent orientations. However, the existence of frequent objections from a manager may also tend to bring the disparate orientation of his or her department—and the reasons for the disagreement—into focus. As a result, other managers may learn not to make a relevant decision "without talking to George first" to assure that he does not object to their plans. At this point, a new differentiation within the structure that serves the flow of information through the organization has been generated, and the consideration of the disparate manager's views provide a potential basis for integration.

With the development of low-level integration, the capabilities of various organizational subunits can become interrelated to enhance effectiveness of organizational functioning. The specific meaning of *effectiveness*, as employed here, may be multiple and can change across time. Strategies and goals may be formulated, tested, and reformulated. Interactions among organizational segments (whether departments, informal groups, or individuals) may shift from task to task or from time to time. Both formal and informal information-flow patterns through the organization may begin to be used. The organization may begin to function in a more flexible and adaptive fashion—in part because the cognitively complex cognitions of individual managers have been communicated across organizational segments and have been matched by equivalent or similar differentiated and integrated processes in the organizational structure and in organizational information flow. Further, the integrated functioning of the organization may be enhanced by the development of concepts that have become part of a common organization-specific language and/or common organizational culture (see the "old friends" argument of Simon, 1979). The key is communication of integrated views across the boundaries of organizational subunits.

Effective integrative cooperation requires that managers and their subordinates both communicate and understand the need for an integrated processing. A cognitively less complex manager who constantly insists that he or she is right (no matter what) (i.e., a manager who employs a unidimensional approach to organizational problems) will tend to be ineffective in an otherwise integrated organizational system. Where the approach taken by this manager happens to be successful—either by chance or because the task environment for this specific decision is simple—he or she may receive considerable credit for excellence in decision making. However, if the decision turned out to be less than optimal or detrimental (which is likely to be the case for unidimensional decision making in complex and fluid environments) that manger may be rapidly replaced. Even success in the short run may not be an adequate defense against likely failure in the long run.

Of course, the astute manager knows that the world is not simple. He or she presumably understands that it is short-sighted to operate an organization on the basis of a single (unidimensional) principle. After all, numerous external and internal events, their specific characteristics, their potential consequences and, most of all, their interactions with organizational characteristics must be considered.

Managers who are high-level integrators not only understand the integrated functioning of their organization on the basis of multiple potentially interrelated factors, they also consider information shifts and conceptual changes across time. They are able to develop multistep contingent strategies without losing sight of general flexible goals (see the section on strategy in this chapter) and are likely to lead the organization into a highly integrated period of functioning. Yet these same managers are not people who can honestly tell you exactly what will happen tomorrow, what goals the organization will achieve next year or next decade. All they can do (if they are speaking truthfully) is to generate a tentative estimate. The same holds for the many separate decisions they must make. They can only reach guesstimates—and the degree of guess is in part dependent on the level of remaining uncertainty. In part, use of guesstimates and fuzzy definitions of distant goals allows them to be more open to novel and potentially inconsistent information, to continue to flexibly integrate actions and sequential problems, and to adapt their organization to successive changes in task environments. It is these same managers who can lead the organization through periods of growth that defy rigidification and inertia as structural management properties.

To many, such an apparently loose management style may imply indecisiveness. These critics might raise the question whether it is not possible for managers to assemble the various components that underlie organizational decision making into a meaningful system and to derive orderly and utterly rational (they might also say, maximally correct) decisions. A manager who is looking for a single correct solution to organizational problems may well agree. However, the multiple considerations that may be important in deriving the correct solution must all be sorted and weighted and related to one another. What form should such an optimally weighted solution take? How can one appropriately integrate the various aspects and interactions that exist in a given situation? If one could accurately specify all their relative probabilities and effects on organizational functioning that should be considered in a given situation; if one could mathematically describe all the possible interactions among these events and their effects on organizational functioning, components and outcomes, then one should be able to develop an algorithm to test each potential decision before it is made. One would then be able to compare potential decisions and select the one that is most likely to lead toward organizational success. If such a process were possible and selected, the decision makers who are seeking the most correct solution via a mathematical decision process would be engaging in a form of organizational decision making which, in the terminology of complexity theory, is based on hierarchical integration.

Many managers and management training institutions have championed this form of programmed decision making. After all, if all events that might affect future outcomes and their interactions were known, and if one were strictly rational (logical might be a better word, particularly where deductive logic is used[5]), then many event-driven uncertainties could be predicted and eliminated. Managerial decision making by supposedly imperfectly functioning human brains could make room for the (most of the time) perfectly functioning and much faster genius of the computer.

Such arguments have led to the widespread use of computer-based management decision-making algorithms, designed to achieve optimal outcomes. Indeed, hierarchical integration and the computer models reflecting that process should work: (1) when unanticipated changes in the environment will not occur, (2) when all contributing factors in the organization's environment, the organization itself, and in the likely outcome are well known, and (3) when the precise interactive effects of these factors are sufficiently understood to be specified as unchanging parameters. Where that is the case (through the use of high-speed computers and the elaborate mathematical models that decision theorists and mathematicians provide for us), decision making in complex organizational settings should be easy.

But is it? Many a theorist and researcher has strongly—and indeed, quite appropriately—disagreed with the effectiveness of the rational hierarchical integrative approach. Hierarchical integration is based on the inflexible classification and placement of stimuli on specific dimensions and on the assumption of a fixed or, at least, predetermined relationship among these dimensions across situations, tasks, and time. Through the use of hierarchically integrative principles, a reductionistic and analytic simplification of the decision-making process is attempted. When additional environmental or task-relevant events occur, are sensed and considered, they will have to be viewed and organized in terms of specified preexisting parameter characteristics and interactions. With this approach, mathematically based decision theory and its applications are employed in lieu of flexible integration.

An excellent comment on mathematically based techniques was provided by Wohl (1981). This author stated that

> Decision theorists have tended toward prescriptive definitions based on the concept of a decision as a selection from given alternatives, while commanders and corporate executives have tended toward descriptive definitions involving statements such as "It seemed to be the best thing to do at the time". . . . Nearly all classical decision theory, including its statistical (Raiffa and Schaiffer, 1961) and sequential (Wald, 1947) branches assume that the options are given. Optimal choice usually has to do with the degree of uncertainty in the information input, the relative costs and gains involved in each of the possible choices (including the cost of either waiting for more information or taking action to decrease

---

[5]See our discussion of rationality in Chapters 1 and 4.

uncertainty) or the "utility function" of the decision maker (i.e., the relative value or weight subjectively assigned to each of the alternatives; for example, see Edwards, (1954a, 1954b, 1965). The preponderance of work in decision theory has concentrated on techniques for option *selection* with little research on those portions of the process which are of greatest interest—namely, the *creation*, *evaluation*, and *refinement* of both hypotheses (i.e., what is the situation) and options (i,e., what can be done about it.) [emphasis in original].

We should emphasize, as stated earlier, that decision-making situations exist where a hierarchical approach can be useful and appropriate. Keen and Scott-Morton (1978) have described three different categories of decisions that require diverse approaches: (1) fully structured decisions that may be delegated or automated, (2) semistructured decisions where part of the problem can be solved by rational approaches (e.g., via computer assistance) but other components require human cognitive intervention, and (3) unstructured decisions where dimensions of the problems involved are poorly or not at all understood and human intuition[6] and judgment are required.

It is our thesis that dimensional human judgment and intuition are best applied via a flexible integrative cognitive process. Let us return to the arguments of Wohl (1981). That author argues

> Where options are clearly prescribed and input data are of high quality, a system can be designed which directly "maps" input data into output or response so that only key observables are considered in the mapping process (e.g., as with a highly trained pilot carrying out an emergency procedure). Where options are more or less clearly prescribed but input data are of low quality (e.g., as in military intelligence analysis), a premium is placed upon creation and testing of hypotheses (e.g., where is the enemy and what is he doing?). Where input data are of high quality but options are open-ended (e.g., as in the Cuban missle crisis), a premium is placed upon creation and analysis of options and their potential consequences (e.g., if we bomb the missile sites or if we establish a full fledged naval blockade, what will the Russians do?) (Allison, 1971).

Wohl also considers situations where input data are of marginal quality and where decision options are open ended: settings that clearly require complex flexible integrative activity.

The greater the uncertainties, the less the potential for providing predetermied solutions, and, finally, the greater the number of issues, strategic steps and/or length of time involved, the greater is the necessity for a flexible highly integrated approach to organizational functioning. Clearly, the greater the number of units within an organization that may be affected by decisions, the greater the necessity for their involvement in an integrative

---

[6]We consider the concept, *intuition*, later in this chapter.

decision process. If, in addition, it is not clearly known what the consequences of potential organizational actions might be (which, in turn, might be quite different in implication for the various organizational components), the consideration of the views of those components might be even more vital.

Given a fluid, uncertain organizational environment that requires successive adaptations to unanticipated external and internal events, an organization that uses differentiated and integrated decision processes should be considerably more successful than its less differentiated and integrated counterparts. We propose:

5.7 *Differentiation and integration in young (and small) organizations that function in highly competitive environments are often based entirely on the cognitive differentiation and integration of their managers.*

5.8 *Increasing organizational size may lead to increased specialization and with it to a more differentiated organizational structure. Differentiation without integration may, however, lead to fractionalization and inadequate organizational functioning.*

5.9 *Recognition of disparate tendencies in different departments of an organization may lead to more effective communication and rudimentary low-level integration, potentially first via compromise and later at a joint-purpose level.*

5.10 *Where integrative processes become fixed (hierarchical), organizations are less able to deal with unexpected novelty and can no longer adapt adequately to changes in their environment.*

5.11 *Existence of considerable uncertainty, absence of adequate predetermined solutions to organizational problems, multiple problems with multiple effects on organizational components, and flux in organizational environments require organizational functioning at highly integrative levels. Where such conditions prevail, an extensive understanding of views and needs of the organization's structural units and of their interplay within the "Gestalt" of the overall organization is required.*

5.12 *Highly integrated organizational functioning implies the consideration of information on a sufficient number of dimensions (whether obtained via openness to events or via scanning and search). It requires the integrative consideration of that information across organizational segments (ranging from the level of individuals to divisions), the conceptualization of both the present situation and future anticipated conditions (including strategies and goals) and the use of the integrative processes in flexible and contingent decision making. It requires the consideration of interactions among these dimensions to chart the course toward optimal outcomes. It requires periods of openness to information on all relevant dimensions and it requires the capacity to close temporarily for new or revised conceptualization and, at times, for decision making. Where applicable, it requires subsequent reconsideration and corrective action, if needed. Finally, it requires extensive communication among organizational units and the development of a shared but flexible organizational culture that is based on integrative processes that continue to be established, adaptively modified, and used.*

Differentiated and integrated information processing is often highly visible in the characteristics of organization cultures. When we speak about *organizational culture*, we are referring to a shared set of beliefs, behavior patterns, concepts, and communications that are more or less unique to persons who are members of a specific organization. Such a culture may develop naturally or may be forced on an organization and/or its members by internal or externally imposed constraints. The culture may be encompassing or limited. Whichever form it takes, it is likely best understood by those who are members of that organization.

When Peters and Waterman (1982) discuss guiding beliefs of organization, they speak about one aspect of organizational culture. They emphasize that organizations with the best defined and most quantified belief systems often do not perform as well as organizations with broader, less precise and more qualitative (rather than quantitative) beliefs and values. From our point of view, their observations are not surprising. Where a company, for example, has only a single guiding belief (e.g., that profit should be maximized at all costs) it functions on a unidimensional basis. All components of the structure are directed towrd that single goal. Where an organizational culture contains closely related and quantified values, we may be dealing with the culture of a hierarchically integrated organizational system. Neither is optimally effective in a complex and fluid environment.

In contrast, more qualitative (i.e., less precise) cultural views with broader, more qualitative perspectives permit alternate interpretations that permit openness in the face of novelty and fluidity.[7] More qualitative views also suggest that goals are less precisely defined—that is, they are more general in nature. That generality or fuzziness may be even more pronounced where organizational goals are considered that are multiple steps

[7]If we conceive of the United States of America in organizational terms, we see that the looseness and qualitative character of the U.S. Constitution has allowed for interpretations of that legal document to change with the changing needs of this society over many years, resulting in adaptation, yet in stability of the American form of government and of the national culture as a whole.

away from realization. This apparent lack of precision is highly useful to the flexible integrating manager. It allows the interpretation of unexpected and inconsistent input via reintegrations, resulting in possible modifications of strategies, plans, and goals that are adaptive to changes in the environment. As goals are approached (i.e., as they are fewer and fewer steps away from realization), they would, of course become less general and less fuzzy. Greater clarity is now possible because more information about the antecedents of achieving those goals is now known and the arrival of inconsistent information has, therefore, become less likely and/or frequent. In other words, the organizational culture may be redefined to include clearer goal structures as goals are about to be achieved—with potentially new and fuzzy goals added that are still years from realization.

Organizational culture is not restricted to goals and belief systems, of course. It involves many other aspects, such as fluidity of communication among persons and departments (including informality vs. formality), and the sharing of concepts that allows members of different organizational segments to empathize with each other. We do not wish to discuss organizational culture extensively because others have done so in considerable detail (e.g., Pettigrew, 1979; Van Maanen and Schein, 1979). We want to emphasize, however, that the cultural characteristics of an organization can have major impact on the degree to which integrated information processing is possible an achieved throughout the organizational structure.

INTUITION AND MANAGERIAL FUNCTIONING

We have discussed some characteristics of differentiative and integrative processes in organizations, their development, and their effects. Before we consider their relationships to other partly related concepts, such as leadership and the use of strategy, we explore the concept of *intuition* as a basic component of organizational management. Sometimes that phenomenon has been applauded, sometimes criticized as evidence of irrational behavior. Managers use intuition when tasks are difficult, when past answers are not immediately available, when uncertainty is considerable. Intuition, on the surface, appears to be synthetic, supposedly irrational rather than an analytic rational process. What is intuition?

Researchers and observers alike have used the term *intuition* to describe a cognitive process that cannot be easily conceptualized, described, or quantified. One may raise the question whether lack of understanding of cognitive processes has led to the use of this rather vague and descriptive term or whether the described process itself is vague and unknowable. If we ask managers why and how they reached conclusions, they are likely to tell us more about the components of that process and about the interrelationships among those components than an outside observer would be able to do. To the outside observer, only his or her conceptualizations of those cognitive components exist, and only the given interrelationship among those components. In other words, the observer, in many cases, cannot empathize with the supposedly intuitive process. Even the manager who engages in intuition may not be able to do so. We suggest that our intuitive manager may be involved in the differentiation and the integration of events, concepts, organizational components, and so forth. He or she may be trying out a number of interrelationships among differentiated aspects of a situation or task until he or she suddenly arrives at an (at least tentative) solution. In other words, the intuition is likely the result of an integrative process.

If our argument holds, should it not be possible to ask the manager to report on that process (i.e., to tell us how a conclusion was reached)? Probably not, at least not in normal organizational task environments that are not specifically designed to identify intuitive processes. As individuals, we learn quite early to understand and describe what we think. We are not trained in understanding how we think. Typically, we cannot describe how we reached any one conclusion, unless that conclusion was based on a simple unidimensional process, or, at the minimum, on simple forms of differentiation. Consequently, we are at a loss when we are to describe our thought processes and we tend to shrug off requests for such a description. An outside observer will find it even more difficult to understand that process and will, most likely, agree on the vague interpretation of the process as intuitive.

Indeed, excellent managers use intuition. It is not the kind of rational process that is easily described by mathematical models. Mathematical models are not able to add or modify judgmental dimensions when new and inconsistent information becomes available (at least the programs typically devised to aid decision makers cannot do so). On the other hand, the intuitive process is not irrational in the sense of irrelevant, meaningless, or unreliable. It is rational in the sense we have described in an earlier chapter. Generally, it provides one or more potential differentiated or integrated interpretations or solutions to problems in uncertain settings.

When we study intuition by managerial decision makers we find a set of partially diverse yet interrelated kinds of intuitive processes that are well described by the differentiative and integrative mechanisms of complexity theory. For example, at the simplest level, intuition is merely the recognition of familiar (previously integrated or learned) patterns from experience; a kind of deja vu that relates a current problem or stimulus array to a similar event in the past. Here the manager intuits that the previous successful solution may, again, be applicable. The more sudden or delayed the insight, the more likely the term intuition may be applied.

A second form of intuition involves differentiation, either in perceptual or decision processes. For example, a manager may attempt to analyze information that was received but does not fit with expected information patterns. Invoking other potential interpretive dimensions may lead to the discovery or identification of a dimension on which the information suddenly makes sense.

In other situations, intuition reflects more integrative processing of information. At the lowest level, an integration may be fixed (i.e., hierarchical) and may generate the deja vu experience discussed earlier. At a more complex, but still partially hierarchical level, a practiced and fixed hierarchical integrative pattern of cognition may not fit with incoming information (e.g., information that is somewhat changed from usual patterns). Rearranging the relationship among locations of stimuli on dimensions or rearranging relationships among cognitive dimensions may suddenly yield a meaningful conceptualization of events, e.g., the insightful intuition "that's why they are doing it" which , in effect, reflects a modification of previously established integrative patterns.

On the other hand, where considerable novelty and uncertainty is encountered and where no previous integration experiences are available, intuition describes the process of differentiating and integrating to establish at least a tentative set of insights, assumptions and/or exploratory actions. Here, problems may be redefined or new relationships between the meaning of inputs and outputs may be generated. Clearly, the latter kinds of intuition we have described involve more complex differentiative and/or integrative processes. Consequently, their process characteristics would be more difficult to identify by a manager and, especially, by an observer. As a result, these latter processes would probably be even more frequently identified as intuitive.

Intuition may serve well when managers function as leaders of their subordinates and when they develop strategies and goals. In other words, they use, in part, differentiative and integrative processes as they engage in these activities. The next sections of this chapter explore the application of those processes within the organizational setting.

ORGANIZATIONAL LEADERSHIP

Much has been said and written about leadership. A wide variety of leadership characteristics have been defined (e.g., Fiedler, 1964, 1965; Stogdill, 1948, 1962), researched, doubted, reconsidered, and either laid to rest or added to the many other descriptions of the leader that are already part of the literature. We now have many pictures of "good" and "bad" leaders, most of them relevant to specific tasks and situations. We do not wish to add to all those descriptions. Writing in detail about leadership, as is the case with so many other characteristics of organizational psychology, requires major effort. For the present purpose, we merely wish to explore some structural characteristics of leadership in an organizational setting, and even that to only a very limited extent.

First, let us make a relatively categorical statement. Many researchers and theorists have stated, implied or acted as if leadership quality and decision-making quality are a single phenomenon. We strongly disagree with that notion. Indeed, these qualities may be found in the same person (or the same organization). They can, in certain settings, tasks, conditions and for specific events be based on the same underlying structural processes. However, the two phenomena may occur independently of each other as well. There are excellent decision makers who are terrible leaders. There are leaders of high quality who are poor decision makers. And, of course, there are individuals who excel in both; others, who perform poorly in both categories.

Consider, for example, a low-level leadership position, possibly a military platoon leader or a foreman on an assembly line. He or she does not necessarily need to be an outstanding decision maker. Probably he or she needs the interpersonal skills and the task competence to be trusted. However, decision making at higher levels are not part of the job, and the absence of that competence does not distract from the potentially outstanding leadership qualifications of that individual.

At advanced execcutive levels, the two functions are not necessarily identical either. We argue that higher-level structural processes are needed in either case. However, a particular executive's ability to use multidimensionality, whether differentiation and/or integration, in one content domain is not (see Chapter 4) necessarily identical to that person's dimensionality in a different domain. We may, in many cases, hope that a high-level executive would be able to apply differentiated and integrated approaches to *both* the leadership *and* the decision-making domains. However, in analyzing an executive's performance, we may find that his or her cognitive complexity is specific to either domain or that it generalizes across both performance domain areas.

If we were to list several ideal characteristics of a leader, they would only partially overlap with ideal characteristics of a managerial decision maker. Let us consider one example: an effective leader must be able to relate to subordinates in part emotionally (when appropriate) (e.g., with warm affect). People want to feel that they are understood, appreciated, liked or loved, and needed. The experience and expression of affect is one effective way of communicating to people that they are important.

For the high-level managerial decision maker, affect is generally inappropriate. He or she must generally function on the basis of cold cognition to optimize information processing and organizational outcomes. Indeed, he or she will have to (cognitively) consider affective components of people in the organization. Nonetheless, the decision-making function will remain generally cognitive.[8] If a manager is effective as a leader as well as in the decision-making role, he or she may have to switch to affect from time to time, only to return to cognitive information processing when decisions need to be made.

Our example of affect as a potential distinctive characteristic of leadership versus decision-making functions was only presented for convenience. There are many other dimensionally based requirements that predict excellence of leadership and decision functions separately, even at the highest organizational levels. Of course, there are many common antecedents of performance quality as well.

We do not deal specifically with the characteristics of lower levels leaders in this chapter. Fewer structural characteristics may be involved in the prediction of leadership at lower echelons.[9] Instead, we focus on leadership at relatively advanced organizational levels. Where a company markets a product that is in high demand and has no competitors, where cost is no issue, where resources are and continue to be available and where sales are expected to continue to be high for the foreseeable future, leadership will likely involve few problems. In such situations, various kinds of leaders may excel. After all, even some lost opportunities, strikes, decrements of performance due to lower worker satisfaction and morale are not likely to take the company into bankruptcy.

However, in a highly competitive market, leadership requirements can be quite different and quite specific. Success may depend on high productivity at low cost, on considerable profits from limited profit margins and on a number of other (on the surface contradictory) aspects of organizational functioning. Under these conditions, a leader must be able to motivate personnel optimally. What, then, should we look for in an organizational leader or in a leadership team that must function in complex, fluid, and competitive situations?

---

[8]It is interesting to note (see Fiedler, 1984) that managers often think of themselves as accessible and liked by their subordinates, a view that is often not shared by the latter group.

[9]Note, however, that this limitation is restricted to requirements for successful leadership at such levels and does not refer to the characteristics of any specific leader who currently or permanently functions at that level.

First, let us consider the concept of appropriate dimensionality. To lead people and to lead an organization in complex environments, the leader(s) must possess a sufficient overview of the organization and the environment within which the organization is placed. Leaders must be familiar with and/or be open to the needs, views, concepts, vocabulary, and culture of the various organizational segments. The leader must, to the extent possible, understand the perspective of both assembly line worker Smith, and Vice President Jones. But understanding is not enough. The leader must be able to reach out and obtain information as necessary, making sure that the source of that information is made to feel legitimate. The leader must demonstrate legitimacy by (at least apparently) seriously considering that information and its implications for the organization.

Effective leaders in higher managerial levels must learn to understand the motivations, needs, abilities, and limitations of their subordinates. Such an understanding permits them to optimize the capabilities of these persons and to optimize the interactive processes among them. Again, empathy plays a major part. Another part of optimal utilization of personnel is viewing them on a multidimensional basis: a person is not simply rejected because he or she is less competent in some specific task area or is not pleasant to deal with when criticized. Rather, people are viewed, optimally employed, and rewarded in terms of what they do best. In considering the optimization of people, the excellent leader would develop his or her own actions in terms of the structural processes that would achieve interpersonal goals. Kinds and flow of communication to, and information search from subordinates, tasking characteristics, rewards, and (where necessary) punishments would be designed to reflect an optimally integrated process that is most likely to achieve the desired results. As actions are taken, the effective leader would remain observant to add or modify interpersonal processes and communication flow, correcting leadership outcomes where they are less than desirable.

The leader must be able to assemble obtained information from and about subordinates into tentative conceptualizations (tentative, because they may have to be tested and revised in the face of subsequent information that may become available). Further, a leader must be able to reach closure for action, make decisions, and put his or her weight and prestige behind that decision. The appearance of indecisiveness can have disastrous effects on the morale of those who are led. Yet, despite the decisive action, the leader must also be able to reconsider an action, if reconsideration is appropriate (particularly where the previous decision was only partly successful or resulted in subordinate dissatisfaction), and may amend or modify decisions and strategies, as appropriate.

Once a decision has been implemented, the leader should be able to communicate effectively with subordinates and with other leaders and should be able to heal wounds where the decision has created them. In other words, a leader must be both hard (in making decisions to optimize the functioning of people and of the organization), and soft (in dealing with the sensitivities of people in the organization). He or she must be decisive (particularly on the surface) when it is important to defend decisions and/or organizational systems that are not changeable. Yet, he or she must be willing to adapt and make changes in the organization and/or his or her own conceptualization when changes are potentially of strategic advantage or when there is a need for experimentation and creativity. A leader must be able to communicate both the pleasant and the unpleasant—in a way that is clearly understood and in a way that is not detrimental to the leader's relationship with subordinates.

In summary, a leader at advanced organizational levels must understand his or her people and his or her organization as they function interactively, and must be able to motivate and communicate. In dealings with people and with structural components of the organization, a leader will encounter many conflicting thoughts, needs, demands and requirements. He or she cannot simply make a choice. The entire organization and its components, from the individual worker on up, must be considered. Such complex activities require high levels of flexible integration. They require sharing between leader and subordinates, a process that must be initiated through actions of the leader. It requires the development, for example through organizational culture, of the organization into an organismic symbiotic whole. In this whole, productivity and people, for example, can no longer be separated from each other but become interacting parts of an integrated organizational structure. Such an integration, in turn, may be supported by developments and or changes in the organizational culture—for example, in legends about "what happened 3 years ago when we all chipped in at a time of trouble" and "what happened a year later when the company did particularly well and all its people benefited." The process of organizational integration, developed by astute and cognitively complex leaders can, in turn, generate a situation where the majority of employees feel motivated to support the organization because it supports them—and where they feel that they are the company. We propose:

5.13 *While both leadership processes and decision processes are affected by the dimensionality of structural information processing, and while both qualities may be present at excellent levels in the same manager, excellence in leadership and excellence in decision making cannot be considered to be identical.*

5.14 *Integrated leadership processes, including affective and cognitive di-*

mensionality, are of particular importance at higher levels in organizations where optimal motivation and optimal application of skills are required for successful organizational functioning.

ORGANIZATIONAL STRATEGY AND PLANNING

When researchers speak of strategies employed by organizations, they typically speak of goal-oriented activities. Where the goal is easily achieved—that is, where the world is constant and events can be easily predicted, where the same or similar goals have been achieved in the past—the strategy can be based on previous experience. For that matter, the organization may wish to enforce adherence to an established and prescribed method of goal attainment (see March and Simon, 1958). From our perspective, such a fixed path toward a specific goal is not actually a strategy, although it may have been at one time. Rather, it represents an established way of doing things, a habit, maybe even part of an organizational culture.

Another view of strategy and strategy development that we do not share concerns a specific path toward specific and fixed goals, a path that could well be described or developed via mathematical decision models. Some writers who have suggested that managers are not strategic have had such models of strategy in mind. Indeed, if strategy were a rational rather than intuitive approach, we would have to agree. However, when we speak of strategy in subsequent pages, we are not concerned with organizational functioning in constant and utterly familiar environments. We are not concerned with repetitive operations. We do not talk about strategy as a hierarchical approach to fixed action sequences toward fixed goals.

In our definition, strategy employed by an organization is, in effect, similar to a strategy employed by an individual. It implies flexible planning—usually across a number of steps including actions with potentially uncertain outcomes—toward one or more goals. It involves the consideration of alternative actions and potential alternative outcomes of actions, *and* their use in the next step toward more or less general goals. Strategic planning, in other words, encompasses the consideration of several steps of anticipated future actions and events, steps that include both actions and planning: enough to move forward toward a goal, but not so many steps that confusion and disorientation result.

Organizational strategy—at least in organizations of reasonable size and with a number of influential managers—typically develops from an interaction of integrated concepts and plans, provided—to varying degrees—by several individuals. The number of individuals involved in strategy development sometimes produces a problem: Not every manager is able to think in strategic terms.[10] Even where integrative capacity as the basis for strategic planning is present in all persons, that strategic capacity may not exist within the same cognitive domains. One frequently encounters some managers who—based on more unidimensional thought processes in some specific domain—will rigidly and dogmatically hold onto the old way of doing things and will not understand that a changed or changing environment may require modified organizational responses. In the absence of a consensus—and particularly where unidimensional thought has been the typical approach to planning, organizations may fail to generate appropriate strategy. Pettigrew (1973) has referred to the inertial characteristics of such organizations. Management staff of organizations characterized by inertia tend to maintain a view of their world that may be quite outdated despite strong evidence to the contrary. Under such conditions, strategy does not exist: What may be called strategy is merely a replay of old (and often increasingly ineffective) methods of operating.

To avoid the pitfalls of inertia, organizations need not only an integrative system of strategy development; they also need a considerable level of flexibility with which that integrative system is developed, used, reevaluated, modified, monitored, and so forth. Failure to employ strategy, where strategy is useful, does not only occur in organizations that hold onto the old ways; it also takes place in others that hold onto a new way.

For example, 5-year plans often sound good, but they generally do not work. Organizations and nations that announce 5-year plans rarely achieve the goals they have set for themselves. There is nothing inherently wrong with planning over years (1) if those plans remain sufficiently flexible to permit adaptation and change where necessary, (2) if the number of planned actions that are directed toward the outside world are relatively few, and (3) if a very limited number of feedback responses to the planned actions can be expected. Unfortunately, none of these conditions are typical of the experiences of most modern organizations. As a consequence, 5-year (or other fixed length) plans often become rigid and may contain detail or goals that are soon outdated.

While detail may be appropriate when it was first conceived, it can become irrelevant by the time feedback to an organization's initial strategic action is received. In other words, lengthy and fixed advance planning frequently may contain components that do not adequately allow for integration of subsequently received information. It does not permit the adjustments that are possible when openness to information aids in the

---

[10]A recent survey by the American Management Association (Margerison and Kakabadse, 1984) found that CEOs view strategic planning and decision making (in that order) as their most important activities, yet planning was also rated as causing the most difficulty.

interpretation of the outcomes that are generated by successive planning–decision–planning–decision sequences.

Limitations to organizational strategy development and strategic action are, in part, due to limitations of organizational personnel. Two *kinds* of limitations should be considered. First, there are limits to an individual manager's capacity to employ differentiated and integrated strategies (as discussed earlier). Secondly, the human capacity to consider various alternatives simultaneously is restricted (probably to the seven plus or minus two values, which Miller, 1956, has established; an integrator will probably process only about seven concepts at a time and may then proceed to the next (potentially overlapping) seven concepts [plus or minus two]. Some "integration error" may occur due to the particular sets of seven concepts (or already integrated components) that are chosen for differentiative or integrative consideration at any one time.

Similar problems can occur at the organizational level. Organizational plans developed by several managers in interaction often do not consist of more than seven concepts or dimensions per integration. That, however, is very little, if we were to demand that all aspects of an organization's problems, task conditions, future potentials, and more must be considered in each integration that forms part of a strategy. The same errors that are generated by individuals who employ sequential integrations in the development and application of strategy are also encountered in organizations.

What solutions can be devised to address the limited capacity for strategic planning? Many mathematical decision theorists would argue for computer-generated solutions. Certainly, the computer is not limited to Miller's magic number seven. However, we have already expressed our strong reservations about this approach. Computer-based decision making, as Peters and Waterman have suggested, is often wrong headed—that is, too complex to be useful. Even more important, it is too static and unwieldy to be flexible and adaptive. It is often negative and counters adaptive innovation (see Drucker, 1969). Although it may permit planning for complex hierarchically organized processes in a fixed world, it cannot be emancipated toward more flexible strategic orientations in complex and ever-changing organizational environments. It certainly does not permit the intuitive differentiative and integrative processing we have described. On the other hand, as we discuss in the last pages of this chapter, the so-called rational approach may be used as an aid to the manager.

The other personnel-based limitation on strategic planning that we mentioned (i.e., the specific structural limitations of individual managers) may be equally difficult to resolve. Use of strategy can mean something quite different to the cognitively complex and the less complex manager. We have considered strategy in terms of multiple, flexible integration. To a less cognitively complex manager who is not able to differentiate or integrate in multidimensional fashion, strategy may mean somethig considerably more simplistic (e.g., the use of power toward an end or some single approach toward a goal). To a differentiating manager, strategy may imply pragmatism. Try approach A and, if that does not work, try B, then C, and so forth, until either something works or the fixed options are exhausted. Daft and Weick (1983) might say that organizations led by such differentiating managers play the game "20 Questions."

To the hierarchically integrating manager, strategy would imply something much more comlex (i.e., a stepwise and possibly multiple and complex integrated [interrelated] sequence of approaches toward one or more goals). However, the approach would likely be based on established and likely proven procedures that are fixed and invariant. For example, let us say that a company has repeatedly employed a complex strategy to diminish the sales of a competitor in a market of interest to both companies. The strategy might be primarily aimed at diminishing the reputation of the competitor. However, such an attack, if not controlled, could drive the competitor out of the market entirely and generate a complaint to a federal regulatory agency. To avoid that possibility, the hierarchical integrating manager may have wisely planned an action that would let the competitor save face and retain a (smaller) part of the market. However, if the competitor does not act as expected (e.g., if the opportunity to save face is not used, and, instead, an approach to a regulatory agency is made), our hierarchical integrating manager may be at wit's end. An alternate strategy to deal with the competitor was not developed and, consequently, is not available.

In contrast, a flexible integrating manager might have considered a number of potential outcomes of the earlier action. Strategic options of dealing with conceivable alternate responses of the competitor would have been developed and would have been ready as their response became known. For that matter, actions that could potentially result in unacceptable responses may not have been taken in the first place, or, at the minimum, would have been seriously considered in terms of potential risks and consequences.

Regardless of their complexity level, organizational decision makers are limited by both the number of concepts with which they can deal at one time and by the quantity of information which they are able to process. Unfortunately, many organizations and managers believe that decision makers need all available information to develop useful strategies and to make optimal decisions. We argue against such a view. Too much information results in overload and in subsequent decisions that tend to be simplistic and inflexible (we deal with the effects of load and overload later in this chapter). Attempting to consider too much information, establishing too many (especially fixed) goals and generating overly complex (especially static) strategies, all at the same time, can result in overplanning, something that Peters and Waterman have called, in part, the "paralysis through analysis" syndrome. Obviously, important and relevant information needs to be considered in strategy development and in decision making. However, much obtained information is marginally relevant or not relevant at all. Considering all that information does not allow the time and flexibility to remain open to continuing changes in a task environment. Everything stops while that kind of planning proceeds. Rather than developing strategy by actions that, in part, test the waters, precise and detailed plans may be developed that are inflexible and founded on a multitude of earlier events, ignoring information that arrives during the planning process. It is not surprising that this kind of overplanning is soon outdated and ineffective.

Strategy development via flexible integration, by contrast, continues to be open to novel information. While several steps toward general goals are considered at the same time, they are open to modification as the process in which initial planned decisions are tested for effectiveness, followed by modifications of strategic plans that are again expressed in decisions, and so forth. Continued openness permits the fluid development of adaptive planning, decision making, revisions of plans and strategies in response to decision outcomes (where appropriate), and repeated closure for sequential decisions at times when those decisions appear to be maximally effective. While those later decisions may no longer be highly similar to planned decisions, they are part of the overall process that leads from initial plans toward overall and often (at least initially quite) general goals. To put what we have said into other terms: Optimal strategy development relies on continued information flow into an open organizational system that reconsiders and reintegrates events, strategies, and goals as information characteristics change.

If, in retrospect, an earlier decision turned out to be wrong because it did not obtain the desired outcome (and, again in retrospect, it became evident that another decision might have achieved that outcome), a flexible integrator would consider whether the decision contained errors that might have been avoided. For example, if important information was available but not obtained, or if a flagrantly faulty assumption was made, then strategy development and planning activities were indeed poorly performed. If, on the other hand, a decision was forced on the decision maker at a time when it would have been better to delay, if uncertainties could not be eliminated, or if unknown factors produced an unforeseen event, then the undesirable outcome may have provided information that can be useful in a similar future situation. In other words, the decision was not wrong or a mistake. Possibly it was a necessary risk, a good try, or one of many exploratory steps toward achievement of a desired goal.

Organizational decision making in uncertain environments by necessity implies risk taking. However wherever possible, one would hope that calculated risk taking will produce high risk–low consequence or low risk–high consequence decisions. Unless an organization is in a desperate position, high risk–high consequence decisions would be undesirable. Where risk levels are appropriate for an organization's goals, temporary setbacks in goal achievement may be acceptable. Undesirable outcomes can be viewed as a learning experience for more appropriate (and error-free) subsequent actions. Where organizational management is flexible and where managers are cognitively complex, acceptable risk–consequence levels should emerge. Possible negative consequences of such risky plans and strategies should be acceptable—and should not result in punishment of the planners and decision makers involved.

Levels of Organizational Strategic Decision Making

Thus far, we have emphasized flexible integration as a decision-making style in both persons and organizations. However, as discussed in Chapter 4, there are differences in levels of flexible integration. For convenience, we do not consider all of the levels that could be specified.

At the lower end of organizational strategy development, we might observe the consideration of several alternatives. For example, organizational segment A may want to do X and segment B wants to do Y. One is chosen. If the choice is based on power, chance, or some other nonintegrative process, then we are dealing with unidimensional actions or, at best (if the alternative dimensionality is understood) with pure differentiation. As suggested earlier, we would consider selection from alternatives to be barely within the realm of strategy. Nevertheless, differentiation (i.e., understanding of the alternate views, needs, conceptualizations, etc. of diverse organizational segments) is a necessary precondition for integration. Although differentiation may aid in achieving higher levels of integration, excessive differentiation will tend to hinder that process. Too many alternative views may, in effect, operate like any other load variable (see later): at excessive levels it may overwhelm the planning process and discourage, diminish, or even eliminate strategy development.

Development of strategy, from our point of view, begins with integration. Low levels of planning and strategic development may represent primitive integrative processes: For example, "Which of the alternatives would likely produce the best results for the organizations?" However, most persons familiar with organizational decision processes would view such a minimal integrative approach as insufficient. In various situations that require the development of strategy, there may be parts of each alternative that can be combined toward a more effective strategic plan. Possibly, multiple goals can be achieved simultaneously or sequentially by interrelating conditions, actions, and goals. This process of organizational strategy development represents low-level flexible integration; *low* because planning, although multidimensional, takes the organization only one or a few steps into the future; *flexible* because contingent planning and openness to the requirement for a potential change in plans does exist.

Higher levels of strategic planning are achieved when plans extend beyond the immediate step(s) toward subsequent actions (which may or may not be farther removed in time). Often the advanced stages in this kind of strategy no longer integrate events, action decisions, and specific anticipated outcomes but generate conceptual integrations (contingent, of course) of anticipated goals or results. Often these anticipated goals are vague and limited in number. They provide highly flexible overall principles that allow the organization and reorganizations of events and concepts as they are developed, explored, maintained, rejected and, finally, interrealted with each other.

In other words, higher-order integrations involved in strategic planning permit a second level of integrations that serves to interrelate previously integrated concepts. To put it in another way: High-level strategic planning includes multiple contingent plans and actions carried out in sequence, designed to achieve a few, typically interrelated, general goals. It is likely that a number of alternate strategies leading toward those goals are considered and applied. These strategies would interact with each other or provide alternatives to each other, in case one or more of these strategies do not work or do not work well enough. Continuous checking and rechecking of progress occurs. New information, new integrations of information, decisions and feedback based on actions and decisions are related to overall general goals and generate modification or replacement of strategies or strategic elements. Most of all, the stepwise sequence of actions toward goals is tentatively planned: The further removed an anticipated action may be, either in time or in terms of actions that must be completed beforehand, the more the planning will be tentative and conditional and the more the strategies may be designed to create general conditions rather than specific outcomes.

At the very highest levels of strategic planning, more remote and consequently even more general goals will be evident and will help to control overall integrative processes governing sequential activities. The higher the process, the more sequential groupings of potential actions will be included in a strategic plan. Planning no longer occurs across a limited range in time and focused on a single set of goals, but will become a truly continuous process. It may involve reconsideration of previous actions and their outcomes and the relationship of previous plans to present and future plans.

It will involve learning from the effects of previous actions in the development of current strategies. As distant goals become less distant (i.e., as they are fewer action-steps removed from achievement), they will become less general, and strategies designed to achieve them will be more focused on specific outcomes. In turn, new and, again, more vague subsequent goals, which can serve as general overall principles that organize subsequent events, concepts and actions, may emerge.

Establishing higher levels of integration (i.e., integrations of integrated concepts), allows planners and decision makers to reduce experienced task and/or information load toward more acceptable levels. As overload is decreased (see Chapter 4 and the following section on the environment), respondent actions that would only deal with immediate emergencies are decreased in frequency. Lack of overload may make tasks more manageable. In fact, integrated and strategic actions are likely to increase. Meaningful priorities can be set to complete actions that could reduce load even further. With more available time, flexibility, useful experimentation, and meaningful information search can increase. In effect, high-level integrative efforts in strategy development and decision implementation are self-serving: They tend to produce situations that make subsequent integrative efforts more likely. Stated in another way, integrative activity can function to simplify task demands.

Certainly, some organizational planning can be accomplished at lower complexity levels. Certain plans can be adequately addressed via differentiation and others may require only low levels of integration. Some particularly complex multistep strategies may require the highest levels of integrative effort. Clearly, organizations and their personnel differ in the degree to which they can (or should) apply complex integrative processes to strategy development. In some cases, where high levels of integrated strategy development are attempted, failure may ensue if the integrative planning fails to be flexible, or where strategies try to deal with multiple current/or anticipated events without adequately integrating them with applicable organizational goals. In the latter case, the result is likely confusion and duplication of effort, resulting in a load level that is prohibitive and counterproductive. Observation of this problem resulted in admonishment by Peters and Waterman to keep things simple and to avoid extensive planning. Where flexible integrative processes are not available during planning, Peters and Waterman are probably quite right. Keeping things simple (and flexible), at least allow an organization to respond to current conditions. However, where integrative processes are available and appropriate, and where integrative efforts themselves result in a kind of simplification process, an organization should be able to respond to current conditions in an effective manner *and* should be able to prepare more extensive strategic plans to deal with events. Integrative processes, thus, despite their concern with multiple organizational processes, keep things simple in their own, unique but effective fashion. We suggest that:

5.15   *Effective organizational strategy (similar to individual strategy) involves the process of planning subsequent actions across several steps toward desired (often general) goals. It involves the integration of differentiated plan components and inclusion of adequate contingencies. The number of useful steps and the specificity of steps in the planning process is, in part, determined by the experienced and anticipated degree of uncertainty about the environment's response to each of the sequential aspects of the strategic plan.*

5.16   *Mismatches in strategic thinking among responsible personnel can lead to a lack of overall strategy and to rigidity of organizational actions.*

5.17   *The level of strategy development is limited by the capacity for integration of individual managers and by the apparent limits in the conceptual functioning of the human central nervous system. Where, more than seven (plus or minus two) items must be simultaneously considered and integrated (related, compared, etc.) at the same time, errors of omission or integration error may occur and may, to some extent, flaw the resulting strategy.*

5.18   *Complex but fixed planning (e.g., that based on mathematical decision theory) is likely to fail when unforeseen events occur. Optimal organizational strategic efforts would employ a moderate number of flexible integrated steps with contingencies toward one or more potentially flexible goals. The appropriate level of flexible stepwise integration would increase with the complexity of task and task environment, but would likely decrease with increasing fluidity and uncertainty.*

5.19   *Cognitively less complex managers who function in structurally unidimensional fashion may conceive of strategy as the fixed application of a given principle to a specific problem. Managers who employ structurally differentiated styles typically employ a pragmatic (one-at-a-time solutions) approach. Managers who are flexible integrators tend to plan across several steps toward a goal, keeping alternative steps in mind as contingencies.*

5.20   *Organizations that are characterized by flexible integrative strategic planning may view a moderate number of (subsequently identified) mistakes in strategic planning as outcomes of reasonable risk taking and as sources of information for future plans. In contrast, organizations where planning tends to be based on unidimensional considerations may not tolerate mistakes and may punish or fire managers who are deemed respon-*

sible. As a result, such organizations may not process sufficient environmental feedback and may not adapt successfully to changes in their environment.

5.21   *While differentiation is a necessary but insufficient condition for integration, and while moderate increases in differentiation beyond the minimum may be of aid to interactive processes, excessive differentiation may diminish potential levels of integration and strategy development.*

5.22   *True strategy development is not possible without integration.*

5.23   *Low levels of strategy development are limited to a single or very few sequential steps toward goal(s).*

5.24   *More advanced levels of strategy development imply the development of tentative and contingent sets of potential goal-directed actions in more extensive sequences, leading toward general goals. The further removed in terms of steps and feedback an action is from the present, the more tentative and contingent the planning must be. Strategies will, by necessity, have to be less precise and goals more general the farther (in steps to completion) they are removed from the present.*

5.25   *Strategy development requires consideration and reconsideration of current and potential events, conditions, and outcomes. To avoid the information overload that may be associated with this process, integrative efforts that transform these events, et cetera, into composites will effectively lighten the load, allowing strategy building via higher-level integrations of previously integrated concepts.*

5.26   *Where integrative processing in strategy development is not available or appropriate, a consideration of multiple events, et cetera, will likely generate information overload and will likely have detrimental consequences. Calls for keeping planning simple and free from excess informational baggage have arisen from the observation of lacking or inappropriate integrative processes.*

Experimentation

So far we have considered mistakes as a necessary evil in the pursuit of complex strategy—yet something to be avoided, where possible. Mistakes can be errors in integrative planning, often based on uncertainties that remain as a decision is made (i.e., uncertainties that could not be eliminated prior to decision making). To the degree possible, managers will eliminate uncertainties before a decision must be made. However, there are times and situations where uncertainties predominate, where the novelty of the task is encompassing, where information cannot be easily obtained. Such situations, for example, may be ideal for experimentation. Experimentation effectively invites error, but it also invites necessary information feedback. Sometimes it may even be necessary to behave in ways that appear (to the outside observer) to have no rationale (see March, 1980) in order to develop a rationale for future action. Experimentation is—and often must be—a necessary tool of flexible integrative strategy. Sooner or later—and sometimes much later—experimentation can point the way toward needed solutions. Of course, experimentation as a component of strategy should not, under normal conditions, be used in situations where high risk is combined with potentially high levels of negative consequences.

Many organizations, unfortunately, restrict, or even abhor experimentation. Often an organization permits only those actions that can be viewed as maximally correct. Experimentation is nearly antithetical to the structure of such organizations. Acceptance of experimentation by an organization, on the other hand, may be generated by more fluidity in the organizational structure, or by integrative processes that call for assumptions and information, where tentative decisions need to be made in the face of uncertainty. Permitting experimentation within an organization has some similarity to permitting creativity to flourish in some corners of an organization (we return to the concept of organizational creativity).

We suggest that

5.27 *Where uncertainty is considerable, and risks of negative consequences are not excessive, experimentation can provide information that may aid in the development of organizational strategy.*

The Negative Side of Strategy

We have previously discussed various problems that limit strategic action, such as different cognitive complexity levels among managers or among organizational subunits (domains), inertia (habitual action tendencies), and more. Whatever the reason that an organization is not developing strategy or adequate strategy might be, the concept *strategy* is typically attractive to management. Managers feel that being strategic is a positive attribute. As a consequence, managers often wish to develop strategies for their organizations.

However, strategy development for its own sake can be counterproductive. We have already mentioned the fact that 5-year plans are often of marginal use, due, primarily, to their inflexibility. In addition, situations exist where strategies may be inappropriate when first conceived because they were developed in a vacuum, because they were based on faulty assumptions or, simply, because enough useful information to develop strategy was unavailable. Unfortunately, organizational strategy development has often taken the place of experimentation, although experimentation, as a first step, may have provided information at a more rapid rate and at a lower cost.

Another typical hindrance to successful (appropriate) strategy development involves fixed inflexible planning across too many steps in uncertain environments. The greater the environmental uncertainty, the fewer precise sequential steps can be meaningfully incorporated into a strategic plan, and the more alternative and flexible contingencies for subsequent steps must be included. For example, although Jaques (1984) discusses organizational planning across decades, the utility of achieved plans would probably be marginal if events in the first few years could not be predicted with sufficient accuracy. As we have stated previously, quality of strategic planning is, in part, a function of the number of steps in a plan, not a function of the absolute amount of time involved. It is then not surprising that some writers have rejected the idea of strategy and have argued for keeping things simple (e.g., Peters & Waterman, 1982). We would like to modify their admonishments:

5.28   *Strategy development may be of little benefit (1) if it is inflexible, (2) where, based on current conditions, it extends over too many steps, (3) where too few contingent and flexible alternative actions under conditions of excessive uncertainty are considered, or (4) where strategy development occurs in a vacuum–that is, remaining apart from sensitivity to continuous information flow.*

Organizational Creativity

We have discussed mistakes and experimentation in organizational settings. Some acceptance of mistakes as an aspect of strategy development and acceptance of experimentation as a means to obtain needed information, can move organizations a good distance toward fostering organizational creativity. In dealing with the creative individual, we have emphasized that the novel and remote views or actions of an individual may be integrated with components of an organizational setting and with task demands. Creative thoughts that are useful for an organization emerge from individuals with these novel and remote views, from individuals who relate these views to organizational events, to the functional parts of the organization, and to the organization's needs. Creativity is not an everyday occurrence. Creative thinking typically requires time, freedom from demands, and then more time. Creative attempts engender mistakes as well as perfectly good ideas and products that—initially—may not even seem to work. An organization that fosters creativity is, therefore, an organization that is, to some extent, tolerant and patient.

Most people are—probably fortunately—not creative. Few organizations would be able to have the tolerance to allow large numbers of employees adequate time and resources to engage in lengthy creative efforts. If an organization did, its resources would soon be exhausted. Some organizations set up internal think tanks and laboratories, where presumably creative individuals are encouraged to develop ideas, products, services, or concepts. Sometimes they do. However, there are many other employees in other parts of these organizations who are not expected to be creative. It is quite possible that some of these individuals may have a useful idea—and/or even the skills to develop and test that idea. Successful organizations take advantage of such abilities: Their tolerance and patience allows the creative individual his or her niche for some time to develop the promising idea—without threat of punishment if the idea is not useful. Most ideas do not work. However, many that could work and might be profitable are never seriously considered because the organizational structure does not have a place for the potentially creative genius—or for the average employee with a once-in-a-lifetime idea.

Creative products and solutions to organizational problems are defined as *creative* because they operate in new and unexpected fashion. One might say that they violate previous assumptions or conceptualizations. Organizations (especially those that are restricted by inertia) find it difficult to cope with the unexpected. While they may not object to the end product of creativity (particularly if it is a marketable product), they may experience considerable difficulty in dealing with the procedures necessary to develop such a product. Peters and Waterman have discussed the existence of champions in organizations where the creative individual is protected by others who are sufficiently powerful. Including the champion process is one means of fostering creativity in less flexible organizations. However, in the more flexible informal and structurally integrated organizations, a creative individual can typically obtain a niche, at least part of the time, without fear of the punishment that he or she would experience in more rigidly structured unidimensional organizational settings.

5.29 *Structurally unidimensional organizations tend to punish creative efforts as inappropriate and unproductive.*

5.30 *Support for organizational creativity requires that creative individuals be provided time, freedom from demands, resources, and freedom from the threat of punishment in case of failure.*

5.31 *Creativity is more typically found in structurally less formal, more highly integrated and generally more tolerant organizations.*

ORGANIZATIONAL FUNCTIONING
AND THE ENVIRONMENT

Two aspects of the environment affect organizational functioning: the world inside the organization and the world outside of the organization. For simplicity's sake, let us consider the effects of information load within these environments on organizational performance. We deal first with load engendered by the organization's internal characteristics and functioning. Later, we turn to external load effects.

Internal Organizational Environments

We have suggested that individuals in organizations are necessarily limited in their unique information-processing capacity. Limitations applicable to individuals also apply to groups and organizations. The quantity (amount) of internally determined information load per unit of time with which an organization and its personnel must deal is, of course, in large part a function of the information-processing characteristics of the organization. If we consider how different organizations are structured, we may see that equivalent decision makers in various organizations often deal with quite different kinds of information and, of course, quite different quantities of information per unit of time. The more complex the organizational structure, and the greater the number of diverse task demands at any given point, the more overload may occur. In other words, excessive organizational complexity can itself be quite detrimental to overall organizational performance.

One might therefore suggest that it would be preferable to keep things simple. Would it be? The observations of Peters and Waterman on this point are quite appropriate: They have noted that excessively complicated organizational structures are not useful. However, simplification to the extreme can be just as disastrous. At the extreme it would lead us back toward the problems observed in many family owned and operated companies: too little diversity of opinion, too much work for and too much control by the central decision maker; making all the decisions without much input from others is quite an overloading task for any one person (or even a very few persons). We would argue that it is important to keep the organizational structure simple, but not too simple.

Indeed, it is necessary to vigorously avoid formal or informal organizational structures that foster overload, which, in turn, would generate respondent rather than integrative decision making. As suggested, overload could be generated both by excessively complex and by excessively simple structuring of the organization. Yet, one can move too far into the opposite direction as well. The receipt of too little information (i.e., information deprivation) should be avoided as well. With too-limited information resources, with limited scanning or openness and with restricted information search, decision makers and the organizations in which they function may become ineffective as well.

Ideally, the expected information level should be matched (via consideration of an organization's optimal information-processing capacity) with organizational structure. Indeed, very large organizational staffs at multiple levels often produce confusion, conflict, and lack of communication. Excellent organizations, by contrast, tend to create systems of a size that permit differentation and integration to occur (i.e., they generate a level of organizational complexity that is manageable). Often the number of departments is large enough to clearly differentiate functions, but small enough to maintain an integrated overview of their interactions. The number of senior-level personnel in excellent organizations is limited so that communication among that group is not overly complicated. Yet, enough senior-level persons exist to generate diverse (and potentially integrated) points of view. Enough general goals exist to permit adaptive dealing with events, but the number is small enough to prevent chaos.

Size and diversification of organizational elements in excellent organizations are not simplistic as Peters and Waterman have suggested. Rather, we would say that size and diversification should be optimal. *Optimal* means that the organization is differentiated and integrated to the point where management personnel can maintain an overview of the organization, of its functions, and of the key personnel in these functions. Optimal also implies that the structural characteristics of an organization are matched to the structural complexity of relevant personnel in that organization. Optimal means that information flow is controlled so that relevant information is available, but not overloading (see the next section). Finally, optimal means that the seven-plus-or-minus-two items-of-information rule per unit of time is not widely violated. In other words, the degree to which optimality is present reflects (with the exception of external environment effects) the extent to which information-processing activity is sufficiently under the control of the organization.

External Environments

Relevant information that impinges on an organization from the outside varies, of course, in terms of quality and quantity. External load cannot be entirely controlled. To some degree, internal search and scanning can add to information where load is suboptimal (particularly, where relevant information is insufficient and considerable uncertainty exists). To some extent, elimination of some information from consideration can reduce external load to an acceptable level—but at the potential cost of losing important information. In other words, merely adding or subtracting information to achieve optimal levels is not necessarily appropriate.

Before we can consider how load optimality can be achieved, let us take another look at the concept of optimality. We have previously stated that organizations are people. People process information for organizations. We have emphasized that the processing limits of individuals and interacting groups are restricted by the limits of the human central nervous system. How, then, can information flow into and through the organization be optimized?

In some cases, of course, it cannot. Where, for example, an organization is suddenly faced with an unfriendly take-over attempt, it may be virtually impossible to reduce load levels. In such a crisis, multiple events must be immediately considered and immediate responses must be generated. Superior strategy, under these conditions, may not emerge. Stress, where it is serious in nature, is not a good precondition for strategic integration. One would hope that the resulting respondent decision making will be sufficiently effective to avert the immediate crisis.

Under more normal conditions, however, means can be developed to reduce load effects. We have already discussed the simplifying effects of sequential integrations where, initially, too many items had to be considered. Such sequential integrations can be separated across the structure of an organization.

Figure 5.1 shows examples of three different information flow patterns through two segments of an organization. In the first example, (Pattern A), all information is demanded and processed at the higher of the two segments. Even if optimal information levels (e.g., 7 plus or minus 2 items) would flow into each of the three lower-level organizational segments and then would be forwarded to the higher segment, that higher segment would have to process 21 plus or minus 6 items—a distinct overload if all items are considered at the same time.

In the second example (Pattern B), preintegrations occur at the lower segments, reducing information flow from each lower level to two or three integrations, which are then forwarded to the next higher level. Where these forwarded information items indeed represent *integrations* (and not merely distorted or selected items of information) the higher organizational segment may receive an optimal load level, permitting integrative activities at that level. Nevertheless, at least one problem remains. We have already discussed potential integration error. Some information received at each lower organizational segment may have been overlapping and relevant to more than one of the lower level segments of the organization. Differential integrations by these lower segments may have used that information in di-

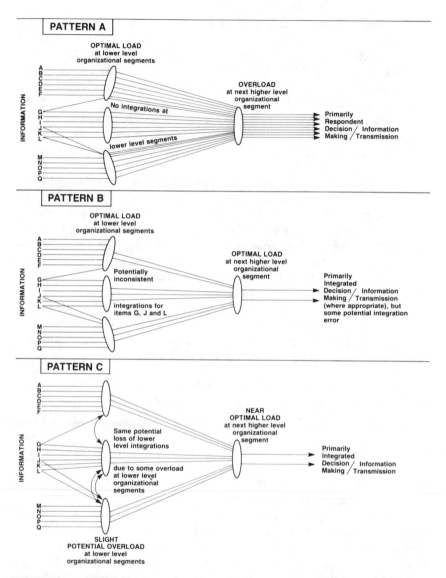

FIGURE 5.1.   Effects of information flow on load and decision making through organizational segments.

verse and inconsistent ways, something that may not become evident when integrated views are presented to higher organizational segments. For that matter, even nonoverlapping information items may produce lower segment integrations that are incompatible with the needs and requirements of other segments and may, consequently, diminish the effectiveness of overall organizational functioning.

A third information flow pattern (Pattern C) allows communication among lower-level segments prior to integration. Although this pattern may serve to diminish integration error, it may have the disadvantage of increasing information load for lower organizational segments—an increase that could be detrimental where load is already too high. However, this information flow pattern has the advantage of encouraging overlapping and interrelated integrative activity across segments, forwarding more generally relevant integrations to higher organizational segments. To the extent to which load at any point in an organization's information flow structure becomes excessive, sequential processing of information at that level becomes necessary, again permitting possible integration errors. Communication across segments may, to some extent (where there are common interests, activities, etc.) aid in diminishing that possibility.

We would propose:

5.32   *Load is meaningful only when considered in terms of the unit of time to which it is applied. Load within organizational units is, in some part, a function of an organization's information-processing structures. Excessively complex organizational structure (both in terms of the levels of an organization and in terms of the number of relevant personnel) is likely to result in overload and may decrease potential integrative processing of information.*

5.33   *Excessively simple organizational structures (in terms of the number of levels in an organization and/or the number of relevant personnel), may generate insufficient quantities of relevant information and consequent underload, or may generate overload where excessive quantities of information must be handled by too few persons or organizational segments. In either case, lack of integrative activity may result. Appropriate levels of organizational integrative functioning are typically maintained at structurally optimal (i.e., intermediate) levels of organizational information processing.*

5.34   *Where large quantities of relevant information are fowarded by lower organizational segments to higher segments, the higher segments may experience overload and may be prevented from integrative functioning.*

5.35   *Where information received by lower-level segments within an organization is integrated into higher-order concepts before it is transmitted to higher-level segments, load at higher levels will be reduced, and integrated information-processing activity at those levels will be facilitated.*

5.36 *Where integrations by lower-level segments are made without com-munications among segments, communications transmitted to higher levels may contain integration errors that may not become evident at those levels. Communication prior to integration among lower-level segments may di-minish such an effect but may increase the load experienced by the lower-level segments.*

5.37 *When information load received by an organization is temporarily or permanently low, less information should be filtered or preintegrated at lower organizational levels so that optimal loads can be maintained at higher levels.*

Reducing Load Effects

Where it is impossible to reduce load toward more optimal levels, pro-cedures must be developed that aid decision makers in dealing with overload conditions. It is probably impossible to learn to handle excessive load levels adequately. In other words, the solution to overload must be found in meth-ods of reducing effective load. We have already spoken about the decrease in load impact via filtering procedures and via higher-level integrative proc-esses. Although we did not specifically emphasize its impact on load, we have at least suggested that the existence of general overall goals can permit greater ease of integration, which, again, may serve to reduce load effects. Another means of reducing load is sharing it. While any group of persons who jointly (interactively) deal with a problem or task are, if anything, increasing the effects of load as they interact with each other, a division of the task among various persons (who, for some part of the time, function coactively, i.e., separately or in smaller subgroups) may decrease load ef-fects. However, integration error may occur when the integrations resulting from efforts of the various individuals or groups are combined.

Finally, another method of reducing load is achieved by ignoring some of the incoming information. Where such information is of importance, discarding it can have serious consequences. However, frequently much of the information reaching organizations is, in fact, redundant. It can be sorted by trained personnel even before it reaches a potentially overloaded group of decision makers. However, it is important that novel, unusual or inconsistent information is not eliminated in that process. Information that brings astonishment to a recipient suggests that something has changed, something has not been previously considered or that previously established integrative conceptualizations are at least partially inapplicable, incorrect, or incomplete.

The astute decision maker neither ignores nor discards inconsistent information as faulty, nor attempts to change its meaning to fit previous conceptualizations. It is this kind of information that provides an opportunity for reintegration (i.e., for readjustment of the organization and its management to potentially changed conditions). It is the response to novel or inconsistent information that most often distinguishes organizations that are adaptive from those that have become subject to inertia. Inconsistent information, even in the presence of overload, may require appropriate search activities to confirm or refute the viability of reconceptualizations, of rethought strategies and of newly discovered opportunities and goals.

Another look at the computer as an aid to decision makers may be in order. We have previously stated our objection to rational computer-based models as a replacement for the manager. Nonetheless, the computer can be of help. Well-designed and extensively tested software progams can aid in the assembly and organization of expected information. They can be useful for making decisions about simple problems where the potential interrelationships among incoming items of information and their outcome implications are fixed and known. However, as managerial problems become more complex and as uncertainty increases, the usefulness of computers and computer models diminishes.

Consider, for the moment, a situation where a standard managerial procedure to deal with a recurring problem was developed. A current event is mismatched with the assumption underlying the rational model that provided the basis for the established preintegrated procedure. This is a situation where an intuition (i.e., a reintegration) is required. In this kind of situation, the rational model on which the computer bases its decision processes can continue to be helpful, if the model not only generates proposed decision outcome(s) but also shows how and why concurrent information does not match the model and the program-generated outcome.[11] Such a procedure would serve to highlight the inconsistent information, potentially aiding necessary adaptive processes. In addition, it may serve to reduce the load of dealing with some of the information that might be redundant (as long as that information need not be considered in a reintegration that has become necessary with the inconsistency of some current events).

Where decision tasks become even more undefined, where multiple novelty and high levels of uncertainty are present, and where exploration and experimentation would likely be more appropriate than a (partial) application of preintegrated views or concepts, computer models cease to be of

---

[11]Communication from the computer to the manager should not be excessively complex and, in effect, overloading. Unfortunately, many software systems that are inappropriate are used and some that are appropriate are not used by managers, because the manager does not understand the process on which computer solutions are based.

value. With less-complex decision problems, however, the aid of computers is of some value, if managers do not rely entirely on the computer program's integrative efforts. Even the best computer programs are based on hierearchical integration. If not checked, they may support organizational inertia. Where managers would depend entirely or even primarily on computers in arriving at complex decisions (i.e., where they would not reconsider whether the program's integrative processes are sufficiently appropriate), computer assistance in complex decision making may become a hindrance rather than a help (see also, Keen and Scott-Morton, 1978).

6

The Measurement of Differentiative and Integrative Complexity

In the preceding two chapters, we have discussed various aspects of complexity theory. We have been concerned with differences among individuals and differences among organizations. We have emphasized differentiation and integration as structural processes underlying both the acquisition and the utilization of information and its sequels, such as decision making, creativity, and leadership. Where differences in cognitive complexity among persons, or where differences in information processing complexity among organizations exist, they should be subject to measurement. In this chapter, we discuss structural measures for which reliability and validity have been previously established. In addition, we spend some time on measures that appear promising but are still under development. Again, we proceed by dealing first with efforts to measure differences among individuals. It is in this area where most empirical efforts at complexity measurement have been reported. Subsequently, we discuss the measurement of organizational complexity—an area where we report more on developmental than on established efforts.

MEASURING INDIVIDUAL DIFFERENCES
IN COGNITIVE COMPLEXITY

Early theorists who were concerned with cognitive complexity tended to develop and employ measurement techniques that were primarily concerned with social perception. That orientation is not surprising: Complexity theory itself was thought to describe only how people differentiate information about others. For example, the Role Concept Repertoire (REP) Test of Kelly (1955) was extensively used and modified by complexity researchers. In all of its versions, the test provides a grid where a number of persons are listed vertically and descriptive characteristics (e.g., adjectives) are listed horizontally. Names (or role descriptions) and adjectives can be provided by the researcher or may be generated by the subject. The subject is asked to mark positive associations between persons and descriptors (at least two) and negative associations between the same descriptor and at least one other person. The grid is evaluated (scored) for inconsistency in the placement of the same persons among descriptors. For example, if mother and father are both viewed positively and the boss is viewed negatively on the descriptor "nice," but mother and the boss are viewed as competent while father is not, then an inconsistency exists. Inconsistencies are viewed as indicants of differentiation. The more inconsistencies are obtained, the higher the differentiation score.

The application of REP-related techniques to specifically interpersonal judgments has typically maintained that approach within perceptual social domains. The fact that inconsistencies are scored focuses measurement on differentiation only. For that matter, REP-based techniques often confound integration and absence of complexity: if obtained judgments abut persons in the REP grid already reflect integrations, low (differentiative) complexity scores are obtained.

Streufert and Streufert (1978) have provided an extensive review of measurement techniques that focus on social perception, including efforts by Bieri (e.g., 1955) and associates, Crockett (e.g., 1965) and associates, Zajonc (1960) and others. Their work and measurement methodologies are discussed in that volume in detail. A repetition of that review in this context appears unnecessary. The interested reader is referred to Streufert and Streufert (1978) and to the original sources, e.g., Bieri (1955); Zajonc (1960).

The primary focus of this chapter is on measurement techniques that address both differentiation *and* integration. However, even in this category we omit some measurement systems. Where a measurement system or theory appears unrelated either to flexible integration or to organizational process, it is not considered. For example, the efforts of Scott and associates (e.g., Scott, 1962, 1963, 1969, 1974; Scott, Osgood, and Peterson, 1979) and of Wyer (e.g., Wyer, 1964) have addressed both integration and differentiation on the basis of the *H statistic,* i.e., a measure of uncertainty reduction (see Streufert & Streufert, 1978).

In our view, their measures are not appropriate for the assessment of flexible integrative activity, primarily because reduction of uncertainty on any given dimension (via some form and quantity of information) may well increase uncertainty on one or more other dimensions. Only where dimensions remain independent of each other, or where reduction of uncertainty on one dimension also implies uncertainty reduction on other dimensions, will use of the H statistic be appropriate (e.g., in hierarchically organized environments). Our interest, however, is not in hierarchical integration alone. In fact, we have viewed adequate managerial functioning in organizations as based primarily on *flexible* integrative processes. For this reason we do not devote extensive discussion to uncertainty-based measurement techniques. We begin our consideration of complexity measurement with subjective assessments of cognitive complexity that are sensitive to flexible information.

Subjective Measures

SENTENCE (PARAGRAPH) COMPLETION

The first widely used measure of differentiation and flexible integration was the Sentence Completion Test, developed by Schroder and Streufert (1962) (see also Schroder, Driver, and Streufert, 1967), later, by some authors, renamed the Paragraph Completion Test.

The technique emerged from earlier work of Harvey, Hunt, and Schroder (1961) on four systems of personality structure. In its initial forms, the approach was similar to Harvey's "This I Believe" technique (e.g., Harvey, Reich, and Wyer, 1968). The Sentence Completion Test is subjective. Respondents complete a number of sentence stems (such as "When I am criticized . . . ") and then generate additional sentences on the same topic. Time allowed for completion of each response and instructions to subjects have varied with sample characteristics. Trained scorers (with interrater reliabilities of .9 or better) assess the presence and level of structural differentiative or integrative processes evident in the response paragraphs. Training to become proficient (high interrater reliability) in scoring the sentence completion method takes several days.

Based on unpublished work of Driver and Streufert, Streufert and Streufert, 1978, modified the stems of the Sentence Completion Test to match the previously discussed two-by-two matrix of cognitive areas containing perceptual–social, perceptual–nonsocial, executive–social, and executive–nonsocial domains. As presently used, the Sentence Completion Test contains, at the minimum, the following stems (each provided to respondents on a separate page):

When I am criticized . . . .

When I am not sure what decision I should make . . . .

When two of my friends have a difference of opinion and I am supposed to resolve the conflict . . . .

When I don't know how to interpret a situation . . . .

When someone tells me that I have a characteristic that I knew nothing about . . . .

When there are several decisions I could make and all of them have some, but different advantages . . . .

It seems to me that problems come about because . . . .

When I don't know whether I should follow the suggestions made by a friend . . . .

Two of these stems fall into each of the aforementioned four cells. Additional stems may be added to match the particular characteristics of any sample of interest. The test is usually begun with an additional starter item that is designed to generate particular interest in an appropriate subject population. For example, the stem "Parents . . . " has often been used for high school students and the stem "When people who are only looking out for themselves interfere with what I am trying to do . . . " has often been used for adult populations.

While responses to these stems may also be used to yield clinical information (e.g., degrees of hostility), scoring for complexity is accomplished only in terms of structural characteristics. Let us consider the stem, "When I am criticized . . . ," as an example. Two responses that differ in content but are both low in cognitive complexity (i.e., unidimensional in structure) might be: (1) "When I am criticized I am usually wrong. I appreciate criticism because I learn from it. Most of the time people who criticize me have my welfare in mind. Particularly when the criticism comes from an authority I will change my ways," and (2) "When I am criticized I usually get very angry. I don't do or say anything unless I know what I am doing or saying. They have no right to be critical and I tell them so. Most of the time they are just jealous."

An example of a differentiated response is: "When I am criticized, it typically means that the other person has a different way of thinking than I do. Maybe he grew up in a different environment and learned to think differently. Probably his way of thinking is okay—but so is mine. Most of the time I ignore that criticism."

A low-level integrated response might sound like this: "When someone criticizes me I listen carefully. I don't necessarily agree with all that person may say but there are parts of those views that may be relevant to what I am doing or thinking. Sometimes I combine some of their views with mine."

The Sentence Completion Test is often scored on a 7-point scale. A score of 1 implies absence of differentiation–integration and a score of 3 indicates differentiation. Low-level integration is indicated by a score of 5, and high-level integration by a score of 7. Intermediate values indicate a midpoint between the uneven numbers (e.g., someone scoring 2 would be described as having indicated some capacity to differentiate, although not at an advanced or even effective level). With extensive training of scorers, additional discriminations among structural levels are possible, expanding the 7-point scoring range to 19 values.

Test–retest reliability of the Sentence Completion Test is relatively high, varying from .6 to .95 in various studies. Considerable validity data have been provided via highly significant predictions of various perceptual and performance characteristics (see the next chapter). Cognitive complexity as scored via the Sentence Completion Test does not correlate meaningfully with other structure- or content-based measures. The highest correlations obtained have been with the structurally based construct of focusing–scanning (.2 to .3 correlations with scanning), with the partially structural construct of dogmatism (Rokeach, 1960) at an average level of −.25 and with authoritarianism as measured by the original F test (Adorno, Frenkel-Brunswick, Levinson, and Sanford, 1950) at a level of −.15 to −.2. All other observed correlations, including the relationship with field independence (Witkin, Dyk, Faterson, Goodenough, and Karp, 1962) have remained below ±.10.

The Sentence Completion Test has some distinct disadvantages. First, it is subjective in nature. As a consequence, one can expect that approximately 5 to 10% of the obtained responses may be unscorable. Further, instructions must be varied, and often pretested, to match relevant target populations. Scorers must be trained extensively. Not all potential scorers are able to achieve an interrater reliability criterion of .9 or better. Most of all, however, the test is relatively general and does not focus extensively enough on any one cognitive domain. In other words, the Sentence Completion Test represents a general measure of a person's cognitive complexity, but it provides less information about specific complexity characteristics that may be applicable to specific domains, tasks, or environmental settings.

When responses to various stems of the Sentence Completion Test are correlated, relationships in the range of $r = +.8$ to $+.95$ are typical, if based on the identical cell of the two by two matrix discussed earlier. Responses to stems from related cells (e.g., perceptual social versus perceptual nonsocial) tend to correlate in the .6 to .9 range, while correlations from unrelated cells (e.g., perceptual social versus nonsocial decision making) may be as low as .4 or as high as .85. Such wide discrepancies among correlations for responses to the stems are expected (see the theoretical discussions about differences in cognitive complexity levels across domains in Chapter 4).

To obtain an estimate of a person's general capacity to differentiate or integrate, the two highest scores obtained on stems of the Sentence Completion Test are often averaged. Where it is important to distinguish among cells or domains, the two (or more) scores obtained for stems located within the same cell are averaged to provide a preliminary estimate of cell-specific complexity.

IMPRESSION FORMATION

A less frequently used test of perceptual social differentiation and integration is based on the impression formation task of Asch (1946). In this task, the subject is asked to write a description of a person who has three characteristics (e.g., "intelligent, industrious, impulsive"). Instructions and time allowed to complete the description (as in the Sentence Completion Test) can be varied to be compatible with population characteristics. Next, the subject is asked to describe another person. This person may be "critical, stubborn, and envious." (A number of additional sets of adjectives are available as alternatives; see Streufert and Driver, 1967.) Finally, the subject is asked to describe a third person, to whom all six adjectives apply (i.e., "intelligent, industrious, impulsive, critical, stubborn, and envious").

Scoring of the Impression Formation Test is also based on evidence of differentiation and integration in the response sentences. The restriction discussed for the Sentence Completion Test applies here as well—that is, not all persons can be trained to become proficient scorers. Scoring, as for the Sentence Completion Test, proceeds on a 7- or 19-point scale. Denial of the simultaneous applicability of all six adjectives to a single person is considered evidence of low levels of cognitive complexity. Less cognitively complex persons often form a positive judgment when presented with the first three adjectives. The second set of adjectives (i.e., critical, stubborn, and envious) would tend to generate negative evaluation. An individual who has formed such positive and negative views would find it very difficult to conceive that a single person could be both good and bad. The resulting response may be a denial of the coexistence of all six descriptors.

Differentiators generally have few problems with the simultaneous application of apparently different characteristics. A differentiated impression formation response may, for example, appear as follows: "This person is a good worker who makes quick decisions and everyone at work likes him. But when he comes home to his wife and children he can be very nasty." The positive and negative characteristics were applied but relegated to different time and space.

The integrator has no problem at all with the apparently conflicting implications of the descriptions and can assign them to a live person located within a single time and space. An integrated response might be: "Such a person makes quick decisions. They are usually quality decisions because she is bright and has gained much experience. She is critical of those who work for her because she is jealous of her superiors because she wants to advance quickly—a goal which she pursues relentlessly and with great effort." (Note that all six adjectives are reflected in this statement.)

Test–retest reliabilities for the various sets of six adjectives vary from .72 to .92 and correlations among the groups of adjectives vary from .65 to .84. Correlations of the adjective groups with overall sentence completion scores vary from .41 to .60. However, when impression formation responses are correlated with perceptual social stems of the Sentence Completion Test, correlations are as high as .88 (see Streufert and Driver, 1967).

We have provided a number of response examples for both the Sentence Completion Test and the Impression Formation Test. The reader may have noticed that some of the examples that represent cognitively complex (i.e., integrated) responses were no longer than those scored as less complex. That bias was introduced by us: We decided to cut responses to the minimum essential statements that were required for optimal communication of the responses characteristic to the reader. Length of verbal responses from different individuals can vary considerably. Nonetheless, cognitive complexity, as measured by either of these tests, is uncorrelated with verbal fluency. It is also uncorrelated with intelligence measures, as long as IQ scores are primarily in a range between 95 and 160+ (Streufert and Streufert, 1978). Positive correlations between cognitive complexity and intelligence are, however, obtained when the tested population ranges below 95 on the IQ measures. Jaques (personal communication) has suggested that persons with low IQ levels tend to express their differentiative and/or integrative style, where it is present, in terms of object rather than in terms of *concept* relationships. Existing measures of cognitive complexity are, however, not sensitive to object differentiation or integration. Rather they specifically focus on information processing via cognitive concepts.

Objective Measures

A number of researchers have attempted to develop objective measurement systems where complexity need not be inferred from written text but can be scored directly from objective responses. Considerable difficulty has been encountered in the development of such measures. The problem faced by test developers is difficult to surmount: People generally do not think about the way they process information and consequently find it difficult to respond meaningfully to questions about their own capacity to differentiate and/or integrate. In response to direct questions about their information-processing style, individuals tend to respond in a socially desirable fashion, simply because it sounds good to be cognitively complex. In addition, less-complex persons do not realize that they actually employ a single (or very few) dimensions when they process information (as discussed earlier in the football player example) because they tend to assign diverse labels to dimensional characteristics that are, in fact, highly correlated.

To measure differentiation and integration, one must base one's conclusions on inference or one must observe performance. At least one attempt has been made to develop an objective inferential measure of cognitive complexity. The (unpublished) Complexity Self-Description Test (C × SD) was initially developed by Driver and Streufert in the 1960s and has been revised by Streufert and Streufert in the 1980s. The test consists of scaled questions about a person's typical mode of dealing with diverse kinds of information. The preliminary factor structure of the revised test appears to classify persons who neither differentiate nor integrate, two kinds of differentiators, low-level integrators, and high-level integrators. However, the relationships of these factors to scores on the Sentence Completion Test are low, and factor prediction of strategic performance in several relevant tasks is at present marginal. Continued efforts to improve this measure are in progress.

MULTIDIMENSIONAL SCALING

Driver (1962) and subsequent researchers have applied multidimensional scaling (MDS) techniques to measure differentiative complexity. For this purpose, approximately 8 to 10 stimuli (which may be sets of information, of events, persons, ideas, or even concepts) are presented in pairs to subjects who are asked to make preference choices. Where n = the number of items in a set,

$$\frac{n(n-1)}{2}$$

represents the number of paired choices. If, for example, a subject chooses item A over item B and item B over item C, then, to be consistent, he or she should also choose item A over item C. If all items are placed (i.e., chosen) in a way that allows them to be ordered in sequence on a single unidimensional scale, consistency is perfect and the assumption of unidimensional choice can be made. However, where choices are inconsistent, either error or multidimensional judgments (differentiation) have occurred. Take, for example, a person who views others in terms of both a moral and a utility dimension. He or she may indeed choose A over B and B over C because A is a very moral person, B is less so, and C may be somewhat immoral. For that matter, D may be completely immoral, resulting in the choice of C over D. Let us, however, imagine that persons A, C, and D are also business partners. D is the most useful because he provides most business; the interaction with C is less profitable and the interaction with A has not generated any profit. Comparing either A, C, or D with B (with whom a business utility relationship does not exist) will result in the expected placement on the "moral" dimension (i.e., A will be valued more than B; C and D less so). In comparing A with D and with C however, C and D are preferred, suggesting an alternate judgmental dimension. Where, in other words, several groups of internally consistent choices emerge, the assumption of multiple dimensionality (differentiation) appears reasonable. To allow a subject to express existing judgmental dimensions via MDS pair choices, task instructions must emphasize comparisons in terms of some relatively vague, superordinate concept that can serve as a flexible guide.

In its usual form, MDS does not provide estimates of integrative cognitions. Integrative activity, where it generates single higher-order concepts may result in interpretation by the scaling technique, which suggest absence of differentiation.

TEXTUAL ANALYSIS

Suedfeld and his associates (e.g., Porter and Suedfeld, 1981; Suedfeld, Corteen, and McCormick, in press; Suedfeld and Piedrahita, 1984; Suedfeld and Rank, 1976) have adapted the sentence completion technique to analyze a wide range of written material (speeches, memos, poetry, letters, etc.) to obtain estimates of differentiation and integration by the authors of that material. Clearly, poems and speeches are not an ideal basis for complexity estimates. While sentence completion stems are specifically designed to create conflicting cognitions that are likely to generate evidence of multidimensional conflict resolution (where present), general material may or may not generate potentially conflicting thought patterns.[1] As a result, lengthy material may be necessary for textual analysis, and scoring

---

[1]Absence of conflicting thought patterns as well as consequent absence of evidence for differentiation and integration may also be due to intentional unidimensionality in certain kinds of written material, speeches, etc. Without understanding the underlying reasons, many politicians, for example, present their thoughts in a more unidimensional fashion to match their statements to the cognitions of less cognitively complex voters. In other words, care must be taken in the selection of material for scoring.

may have to be based on sometimes restricted information. As a consequence, most of the more cognitively complex scores obtained by Suedfeld and associates do not exceed levels of differentiation. Nonetheless, these authors have been able to predict a variety of personal and organizational outcomes on the basis of their measurement techniques (see Chapter 7).

MEASURING INDIVIDUAL, TEAM, AND ORGANIZATIONAL PERFORMANCE[2]

One method to measure the application of differentiation and integration by individuals, groups (teams), and organizations is an analysis of their decision-making structure. Two methods for decision-making analysis have been devised: the retrospective post-hoc interview and a direct analysis of decision and information sequences. We discuss these two methods and some early thoughts on a third method in this chapter.

Actions and their relationships to task environments, task demands, and information flow may be counted, classified, and related to each other. Such counts and classification of actions and of information–action relationships can provide a basis for understanding the reasons underlying action sequences, strategies, and goals. Streufert and associates (e.g., Streufert, 1983a, Streufert and Streufert, 1981a) have developed a time–event matrix methodology that describes the *structural* aspects of an individual's, a team's, or an organization's decision making.

The tasks of an individual or group operating in the organization are rarely limited to dealing with single events within limited contexts. Most decision makers in applied settings must respond to a continuous series of inputs from the environment. Their resulting actions are usually determined, in part, by some plan(s) and in another part by the necessities of dealing with current events. Their decisions may consist primarily of respondent actions or they may reflect some degree of strategy (i.e., decisions that are interrelated and occur in a planned sequence designed to achieve one or more specific or general goals). Whether individual or group actions reflect pure respondent behavior, or whether they reflect strategic planning may be of considerable importance for the outcome of a task effort. The time–event matrix was developed to help researchers or observers identify structurally different kinds of actions (e.g., decision) and their frequencies, as they occur in naturally complex task settings.

The following pages describe how time–event matrices are constructed

[2]This section is primarily based on two ONR Technical Reports (Streufert, 1983a, #12; and Streufert and Streufert, 1981, #3).

on the basis of individual or group performance. Subsequently, a number of formulas describing specific performance measures are provided and explained. The formulas are based on calculations derived from the matrix and reflect generally orthogonal measures of performance style and outcome. Reliability and validity (in predictions of performance) for these measures has been established. Additional measures may be based on the time–event matrix, where needed.

The Matrix

Performance quality, particularly in complex tasks, is determined by at least three components of individual or group effort: (1) appropriate knowledge about what responses are potentially correct or incorrect in a give situation (where possible), (2) ability to develop and employ a plan and to respond at the appropriate time with an optimal combination of responses (including the use of strategy), and (3) the capacity to respond immediately when required. The time–event matrix is designed to assess the second and third of these components. In many cases, the first component (i.e., appropriate content knowledge and understanding of the task situation) can be assumed, as long as the involved individual or organization has sufficient training and/or experience. However, persons with excellent training and ample experience can differ widely on the second and third components.

The time–event matrix is a graphic, two-dimensional representation of action sequences across time. One of these two dimensions represents time; the other represents a nominal scale describing subsets of activities. For example, the second dimension may either represent subsets of decisions, subsets of communication activities, or other actions of interest. Each action is represented by a point in the matrix. Relationships among actions are shown by lines that connect action points.

Time–event matrices may be used to depict a variety of task activities, depending on the interests and orientations of the researcher or observer. Because we cannot cover all of the purposes for which the matrix can or has been employed, we discuss its application for one purpose as an example: decision matrices. It should be remembered, however, that most other performance areas, aside from decision making, could have been selected equally well, At the end of this chapter, we make some suggestions about another application.

The time–event matrix technique was developed to measure interrelationships among actions over time and effects of information flow preceding actions. As indicated, the matrix is not particularly sensitive to action content (e.g., specific decisions) and is not designed to distinguish between correct vs. incorrect action. If the quality of action content is of concern, additional measures (beyond those discussed here) are necessary. The matrix may be expanded into three- (or n-) dimensional space, permitting measurement and prediction of additional relevant variables as they impact on, or interact with, task performance and the measures of task performance that we discuss next.

Establishing the Matrix

The two basic dimensions of a two-dimensional time–event matrix are time and subsets of some specific activity—actions. For present purposes, the activity is decision making and actions are decisions. Each is discussed in turn:

TIME

Time in the matrix is plotted horizontally. There are no particular restrictions on the time intervals used (no matter whether time proceeds normally or is—as in some simulations—expanded or condensed). Events that occur sequentially and independently of each other must be plotted on different time points. The time dimension moves from left to right. Any time scale units may be used, except that decision-making sequences that are to be compared across persons, groups, or organizations must employ the same scale units or must be mathematically transformed to match.

ACTION (DECISION) TYPES

Decision-making tasks and settings differ widely; consequently, types of decisions must differ as well. For example, executives dealing with the potential purchase of another corporation may be concerned with such action areas as establishing the value of the other company, determining potential duplication of effort, et cetera, whereas military decision makers may be concerned with troop movements, air support decisions, and so forth. In other words, groupings of decision types must be established separately for each *general* group of decision-making situations. Selection of decision-making types is best done by experts in the field. The types selected should be inclusive, where possible of approximately equal breadth, conceptually meaningful and consistent. The types should differ clearly in terms of activity, method and meaning, et cetera. Decision types should reflect categories that may potentially be used by decision maker(s) involved in the situation. While some decision makers would likely use one group of decisions, others may use a different overlapping group. In other words, it is not expected that any single decision maker would employ all available decision categories.

While there is no restriction on the number of potential decision types that may be represented in any one time–event matrix, decision types should be selected so that decision makers use, on the average, somewhere between 10 and 20 different types of decisions in any time sequence that lasts for several hours.[3] Note, however, that these suggestions are ideal requirements (which aid in data analysis) and do not supersede the practical character- istics of decision-making situations. For example, if a decision situation requires only one kind of decision, one cannot manufacture other decision types. In effect, use of a decision matrix in such simple situations may not be helpful. For example, if all available actions reflected troop movements, then splitting decisions by the unit moved may not be meaningful for pres- ent purposes.

DECISION POINTS

Once time is plotted horizontally and decision types (as selected, for ex- ample, by an expert panel) are plotted vertically, each decision made by an individual, by a group of decision makers, or by an organization (as desired by the researcher or observer) can be presented by a point placed vertically beneath the time when that decision was made (or announced, or trans- mitted, again depending on the intent of the researcher or observer) and horizontally next to the decision type represented. All decisions can be so placed in the matrix. Decisions made at the same point in time may be connected with vertical lines. Decisions representing the same decision type may be connected with horizontal lines.

INFORMATION INPUT

In the matrix, as used to date, information input is considered only as it relates to decision output (this limitation was chosen for convenience and is not necessary). Any unit of input that leads to an output is marked in the matrix (e.g., by an *) under its appropriate (input) time and in front of (on the same decision-type line as) decisions subsequently made as a consequence of that input. The input asterisk is placed in advance of each output produced—that is, it may occur on more than one horizontal (de- cision-type) line. The horizontal distance between the input asterisk and the subsequent decision point reflects the time elapsed between receipt of in- formation and the relevant response.[4]

---

[3]Because decision makers would rarely, if ever, employ *all* available decision types, the potential for considerably more than 10–20 decision types (as in more general terms action categories) may be provided.

[4]See the section on calculated measures for a discussion of time measurement.

DIAGONALS

As stated previously, we are, among other things, interested in relationships among decisions as they reflect, for example, the development of plans or strategies. Consequently we wish to know whether a decision made at one time is related (leads) to later decisions. Where a decision of one type is made to make a later decision of another type possible, the two decisions are connected across time with a diagonal line with an arrow pointing forward in time toward the later decision.[5] If two decisions show an isolated relationship only to each other, a single arrow is drawn. If, on the other hand, the decision maker(s) decides to engage in decision types A and B at time one in order to allow for action C in the future, and wants to accomplish C in order to allow D to occur even later, and if all these decisions are actually implemented, a longer chain of diagonal connections is established (see Figure 6.1). (Number, length and interconnectedness of forward diagonals are of importance in several of the measures discussed here later.)

Diagonals also may be drawn with arrows facing backwards. If, for example, a decision maker or an organization engages in action E without considering any future action, but later finds that action E is now of use when a later action F is decided on, a backward arrow diagonal between the later action and the previous actions may be drawn (Figure 6.1). As a rule, interconnectedness among backward diagonals does not occur with great frequency.

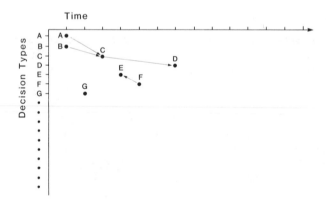

FIGURE 6.1.   A basic time–event matrix. Horizontal and vertical lines were omitted for greater ease of communication.

[5]Such diagonal connections in the matrix are later referred to as integrations.

END EFFECTS

Whether or not a forward diagonal is drawn depends on whether a planned later decision is indeed produced as a follow-up to the earlier decision. Where a decision task ends abruptly, the opportunity to carry out a previously planned decision may not exist. Such an event could arbitrarily limit the number of diagonals generated by decision makers as they are reflected in the obtained measures (see next section). Where decision making is measured in experimental settings, randomization of time periods reflecting or containing potentially differing environmental conditions may be used to avoid a constant error. Calculations of probabilities of diagonal connections may be used as well (see measurement section). In applied settings, various frequencies of diagonal connections among decision points in diverse task segments may reflect current task requirements and may reflect appropriate task performance.

ESTABLISHING RELATIONSHIPS IN THE MATRIX

For purposes of analysis, it is important to establish clear relationships (1) between inputs and subsequent output decisions, and (2) among decisions that are causally or strategically related (as shown by diagonals). The only perfect representation of these relationships exists in the brain of the decision maker(s) at the moment relevant decisions are made. Any measure of those relationships can, consequently, be subject to some error. Clearly, it is important to opt for the least amount of error in both experimental and observational settings. Certainly, the error levels are much smaller in a well-designed experimental simulation than in observations obtained in ongoing free environments. In an experimental simulation, records of planning can be obtained during the planning process. In real-world task environments, that may or may not be possible and less precise techniques (such as post hoc interviews) may be required.

Applications of the Matrix

Ideally, decision maker(s) should be asked immediately (upon making a decision) to indicate (1) any information received on which a specific decision is based, and (2) any planned subsequent decisions that might be employed as a preplanned follow-up to the current decision. Isenberg (1984) has successfully applied a similar method in his analysis of executive decision making by senior managers. With some effort, this can also be achieved in some simulated environments (the participants may have to be persuaded, however, that indicating both the relevance of previously received information and of planned future decisions would be of value to them in terms of long-range outcomes).

In many free simulations (particularly where participants cannot be interrupted and appropriate questions cannot be embedded in the simulation) and in many observations of organizational (real-world) decision-making environments, such questions cannot typically be asked. Collecting data from participants in complex decision-making tasks where large numbers of decisions are made and potentially interrelated in a strategy after task completion, however, may introduce serious bias.[6]

Another viable option requires that experts consider decisions that were made, and judge whether these decisions were responses to previous information and/or were part of a decision-making sequence that should be represented by diagonal connections. In some cases, interjudge reliability for such a task can be high. Previous experience in our laboratory has shown that trained judges tend to produce little variable error in making those judgments. As long as the judges have no particular biases for or against the decision makers they are evaluating, constant errors across samples would tend to produce relatively few errors of comparison for rated decision makers (or decision-making groups or organizations).

Establishing connections between inputs and decisions on the basis of expert judgment is relatively easy. Respondent decisions are typically related directly to the content of received information and are likely relevant to the same physical location of information sources that produced the input. When such commonalities are seen, a connection may be assumed to exist.

Establishing interconnections among decisions is more difficult. Obviously, where one decision refers directly to a previous decision ("Order the unit which we previously moved to quandrant X5 to fire on quadrant Y6") a diagonal connection is appropriate. However, should this be considered as a forward or a backward diagonal? If we had been able to ask the decisions maker(s) about potential future decisions, as the original decision to move the relevant unit was made, then we would know. If we were not able to ask and (in free simulations or in real-world applied decision-making settings that may not be possible), then we cannot know. In such cases, distinctions among forward and backward diagonals cannot be made and directional arrows cannot be drawn.

Let us return to decision-making settings where relationships among decisions (connections) are judged by expert observers of the decision-making

---

[6]Bias may be due to memory error or to social desirability.

sequence. Where no clear relationship is stated by the decision maker(s), aids must be used to determine whether relationships exist. Such commonalities among decisions as addressee, location, action, et cetera, are useful for this purpose. The most reliable of these is probably location. In a military setting, to give a relatively simple example, moving artillery to quadrant X5, asking it to fire on Y6, moving infantry to Y5, and finally ordering the infantry to attempt to take Y6 would reflect a series of interrelated decisions across time. It should be noted here that moving troops to Y5 and other troop units (both infantry) to X5 (at a later time) would not result in a diagonal connection in the time–event matrix: troop movements represent the same decision type. This outcome is intentional: repetitious actions are not necessarily representative of what we have termed strategic actions.[7] If, on the other hand, both units are later asked to attack Y6, diagonal connections between the two movements and the later attack would be drawn.

On rare occasions, decision sequences may be difficult to judge in terms of their potential interconnectedness. To the degree to which a judge can develop a cognitive image of the goals and strategic conceptualizations of the decision maker(s) (or if the judge can obtain advance information about their plans), the determination of strategic relationships will be easier.

In any case, if, after considerable thought, a judge is uncertain whether two decisions are or are not related to each other, it is preferable to err by omission. Uncertain relationships (interconnections) should not be scored because, as the reader will see from studying some of the formulas we present later, some measures would likely be greatly inflated by erroneously scored relationships.

An example of two decision matrices is provided in Figure 6.2. The figure shows decision matrices generated by two groups of organizational managers who differed in their decision-making styles (complexity). Visual examination of these matrices clearly communicates that there are meaningful differences between those styles. These differences are, of course, subject to measurement. A number of measures that have been previously used for research, assessment, and training purposes are provided in the appendix of this book. Many of these measurement techniques have formed part of the methodological basis of research presented in the next chapter.

For the present, let us merely provide short descriptions of the matrix-based measurement techniques we have used. The measures can be grouped into two general categories: (1) simple counts of actions of various kinds, and (2) more or less complex measures of interrelationships among actions.

---

[7]Strategy, as used here and defined earlier, is not necessarily identical to the military application of that term.

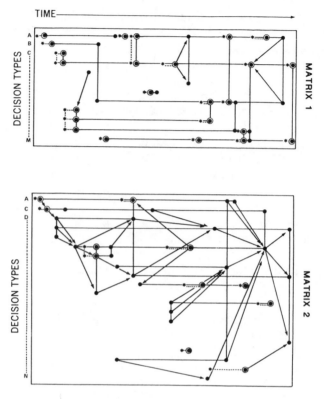

FIGURE 6.2.   Each point represents a decision. Each vertical line connects decisions made at the same point in time. Each horizontal line connects decisions of the same type made at different points in time. Each diagonal represents the strategic integration of different decisions at different points in time. Diagonals pointing forward reflect advance strategic planning. Each circled dot represents a decision response to information received at *. The dotted distance from * to ⊙ reflects the information to decision interval. Each decision type represents a self-selected differentiated decision category based on available resources.

COUNTS OF ACTIONS[8]

Number of Decision Categories.   This measure counts the number of different *kinds* of decisions that a person, group, or organization employs during a specified period of time. Categorization into decision groupings is typically task specific and accomplished by teams of experts.

[8]For the purpose of this short description as well as the more detailed information on calculation of measures we will consider action *decisions* as the unit of measurement. Other actions may, of course, be substituted.

Number of Decisions.   This measure counts the number of specific decisions made by a person, group, or organization during a specified period of time. Subcategories of the number-of-decisions measure may count decisions of diverse content. For example, it is possible to calculate the number of information search decisions.

Number of Respondent Decisions.   This measure counts the number of decisions made in response to (often recently) received information. A subcategory is a count of retaliatory decisions—that is, those respondent decisions that do not form part of a strategy, representing actions that are not related to future decisions that will be made at a later time.

Average Response Speed.   This measure calculates the amount of time that has elapsed between receipt of information and a relevant respondent decision. Other counts may, of course, be introduced when necessary or useful.

COMPLEX MEASURES OF INTERRELATIONSHIPS
AMONG ACTIONS

Number of Integrations.   This measure is the simplest (and most frequently used) measure of strategic interrelationships among decisions. Where a decision is carried out to make a later different decision possible, assuming that later decision is indeed carried out, credit for one integration is given. The total score is the count of the number of interrelationships among decisions that originate during any specified period of time.

Number of Backward Integrations.   This measure considers relationships of the nature just described, except that plans to make a later decision were not made at the time of the original decision. Rather, an earlier decision was later recognized as useful for a current decision. Number of backward integrations are credited to the specified period of time during which the later of two interrelated decisions has occurred.

Integration Time Weight.   This measure counts the length of elapsed time between any two decisions that form the basis of the number-of-integrations measure.

Quality of Integrated Strategies (QIS).   The QIS measure considers the number of integrations that are directly and strategically related to decisions representing the beginning and the end point of any integration. The measure is concerned with complexity of current strategic planning.

Weighted QIS.   In contrast to the previous measure, weighted QIS is not only concerned with the complexity of current strategy but also uses similar calculations to obtain a score for the overall strategic interrelationship among plans and decisions across an entire task.

Multiplicity of Integration.   Multiplicity is similar to QIS, yet drops the concern with the time element of strategic interrelationships among present strategic planning which is part of the QIS measure. As a result, this measure is more sensitive to strategic interrelationships among decisions that must be made in rapid succession to deal with events which also occur with some rapidity.

Serial Connections.   This measure is similar to number of integrations. However, while the number of integrations considers only interrelationships among decisions that differ in their assignment to decision categories, the present measure considers only decision sequences that interrelate decisions within the same category.

Planned Integrations.   The planned integrations measure calculates the number of integrations between current decisions and planned future decisions that are planned but are never carried through. The measure is primarily used to correct end-effect confounds in other measures where measurement must be based on tasks (such as simulations) that continue (or could continue) beyond available measurement periods.

Multiplexity F.   The measure is similar to the weighted QIS but (1) does not consider the time element contained in the QIS and weighted QIS measures and (2) considers only interrelationships with future decisions. In other words, it is concerned with the complexity of the effectiveness of future planning at any current point in time.

Post-Hoc Interviews

In previous sections of this chapter we have discussed how a time–event matrix is constructed and what kind of measures may be derived from it. Can we obtain matrix characteristics that provide information about a person's, a group's, or an organization's decision-making style after a series of decisions have already been completed?

In many cases we cannot and would not wish to control organizational events. Instead, we may want to observe and record what happens as events unfold or as decisions are made in response to events or as part of some strategic sequence. If we are lucky, we may be able to listen to an individual or to a panel of persons as they make decisions. We may be able to watch a decision maker and ask questions as he or she deals with complex issues over time (e.g., Isenberg, 1984). Most often, however, we are not so lucky. We may have to analyze a decision sequence that may have occurred some time ago. The construction of a time–event matrix may have to be based upon a post hoc interview technique.

In a post hoc interview, decision makers may be asked to recount how specific decisions were made and how other potential decisions were rejected. They may also be asked to recount the information that was available at a specific time and when that information became available. They may be asked to indicate what thoughts were generated by the arrival of information and how decisions were based on the information. They may, most of all, be asked to talk about plans they had made, what contingent and/or future actions they had considered and which of these actions were carried out. They may be asked to recount why certain planned actions were taken while others were not. Were earlier plans replaced by later plans? Had some planned decisions simply been forgotten? Did later incoming information make previous plans less useful?

The purpose of the post hoc interview (often checked and substantiated by viewing written records, when available) is to establish whether a decision sequence reflected some degree of planned strategic effort and whether decisions were made in response to specific incoming information. Such an interview should be designed to generate enough data to develop a time–event matrix, allowing calculation of the various measures that we have described.

Without question, post-hoc interviews generate a number of problem areas. Decision makers often fail to recall decisions and decision sequences accurately. Strategic sequences may be reported because they sound good in retrospect yet were never actually considered in the task setting. Errors made by decision makers may be omitted in retrospect in the service of social desirability. The greater an interviewer's access to written documentation that may be used to validate statements, the more accurate the data will be. Where decision makers know that an interviewer has access to written data, they may be more honest about their mistakes. In addition, information that may have been forgotten may emerge from written material.

While the post-hoc interview technique has disadvantages, it certainly has its share of advantages as well. Using this approach, a researcher is able to delve into real decision-making situations, reflecting actual behavior of managers and organizations involved in realistic task environments. In other words, where recollections of interviewees are relatively accurate, a relatively valid representation of managerial and organizational decision making can be obtained. Although this technique has not been extensively researched and systematically employed, it appears generally reliable and predictive of a manager's or an organization's future task performances.

Simulations

Simulations are not unfamiliar to most organizational decision makers. In many settings, both in the private and government sector, they are used for training and performance evaluation purposes.

FREE SIMULATIONS

Early simulation techniques (e.g., those employed by Guetzkow, 1959, and his many followers) have been described by Fromkin and Streufert (1976, 1983) as *free simulations*. In this method, all participants or participant groups begin with an identical problem. Their initial resources, limitations, and opportunities are identical. However, as the participants make decisions, they begin to modify their task environment. After some time, the environment of one decision maker (or group) may show little resemblance to that of another decision maker or group. For training purposes, such a divergence of events and environments can be useful: It clearly demonstrates the consequences of different sets of decisions. However, for purposes of evaluating task performance, this method is not appropriate. Because, for example, early decisions made by a participant in a free simulation can inadvertently make subsequent tasks more easy or more difficult, performance requirements may be drastically modified and valid comparisons among individual decision makers or groups may be impossible. To cope with that problem, Streufert and associates have developed experimental simulation techniques. Experimental simulations and the quasi-experimental simulation techniques suggested by Streufert and Swezey (1985) can be of considerable aid in resolving such measurement problems.

EXPERIMENTAL AND QUASI-EXPERIMENTAL SIMULATIONS

To an individual participant, or a group or team of decision makers, there are no apparent differences between participation experiences in free versus experimental simulations. Participants arrive at the simulation setting and are provided with information about their task and the environment. They make decisions that are designed to affect the situation in which they find themselves across time. They plan, respond, and receive information about ongoing events and outcomes of previous actions. However, while participants in free simulations receive information that is a direct outcome of their previous actions, participants in an experimental simulation receive preprogrammed responses. Although they may think (if the simulation is well designed) that incoming information reflects the effects of their earlier activities, in fact, their actions may have little or no effect on simulation events. In quasi-experimental simulations, the programming of events, to which participants are exposed, is modified to provide some direct effects of previous actions, only as long as those events are not part of an experimental manipulation. Where experimenters wish to measure effects of specific events and/or event frequencies, those events are entirely preprogrammed.

MEASUREMENT OF DECISION STYLE VIA SIMULATION METHODS

If we wish to understand the characteristic decision style of a manager, or of a management team, we can place these persons into an experimental or a quasi-experimental simulation. A relevant environment of appropriate complexity may be generated. The participant decision maker(s) may be asked to deal with that environment over time. Simulation time may be condensed, so that feedback can be accelerated and decisions can be planned and implemented in close proximity. As part of the simulation system, appropriate information (at least, in part, programmed) is provided. The decision makers are asked to state future plans, if any, when a specific action is taken. Further, the decision makers are asked to indicate any previous decisions that have provided a basis for the current action. They also list information they have received that was used to develop the rationale for a current action.

The decision maker(s) must be motivated to provide such information. As an incentive to cooperate, it is often useful to indicate that a record of future plans will speed future actions when they are initiated (e.g., the decision maker's staff is forewarned about potential future actions and will be prepared to implement them more rapidly and more effectively).

The decision categories, number, timing, and relationships among decisions and information that are obtained by this method provide a basis for the time–event matrix discussed earlier in this chapter. Drawing a time-event matrix and calculating the score values based on such a matrix can, of course, be an arduous and time-consuming task. To avoid problems, we have developed microcomputer-based simulation techniques that use com-

puters in the decision-making task. The microcomputer generates preprogrammed information and quasi-programmed responses to decisions made
by an individual or a task group (team). Decisions are entered directly into
the computer.[9] The computer requests and records responses to questions
about future plans, past relevant decisions, and relevance of current decisions to received information, which is stored for later analysis and for
automated calculation of matrix-based scores.

The microcomputer technique allows an experimenter to specify both
content and characteristics (e.g., quantity) of information received by decision maker(s) at any point in the simulation. Consequently, the simulation
technique can be adapted to various task environments and content areas.
Moreover, the technique allows specification of task demand levels that can
differ across time. As has been described for our aforementioned disaster
simulation, a computer-simulated task environment may be generated that
required excellence of planning at one point and decisive rapid responding
at another. Scores are calculated separately for each of these segments, allowing a researcher to determine whether the various appropriate styles are
available to decision maker(s) and whether the decision maker(s) can switch,
where necessary, from one style to another.

Earlier, we discussed free simulations as useful for training purposes and
experimental or quasi-experimental simulations as particularly useful for
research and performance evaluation. We have also indicated that the free
simulation technique is not typically designed for research and may be only
marginally useful for performance evaluation. We should emphasize, however, that the experimental and quasi-experimental simulation techniques
can be extremely useful for training. The fact that they are controlled, and
therefore, reliable across administrations makes them excellent vehicles for
training purposes. Commenting on a specific performance during a pre-
training administration of such a simulation and comparison to performance in a later simulation (with changed content but identical structure)
is not only valuable to demonstrate where a trainee has or has not improved, but is also useful as an evaluation system for the training process
as such.

Experimental and quasi-experimental simulations have been extensively
employed in individual and organizational research. They produce data that
are highly reliable and predictive of organizational effectiveness (where differentiation and integration or other measures obtained are relevant for
specific tasks). Considerable data based on these simulation techniques and
their time–event matrix scores are discussed in Chapter 7.

---

[9]In another version of the simulation methodology, an assistant to the decision maker(s)
operates the computer system. Information is provided verbally by the decision maker(s).

MEASURING THE COMPLEXITY
OF ORGANIZATIONAL INFORMATION FLOW

So far, we have focused specifically on decision making as one example of actions in organizational settings. At this point, we provide a short demonstration of one of many other applications of our time–event matrix methodology. The present example focuses on communications within organizations. We have described the segmentation of organizational structure as a form of organizational differentiation. The number of organizational segments that receive a particular item of information and the number of segments that process that information for their own (separate) purposes reflect the same kind of differentiation into component parts that is encountered in individuals who place and process information on various cognitive dimensions.

We may also, in part, consider organizational integration on the same basis. We have emphasized in an earlier chapter that diverse segments of an organization typically have diverse views, needs, goals, or general conceptualizations concerning the meaning and implications of received information. They may prefer diverse strategies and may wish to pursue diverse goals. The organization as an entity must, in some fashion or another, overcome that diversity. Of course, the diversity may be eliminated by imposition of a single goal and one concerted series of actions toward that goal in unidimensional fashion—for example, by the uncontested decisions of an authoritarian manager. On the other hand, decisions may also be made by considering the needs, interests, and goals of each relevant organizational segment and their respective interrelationships to each other—arriving, one hopes, at a generally beneficial decision. This latter process reflects integration. Where a procedure for integrated processing (whether hierarchical or flexible) is institutionalized in an organization, it should be reflected in (and measureable through) information-processing patterns that are evident in the flow of communications through the organizational structure.

We might, on first thought, wish to describe integrated processing simply in terms of generally applicable (or temporarily employed) interactions among the various organizational segments. Which segments communicate with each other? How frequent is that communication? Is communications restricted to particular kinds of information or is it general in nature? Is the communication mutual or does it occur in only one direction? Is the communication consultative or is one segment reporting to the other?

These interactive communication patterns within organizations across time may be subjected to an analysis via our time–event matrix methodology as well. In this case, we are no longer interested in decision making.

We could now consider organizational segments as vertical entries in a time–event matrix, replacing the decision categories we had placed on the vertical earlier on. The horizontal may remain time. Information input might be represented by asterisks, as before. Communications among segments might be diagonal arrows pointing toward the segment receiving the communication. The diagonals would connect the segment sending the information at the time it is transmitted with the organizational segment receiving the information. Our new diagonal connection would end at the point in time where the latter segment reacts to the information (e.g., by engaging in some form of action, communication, etc.).

Even though this method appears, on the surface, quite useful, it has at least two shortcomings. First, the time component in the matrix has lost some of its meaning. Slow reaction to incoming information may in many cases prohibit effective integration. If so, it is no longer an aid in a strategic process. Secondly, we may want to know more about the particular kind of communication processes occurring among organizational segments. One part of an organization may simply have forwarded unchanged information to another segment. That action would, of course, be considerably different from forwarding information with appropriate commentary and suggestions. (We will not consider the possibility that information might be forwarded with either intentional or unintentional modifications and/or distortions.) Commentary, suggestions and requests, when provided with appropriately transmitted information, can be useful in generating integrated organizational strategies.

To measure organizational communication, in other words, we may employ the matrix in a somewhat different fashion: (1) We may wish to count only communications that include appropriate modifications, commentary, et cetera, as bases for drawing diagonal lines; and (2) we may wish to ignore measures that employ time between the first and the second events as part of the measurement system. In other words, such scores as time weight, QIS, and weighted QIS may not be meaningful for an analysis of organizational communication. Other scores, including the measure for average response speed may continue to be quite valuable to describe the complexity of organizational communication.

While measurement of organizational information flow and organizational decision making characteristics via time–event matrices and related techniques is certainly possible and would likely be of considerable value, the method has not been seriously applied to date. However, time–event-based methods, as well as more standard measurement techniques, have been employed extensively to obtain, for example, data on managerial behavior. The next chapter reports on relevant research completed in our own laboratories.

7

Research Data on the Behavioral and Organizational Effects of Dimensionality

In previous chapters, we have advanced a number of propositions about relationships between cognitive complexity (i.e., differentiative and integrative multidimensionality) and behavior. The present chapter reports on some data collected to test those propositions. In this chapter, we present data in greater detail than was done in Chapter 2. However, a number of hypotheses that we have advanced have yet to be tested, especially those that relate directly to information processing by organizations. The reader in search of research topics can find a fertile field for his or her efforts.

We begin our discussion with research oriented toward the individual and focused on perceptual phenomena. As the chapter progresses, we move toward groups and organizations and, finally, toward data relevant to task performance.

ATTITUDES

Streufert (1966) presented individuals differing in cognitive complexity with information about the views of another person on an important subject. The other person either agreed or sharply disagreed with the views of the subject. Subjects then rated the other person on evaluative attitude scales. Ratings were obtained for three "interaction distances." The subject was asked to consider a situation where he or she would have to spend considerable time with the other person (*minimum interaction distance*), a situation where time and contact was moderate (*moderate interaction distance*) and, finally, a situation where the expected interaction was restricted to temporary visual contact (*maximum interaction distance*). As one might expect, attitudes toward a person who agreed with the subject (conforming message content) were much more favorable than attitudes toward a person whose views were sharply different (deviant message content). The manipulation of interaction distance affected the more and the less cognitively complex subjects quite differently. The least cognitively complex groups of subjects, representing persons with unidimensional cognitive information processing, was not affected by interaction distance. Their judgments were invariate: When the other person was judged positively, that positive attitude tended to be pervasive, no matter what the interaction distance. When that person was judged negatively, the resulting negative attitude was equally pervasive. For three groups of subjects representing higher levels of cognitive complexity, however, attitudes moderated as interaction distance increased (see Figure 7.1).[1]

For the least cognitively complex subjects apparently only one dimension was relevant: the positive or negative evaluation that had been generated by the conforming or deviant thinking of the other person. For subjects representing three higher levels of complexity, information about interaction distance apparently represented a second relevant dimension. In other words, attitudinal judgment of these individuals reflected both dimensions. Because the experimental design presented information on only two dimensions, judgmental discrepancies among the three more cognitively complex groups could not be expected and were not obtained. With the introduction of additional information on other dimensions, these groups may have generated responses that would have reflected their structural differences.

Similar results were obtained by Streufert and Streufert (1969). These authors placed dyad decision-making teams into a complex experimental simulation. Participants received apparently responsive, but, in fact, programmed information throughout the several hours of their participation in the simulation task. Either increasing failure or increasing success was experimentally induced. Decision makers rated their teammates on evalu-

---

[1]The data are supportive of theoretical propositions on attitude development and change advanced by complexity theorists (e.g., Streufert and Streufert, 1978) and indicate that differences in complexity have considerable impact on interpersonal (here, attitude) content areas.

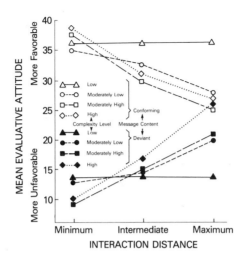

FIGURE 7.1. Effects of cognitive complexity and interaction distance on interpersonal attitudes. (Reproduced from Streufert, S. Conceptual structure, communicator importance and interpersonal attitudes toward conforming and deviant group members. *Journal of Personality and Social Psychology,* 1966, *4,* 100–103.)

ative attitude scales at several points during the simulation. When the teams experienced success, less cognitively complex subjects generated increasingly positive attitudinal ratings of their coworkers. With increasing failure, their attitudes tended to remain constant. As we discuss (in the section on attributions in the chapter), the increase toward more favorable ratings for the success condition, as well as the constant attitudes for the failure condition, reflected subjects' causality attribution in the success or failure experience. For the success condition, less cognitively complex individuals took credit for their team; in the failure condition they viewed causality as external. In either case, attitudes were tied specifically to the causality dimension.

For more cognitively complex persons, attitudes were more varied and, except for moderate success experience, somewhat less favorable than for their less complex counterparts. Apparently the lower levels of evaluative attitudes reflected teammates' frequently different preferences in approaching the task. Results from this research are reproduced in Figure 7.2.

A number of other research efforts on attitude development and change have shown similar results. Less cognitively complex individuals generally tend to generate and maintain attitudes on the basis of a single salient dimension. For more cognitively complex persons, attitudinal judgments tend

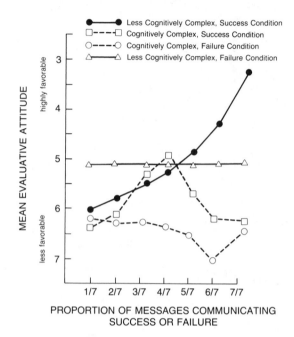

FIGURE 7.2.   Effects of cognitive complexity, success, and failure on attitudes toward team members. (Reproduced from Streufert, S., and Streufert, S. C. Effects of conceptual structure, failure, and success on attributions of causality and interpersonal attitudes. *Journal of Personality and Social Psychology,* 1969, *11,* 138–147.)

to be multidimensionally based. As the salient dimension changes, less cognitively complex persons respond with potential attitude change, a response that varies in linear fashion with the degree of change in the salient dimension. For such individuals, attitude change is unlikely if a change in information (whether relevant or not) is not located on their most salient judgmental dimension. In contrast, more cognitively complex persons may change *less* with modification of any one particular informational dimension, whether salient or not, unless information relevant to other dimensions has changed as well.

In summary: Less cognitively complex individuals are more easily persuaded (where a salient dimension is modified) and less easily persuaded (where the persuader is operating on inappropriate dimensions). In contrast, more cognitively complex individuals change attitudes more easily when new or discrepant information is made available—but that change is likely to be a more moderate one (see Streufert and Fromkin, 1972; Streufert and Streufert, 1978).

ATTRIBUTIONS

We have already mentioned the interactive relationship between attitudes and attributions. People's views of others often depend on the degree to which they consider the other person as causal and/or as responsible for their personal (or their joint) fate. Our research has shown that less cognitively complex persons tend to take credit for success experiences for themselves and their teammates, but typically reject responsibility for failure experience (at least for themselves). More cognitively complex persons, on the other hand, are more likely to view themselves as causal, at least to a point. However, as either success or failure increases to high levels, they will focus on other antecedents of current conditions as well. Data obtained by Streufert and Streufert (1969) on this topic are presented in Figure 7.3.[2]

Nogami and Streufert (1983) and Streufert and Nogami (1984) have extended previous findings on dimensionality and attributions to relationships between message (or question) dimensionality and outcome attributions.

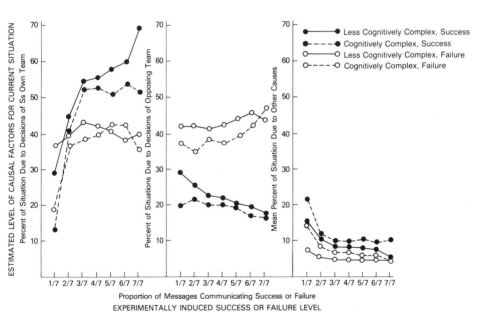

FIGURE 7.3. Effects of cognitive complexity, success, and failure on attributions of causality. (Reproduced from Streufert and Streufert, 1969.)

[2]These data, as well as those on attraction (discussed below), again are indicative of the generality of complexity effects on interpersonal variables.

These authors have shown that specific dimensional cues provided in communications to subjects can produce diverse attributional judgments and decision outcomes. What attributions are made and which decisions are made in task settings is often based on the specific dimension that is made salient by the information. For example, attitudes, jury decisions, or medical decisions may be modified by specific forms of information presentation (see also Streufert and Streufert, 1981b).

ATTRACTION

Attitudes and attributions are, in part, a basis of interpersonal attraction. People tend to like others who they believe are like them, who have similar views, and who are expected to be emotionally or otherwise supportive. For less cognitively complex individuals, similar attitudes are especially effective in generating interpersonal attraction where they reflect the salient dimension relevant to a concern at hand. Research has demonstrated that less cognitively complex persons are likely attracted to each other only when their cognitive *content* is not widely discrepant. Differentiators and integrators, however, are less affected by content. They tend to relate to others who are similar in cognitive structure, even where beliefs and viewpoints may be considerably different.

In a series of research efforts, Streufert and associates (e.g., Streufert, Bushinsky, and Castore, 1967; Streufert, Kliger, and Castore, 1967) asked persons whose complexity level had previously been classified on the basis of Sentence Completion Test (SCT) scores to identify others to whom they felt attracted. Selection occurred for a number of diverse social and task situations. The choices were factor-analyzed to define cohesive groups who selected each other. Less cognitively complex respondents tended to consistently select the same individuals, no matter what social or task condition was identified. Choices varied for more cognitively complex respondents. All groups tended to select partners primarily from their own structural groups.

In addition, the least cognitively complex respondents in some of the analyses tended to split into smaller subgroups (containing two through four persons) that were homogeneous in relevant attitude content. An example sociogram from this research program is presented in Figure 7.4. The obtained factors are shown as graphic (squares, triangles, etc.) symbols representing individuals who made and received choices. Numbers inside the symbols are SCT scores of individual cognitive complexity (simple scoring procedure where 1 = unidimensional information processing, 3 = differentiation, 5 = moderate integration, and 7 = high-level integration). Fig-

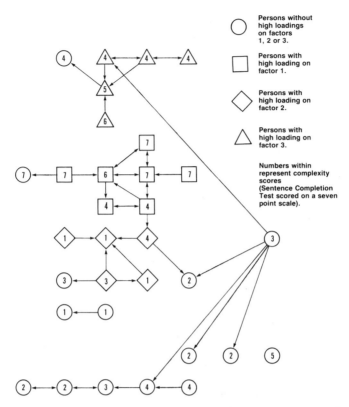

FIGURE 7.4. An example of (social) choices of others by persons representing diverse levels of cognitive complexity (dimensionality). Symbols represent factors identifying groups of persons choosing each other. Numbers are complexity (SCT) scores.

ure 7.4 shows clearly that persons of similar complexity levels clustered together.

PERCEPTION OF OTHERS' INTENT AND STRATEGY

Streufert and Driver (1965, as well as subsequent research efforts by our team) measured perceptions by more versus less cognitively complex decision makers of opponents' strategy. Subjects participated in experimental simulations that included a programmed (simulated) strategic plan supposedly carried out by an opponent. As one might expect, the degree to which the opponents' plans were identified and viewed in terms of long-range pur-

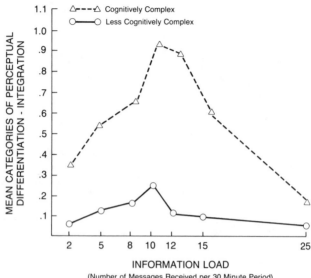

FIGURE 7.5.   Effects of cognitive complexity and information load on perception of the opponent's strategy and intent. (Reprinted from Streufert, S. and Driver M. J. Conceptual structure, information load and perceptual complexity. *Psychonomic Science,* 1965, *3,* 249–250.)

poses and potential outcomes depended, in good part, on the complexity level of the perceivers. In addition, it was a function of the load level of the task setting. More cognitively complex persons (i.e., differentiators and integrators) outperformed their less complex counterparts in all cases. The differences were greatest when load levels were optimal (see the following discussion of task performance). Data on perceptual quality with regard to opponent strategy are presented in Figure 7.5. These results provide support for propositions 4–19 and 4–20, at least as far as perceptual processes are concerned.

LEADERSHIP

The term *leadership* has been used to represent a large number of diverse phenomena. *Leadership,* as it relates to quality of decision making, is discussed in a later portion of this chapter. At present, we restrict ourselves to a consideration of the style of interaction between leaders and subordinates. Streufert, Streufert, and Castore (1968) measured 10 leadership styles defined by Stogdill (1948) to ascertain potential differences between levels of cognitive complexity among participants in a negotiation task. Leaders were rated both by team members and by trained observers. Results generated by the two sets of ratings were virtually identical. Differentiators and integrators were rated higher in leadership styles reflecting tolerance of uncertainty, assumption of the leadership role, consideration of others, and predictive accuracy. Less cognitively complex leaders exceeded their more multidimensional counterparts in initiation of structure, production emphasis, and demands for reconciliation. No differences between the two groups were observed for persuasiveness, tolerance for freedom of action, and representativeness of the group. These data are presented in Figure 7.6. A view of that figure shows that cognitively complex leaders (with the exception of tolerating freedom and demanding reconciliation scores) spread their leadership styles more evenly among the various leadership characteristics. The data support proposition 4–18.

It should be noted that the research data in Figure 7.6 were obtained from groups of persons who were assembled into groups that were homogeneous in their cognitive complexity. In other words, leaders were dealing with structurally similar others. What would occur when leaders must

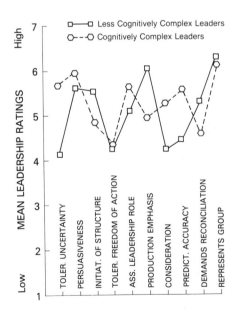

FIGURE 7.6.   Mean leadership ratings on Stogdill's characteristics for leaders of simple and complex conceptual structure. (Reprinted from Streufert, S., Streufert, S. C. and Castore, C. H. Leadership in negotiation and the complexity of conceptual structure. *Journal of Applied Psychology,* 1968, *52,* 218–233.)

deal with more structurally heterogeneous subordinates? While no specific data on that question have been collected, some findings are potentially relevant by implication. In various studies, Streufert and associates have run simulated complex decision making tasks with 2, 4, or 8-person teams. Quite a few participant groups were heterogeneous in team members' complexity levels. In most instances, the more multidimensional persons assumed the leadership role. Often, they achieved the leadership position via a strategic plan. Let us provide an example of this occurrence. In one of these teams, frustration was clearly evident because less cognitively complex team members were unable to understand the differentiated and integrated strategies of their more complex teammates and rejected their thoughts and views as wishy-washy. In contrast, the more cognitively complex team members felt that the decision suggestions advanced by less cognitively complex team members were short-sighted and lacking in strategy (note that the team members were matched for intelligence). At one point in the simulation, one of the more cognitively complex team members insisted (to the dismay of a second cognitively complex colleague) that the team was in need of a strong leader, a point with which the less cognitively complex team members agreed. The speaker then nominated the other cognitively complex individual as the leader. From that point on, the two more cognitively complex persons made all major decisions. Similar occurrences have been observed in numerous decision-making situations, both in simulated and in organizational environments when decision-making teams were mixed in terms of structural characteristics.

The fact that more cognitively complex leaders in the preceding negotiation task (cf. Figure 7.6) typically represented leadership styles of one kind while the less-multidimensional leaders engaged in a different set of styles may suggest that one may want to classify tasks and requirements before deciding what kind of structural leadership style may be preferable in that situation. Where the task is fixed and production criteria are to be emphasized, a less cognitively complex leader may be preferred, at least in the short run. Where a task contains considerable uncertainty and team members must be innovative or creative, however, more-multidimensional leaders would likely be a better choice.

TASK PERFORMANCE

Tasks differ widely in characteristics, difficulty, and requirements. Many do not require cognitively complex performance. Settings that merely require rapid responses (e.g., push a red button when a red light is turned on and a green button when the green light comes on) are not useful for our present interests. Measurement of response latency in milliseconds is not typically applicable to management tasks. Instead, we need to understand how people respond in more complex task settings. *Complex,* as defined here, might mean that several events must be traced, considered, and dealt with at the same time; it might mean that some level of strategy may be required, and so forth. Since the mid-1960s, we have designed several tasks that match these requirements, ranging from visual-motor tasks to complex simulations. The next section of this chapter includes data obtained in visual-motor tasks. Subsequently, we proceed to performance in simulations. Finally, we discuss data from complex organizational settings.

Visual-Motor Performance

Many tasks that are classified as visual-motor occur at relatively low organizational levels (e.g., assembly lines). Generally, such tasks require minimal strategy development. There are, however, some visual-motor tasks that do involve considerable strategic requirements. Consider, for example, the task facing an air traffic controller who must safely guide numerous aircraft that appear simultaneously as signal blips on a radar screen. Strategic coordination is required. Errors, because of the possibility of severe consequences, must be kept to a minimum. Even under highly overloading conditions, excessive risk taking must be avoided.

Air traffic controllers (and others) who engage in complex visual-motor tasks are generally highly trained. It is impossible to duplicate such training with laboratory subjects. In order to avoid the need for extensive training, yet to obtain relevant data on performance in complex visual-motor settings, we have developed a representative task environment. This visual-motor task uses a video-game format, similar to the familiar "Pac-Man." In contrast to Pac-Man, however, careful control has been introduced. Speed of movement and number of antagonists (representing stressor load levels) are under experimental control and can be specified in equal interval steps.

The game uses a series of concentric passageways (see Figure 7.7) that are filled with squares. A subject must scoop up these squares with a horse-shoe shaped object that can be controlled with a handle on a small box that is placed on the subject's desk (i.e., a joy-stick device). Underneath the game matrix on the video screen, the subject's current score, as well as additional information (discussed later), is presented. At the beginning of the game, the participant is provided with 5 (gratis) points. Scooping up each square adds another 5 points to that score. Moving through one unit

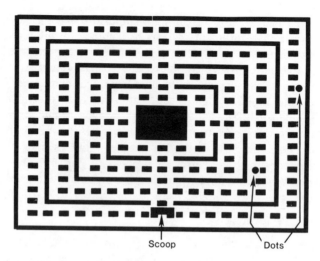

FIGURE 7.7.   Game matrix for the visual-motor task.

of empty space between squares subtracts 1 point. Thus, if a participant were to move in a continuous series through all passageways filled with squares, he or she would obtain $5 - 1 = 4$ points for each square collected.

Unfortunately, a single continuous move is not possible. First of all, some squares are located at intersections of passageways and defy a continuous motion effort. However, by applying strategy, the squares can be gathered in a near-continuous motion effort. If a participant fails to collect any squares at a strategically opportune point in the task, he or she will have to return later through numerous empty spaces which had been cleared of squares by the participant's previous efforts. One point is subtracted for each empty space traversed. These negative points add up rapidly. Good strategy involves effort that avoids the necessity to return through empty spaces.

A second (and more serious) problem encountered by participants is the existence of from one through nine "dots" that randomly move through the passageways of the matrix. As with the scoop, they also cannot cross the solid lines within the matrix. The dots are opponents that are programmed to move in one direction for a while and then, at some random point, to change direction. The dots can turn corners somewhat faster than a well-guided scoop. Collision of the scoop with any dot results in a loud noise, a flashing video screen and an immediate loss of 100 points. After repeated collisions, a participant's score will become negative. After each collision, the offending dot is removed to a different (randomly determined) location in the matrix, making an immediate subsequent collision due to the same error unlikely.[3]

The computer program (used on an Apple II) that controls the presentation of the visual-motor task permits an experimenter to systematically vary conditions for any task period. The experimenter may modify (from task period to task period) (1) the speed of movement (of both scoop and dots) in the matrix, (2) the number of dots that appear and move on the screen, and (3) a constant score that is displayed at the bottom of the subject's video screen. That score represents an experimenter-selected value that indicates the (presumed) average score level that has been obtained by previous subjects while playing the game for the first time, or (optionally) the highest score level that has been obtained by any subject so far. The experimenter can also select the number of task periods in the task.

Each task period continues until the participant has scooped up all squares in the matrix. At the end of the task the final score is displayed on the screen and announced with a fanfare sound. The final score is generally positive for easy load–speed levels, but may become negative as load and speed are increased. (A negative value is generated if a participant guides the scoop through blank spaces about 2.5 times more often than through spaces occupied by squares, and/or if he or she repeatedly loses blocks of 100 points via collisions with dots.)

Four classes of data may be collected from persons participating in the task: (1) scores for strategy, reflecting any movement of the scoop that clearly facilitates collecting squares in off-line locations that, at a later point, could have been reached only by traversing empty space, (2) error scores, obtained by counting the number of collisions with a dot in the matrix, (3) risk-taking scores, reflecting the mean distances between the subject's scoop and an oncoming dot at the times the subject reversed direction. A risk-taking score of 1 implies a necessary collision at the next turn in the matrix if the dot continues to follow the scoop to that point. A score of 5 would indicate that a collision is impossible (distances greater than 5 movement units were assigned the value 5), and (4) the game score, which reflects overall performance of each subject in any one task period. It is the current game score value that is displayed to the subject on the screen throughout each task period.

Pretests of this visual-motor task indicated that a load level of two dots with a moderate speed[4] of motion represented an optimal task environment (even though many subjects preferred higher load levels which, however,

---

[3]The program (Apple II software) for this task was developed by Wise Owl Workshop, Livermore, CA.
[4]Speed Level 3.

typically decreased their performance scores). In our research designs, we selected a warm-up-period that involved a single dot presented at the lowest speed, representing a suboptimal load level. That warm-up-period was followed by four (randomized) subsequent task periods representing optimal (moderate speed, two dots), moderately overloading (moderate speed, four dots), highly overloading (moderate speed, six dots), and extremely overloading (moderate speed, eight dots) task conditions. In a second experiment, both load and speed conditions were varied. Subjects were classified as less cognitively complex versus more cognitively complex (differentiators and/or integrators).

Streufert, Streufert, and Denson (1982; 1985) have reported on data obtained from adults who participated in this task. More cognitively complex persons engaged in considerably more strategic behavior than their less complex counterparts (see Figure 7.8). Increases in load decreased strategic behavior. The data represent a confirmation of parts of proposition 4–17 in a task that differs considerably from other research environments in which that proposition was widely confirmed.

Cognitively complex participants, when compared with less cognitively complex participants, made fewer errors at extremely high load levels. At less extreme load levels, performance differences between complexity groups were insignificant or absent.

Error levels correlated significantly with risk taking (as one might expect,

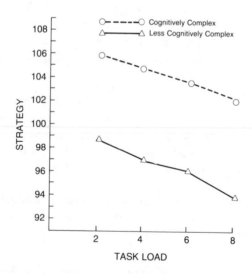

FIGURE 7.8.   Effects of cognitive complexity and increasing overload on the use of strategy in a visual-motor task.

considering the task design). Both errors and risk taking increased with increasing load. An interaction of load and complexity approached but did not reach statistical significance (reflecting a trend toward lesser risk taking by more cognitively complex persons under increasing load levels).

Overall task performance as reflected in the Game Score suggested that increasing load diminishes performance. Game Scores were higher for more cognitively complex persons and discrepancies between the more cognitively complex and the less cognitively complex participants were particularly evident at high load levels.

A subsequent research effort in which both load and speed were varied introduced very severe stressor levels during task periods where both load and speed reached high levels. Performance scores at those levels were generally very low, strategy tended to be absent and errors and risk taking reached very high levels. Differences between more and less cognitively complex participants were rarely evident for the highly overloading task conditions. The data support our proposition 4–22.

In summary, more cognitively complex persons did tend to outperform less complex individuals. Thus, performance in this visual-motor task was clearly aided by the employment of strategic thinking. In other words, where application of strategic thought is useful, more cognitively complex persons may have a distinct performance advantage.

Decision Making

We have previously discussed problems that are encountered by decision theory and mathematical models of decision processes (e.g., calculations of supposedly "optimal" choices) in complex settings. That discussion need not be repeated. In contrast to that approach, Streufert and associates developed a number of experimental and/or quasi-experimental manned simulations that permit the assessment of high-level decision making. These simulations have been used as devices for theory testing, assessment, and applied decision analysis, as well as training techniques. In this section, we are primarily concerned with the application of these decision tasks to research efforts that are concerned with differences among more- versus less-cognitively complex individuals, and with differences in the complexity of information processing by groups and organizations.[5]

[5]While we have described the visual-motor task in some detail, we do not engage in a lengthy discussion of simulation methodology in general or of experimental and/or quasi-experimental simulation tasks in specific. These methods have been discussed at length in the scientific literature. The interested reader is referred to the chapter by Fromkin and Streufert in the Handbook of Industrial and Organizational Psychology (1976, 1983) for a general discussion of simulation research methods, and to Streufert and Swezey (1985) for a discussion of experimental and quasi-experimental simulation research designs.

A number of different content scenarios have been used in these simulations. For example, Streufert, Clardy, Driver, Karlins, Schroder, and Suedfeld (1965) developed a tactical game as an experimental simulation of a military effort to conquer an island. Streufert, Kliger, Castore, and Driver (1967) designed an expanded experimental simulation, named the tactical and negotiations game, in which male and/or female participants make high-level decisions about economic, negotiation, military, and intelligence operations with regard to a small underdeveloped country called "Shamba." Streufert, Streufert, Brink, Cafferty, Krieger, Nogami, and Turner (1972) developed a simulation of an academic environment (Hamilton State University) in which students with middle-of-the-road attitudes attempted to prevent a serious conflict between administrators and radicals.

More recently, our simulation techniques have been developed for microcomputers, which respond in partially or completely preprogrammed fashion to actions taken by participants. Swezey, Streufert, Criswell, Unger, and Van Rijn (1984) have developed a quasi-experimental simulation of an East–West conflict in Yugoslavia. Pogash, Streufert, Denson, and Streufert (1984) have designed a similar, but considerably more complex quasi-experimental simulation that focuses on a potential disaster in a mountainous area of the United States.

Many research designs have been tested in these simulation settings. Several of them have been replicated across scenarios. Replication of obtained data across scenario settings is, of course, advantageous because it demonstrates that results are not scenario or content specific. Some of the many findings relevant to our theroy that have been generated in simulation research are presented here.

Effects of Load on Performance

Performance in complex simulation settings has been measured in terms of both decision *quantity* and decision *quality*. Quantity measures have included (1) number of decisions made, (2) number of decisions designed to obtain information (information search frequency), and (3) number of decisions made in direct response to incoming information (respondent decision making). Quality measures have included (1) differentiation in decision making (the use of different dimensions in formulating decisions), (2) integration in decision making (the frequency of strategy use across time), (3) Quality of Integrated Strategies (QIS), (4) integrated use of information that was obtained through previous search, and (5) presence or absence of risk in decision. In addition, specific performance characteristics (such as the tendency to ignore relevant information) has been measured. The following paragraphs review some of this research.

Streufert, Driver, and Haun (1967) considered a variety of decision-making responses as they are affected by information load. The initial research distinguished among three kinds of decisions: (1) retaliatory decisions, made rapidly in response to incoming information and without application of strategy, (2) integrated (strategic) decisions, and (3) general unintegrated decisions. While overall decision frequency showed a general increase with increasing load (with a dip where integrated responses begin to be replaced by retaliatory responses), strategic decision making reached an optimal level at intermediate loads (i.e., 10 items of information per 30-minute period). That finding supports our propositions 4–19 and 4–20. General unintegrated decision making was lowest at moderate load levels, but higher where load was either very low or excessive, confirming the hypothesis presented in proposition 4–24. Few retaliatory decisions were made when little information was received, but they increased in number toward more moderate levels as load approached optimal levels. As optimal load was exceeded, however, retaliatory actions increased sharply (see proposition 4–23). These data are presented in Figure 7.9.

The majority of work on complexity differences among individuals has focused on integration (i.e., strategic decisions) and, to some degree, on differentiation decisions. The discrepancy between more- versus less-cognitively complex individuals on measures of integrated decision making is especially striking. Particularly, at optimal load levels (as discussed for perception of an opponent's strategy), differentiators and integrators dramatically outperform their less cognitively complex counterparts (see Figure 7.10). The data confirm proposition 4–19 and, in part, proposition 4–32, across various stimulated tasks, group sizes, subcultural and cultural (national) differences, ages and job levels/professions (e.g., Streufert, 1970).

Similar differences have been obtained for decision making under diverse levels of failure (Figure 7.11), success, and information relevance (Figure 7.12). In research on effects of information relevance, load was held constant at an optimal level and relevance was varied as a proportion of load. This procedure allowed relevance manipulation to determine the quantity of load that was designed to be meaningful to task performance. Optimal load levels would thus be expected at 100 percent relevance (10 relevant messages per half hour). Complexity theory would predict general increases in integrated decision making as relevance increased and an even sharper rise in integrated (strategic) activity for more cognitively complex participants in the task. These results were, in fact, observed.

In some research efforts, we have employed measures of highly complex decision processing, such as the QIS measure, which is sensitive to the number of strategically interrelated actions that comprise a general strategy and to the length of time across which strategic decisions are planned. When

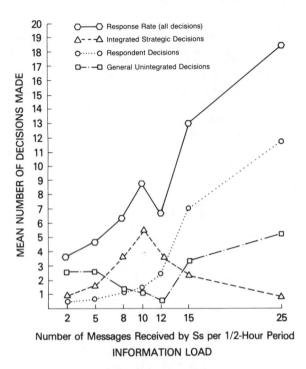

FIGURE 7.9.   Effects of information load on decision making in a complex simulation task. (Reprinted from Streufert, S. Complexity and complex decision making: Convergences between differentiation and integration approaches to the prediction of task performance. *Journal of Experimental Social Psychology,* 1970, *6,* 494–509. Reprinted with permission from Academic Press, Inc.)

such complex measures are used, the general finding, replicated over various subject populations, has been an even greater performance differential between the more and less cognitively complex persons. However, such differences tend to be restricted to a relatively narrow range around optimal environmental load (or success, failure, relevance, etc.) conditions. On measures of this nature, multidimensional differentiators, even though their scores greatly exceed those of cognitively less complex individuals, do not approach scores obtained by individuals who are classified as integrators.

Information Search and Utilization

A variable that has been widely researched by scientists interested in complexity theory has been information search. Generally, more cognitively complex persons, particularly integrators, tend to be more open to (and more actively involved in obtaining) novel–additional information than is

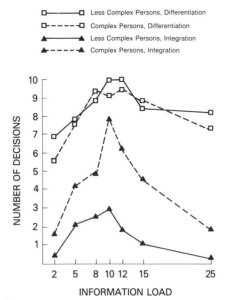

FIGURE 7.10. Effects of information load on differentiation and integration in decision making. (Reprinted from Streufert, S. Complexity and complex decision making. *Journal of Experimental Social Psychology,* 1970, *6,* 494–509. Reprinted with permission from Academic Press, Inc.)

the case for less complex individuals (Karlins and Lamm, 1967). However, the relationship between search and complexity is not a simple one. First, let us distinguish between two kinds of search activities: (1) delegated search, where others are instructed to obtain potentially useful information (an activity that is highly sensitive to social desirability) and (2) self-initiated search, where a decision maker employs his or her own time and effort (at the potential cost of other actions) to obtain desired information.

These two types of search activities appear to be differently affected by task load and by differences in the cognitive complexity of decision makers. As shown in Figure 7.13, delegated search tends to be higher for less cognitively complex decision makers except at optimal load levels. However, self-initiated search by such persons clearly shows load effects. As load increases, these persons are more and more busy with direct responding to incoming information. They have little time left to engage in active search (even though they may still request more information by delegating search activities).

In contrast, active search by more cognitively complex persons (see Figure 7.14) is somewhat less affected by load because all stimuli do not require

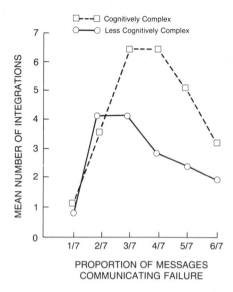

FIGURE 7.11.　　The effect of cognitive complexity and increasing failure on decision integration. (Reprinted from Streufert, S., Streufert, S. C. and Castore, C. H. Complexity, increasing failure and decision making. *Journal of Experimental Research in Personality,* 1969, *3,* 293–300. Reprinted with permission from Academic Press, Inc.)

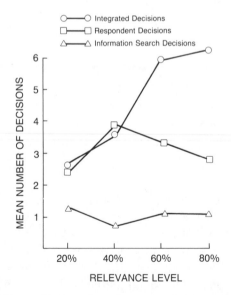

FIGURE 7.12.　　Effects of information relevance on decision making. (Reprinted from Streufert, S. C. Effects of information relevance on decision making in complex environments. *Memory and Cognition,* 1973, *1,* 224–228.)

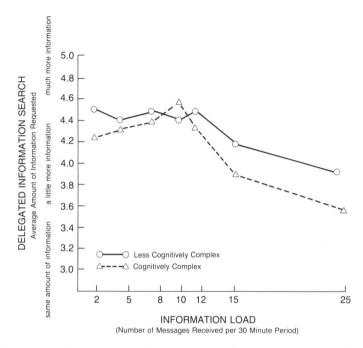

FIGURE 7.13.   Effects of information load on delegated information search. (Reprinted from Streufert, S., Suedfeld, P. and Driver, M. J. Conceptual structure, information search and information utilization. *Journal of Personality and Social Psychology,* 1965, *2,* 736–740.)

respondent decisions, even when load levels are high, and some additional relevant information is typically needed for adequate performance, regardless of load level. The data confirm proposition 4–31. Such information is obtained through search activity. As a consequence, a more moderate slope of search with increasing load tends to reflect the search activities of more cognitively complex individuals.

Additional research (e.g., Suedfeld and Streufert, 1966) has shown that the characteristics of self-initiated search activities also differ between more- versus less-cognitively complex persons. When less-complex persons were searching, they tended to seek information about current events relevant to their task. In contrast, differentiators and integrators tended to seek information more often about emerging changes in task conditions and about potential future events.

Use of information obtained through search has been shown to differ across complexity levels as well. Less cognitively complex persons tend to use obtained information in respondent decisions. In contrast, integrators often convert obtained information into part of an overall strategy. Excessive search, however, often leads to overload and produces poor perfor-

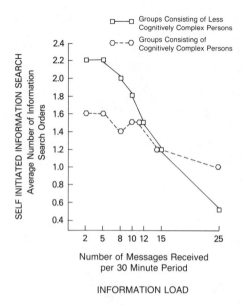

FIGURE 7.14.   Average number of self-initiated information search decisions under changing load conditions for groups of subjects differing in the complexity of conceptual structure.
(Reprinted from Streufert, Suedfeld, and Driver (1965).)

mance, as was suggested in proposition 4–32. This result holds for various
environmental manipulations (e.g., load variation as discussed by Streufert,
Suedfeld, and Driver, 1965; failure variation, e.g., Streufert and Castore,
1971; and other manipulations, such as success or relevance).

Risk Taking

Decision making, particularly in uncertain and complex environments, is
often associated with risk. As a consequence, we have devoted considerable
research efforts to the topics of risk taking and its environmental and structural antecedents. It appears that risk taking is primarily a *cognitive* phenomenon and is consequently relevant to such structural determinants as
dimensionality (cf. Streufert, Streufert, and Denson, 1983, and the next
chapter). Our research shows that risk taking in complex tasks increases
with load, at least until optimal load levels are reached and increases with
time spent on complex tasks (Streufert and Streufert, 1968). The data confirm propositions 4–25, 4–26, and 4–27. They also show that risk taking
may decrease sharply as decision maker(s) near the end of a task assignment
period. Lack of control over a task environment (as perceived by decision

makers) generates increased risky actions (Higbee and Streufert, 1969), and experience of either failure or success often increases risk taking. However, as levels of success or failure become high, risky actions tend to become focused on a single activity. This finding provides evidence for proposition 4-27. For example, if a (simulated) international decision maker must make both economic and military decisions that are risky, a sharp increase in failure or in success generally results in yet higher levels of risk taking that are focused *either* on the military or on the economic realm.

Further, risky behavior appears to be culturally determined. In a simulation of an international conflict similar to the Vietnam War, Chinese and American decision makers represented either a revolutionary movement fighting their national government and its large foreign ally or a foreign nation aiding an allied government against the revolutionary movement. The obtained data paralleled the reasons underlying General Giap's victory at Dien Bien Phu. When Chinese participants in the simulation estimated (in the absence of sufficient information) the strength and capacity of their opponent, they tended to overestimate and, consequently, engaged in very little risk taking. Western (primarily American) participants, on the other hand, underestimated their opponent's strength and, as a consequence, made excessively risky decisions (Streufert and Ishibashi-Sandler, 1973) which, in turn, resulted in unacceptable losses.

Direct effects of cognitive complexity on risk taking propensity per se have not been demonstrated. However, there appears to be a difference in the use of risk as predicted in proposition 4-26: Risk taking by less cognitively complex decision makers tends to be relevant to current task conditions. Differentiators and especially integrators tend to include risky actions as part of a strategy—although they are not averse to employing risky actions in response to current task demands. The overall level of risk taking of persons, however, appears more a function of a cognitive proclivity toward taking chances and a function of a belief in the greater likelihood of success or failure.

RESEARCH WITH ORGANIZATIONS AND ORGANIZATIONAL DECISION MAKERS

Simulation and Organizational Performance

GENERAL PERFORMANCE

Experimental or quasi-experimental simulations have been employed for a variety of purposes and with a wide range of diverse participants. Among the persons or groups who have functioned as decision makers in our simulations were midcareer State Department personnel, midlevel managers from private industry, upper-level managers (e.g., vice presidents) from private industry, banking executives, college and high school students, and adults drawn from various occupations.[6] For some participants at various organizational levels, supervisor and/or peer rating data on job performance were available. Comparisons between simulation performance and job performance have, therefore, been possible. More cognitively complex participants, particularly integrators who held jobs as managers and upper-level executives were typically rated much higher than their less-complex counterparts. The simulation performance on measures such as number of integrations and especially multiplexity F and multiplicity predicted their on-the-job performance even better. A high relationship was also obtained for QIS and Weighted QIS scores with peer and/or supervisor ratings of long-term planning ability.

For college students, grades were not strongly related with measures of complexity or with simulation performance. A minor trend toward improved performance by more cognitively complex college students in subjects such as economics and philosophy was obtained, yet differences between more and less complex students do not appear to exist for such subjects as mathematics and engineering.

COMPARING IDEAL PERFORMANCE AND
MULTIDIMENSIONAL PERFORMANCES

Streufert (1984) analyzed a team of senior executives from various private sector organizations was asked to generate a list of decisions that would typify an "excellent" manager and a list of decisions that would represent a "poor" manager. The hypothetical manager was said to work for a mid-size manufacturing company which had recently projected that a new product would double sales over a 3-year period. A list of relevant information (presumed to be received by the manager during the next 2 years) was also provided. The team of executives was also provided with considerable information about the target company. They were asked to provide the following information (separately) for each of the two (excellent and poor) managers for a hypothetical 24-month period: (1) Specific decisions made by the managers, their timing, and characteristics (such as the general action category), (2) whether and how each decision was related to the manager's overall plan, if any, (3) how each decision was related, or responsive, to information received, and (4) how each decision was related to one or more previous or future decisions in terms of strategic planning.

On the basis of these descriptions of managers' decision characteristics

---

[6]Much of this data has not been published previously.

by the team of senior executives, decision matrices for the excellent and for the poor manager were developed. The same technique that is usually employed to develop decision (time–event) matrices of simulation performance (see Chapter 6) was used for data analysis. The resulting two matrices are presented in Figure 7.15.

Clearly, both the number of diagonals and their interconnections differ greatly for the two hypothetical managers as is suggested by proposition 4–17. Let us take a look at matrices that were based on actual *simulation* participation (Figure 7.16) of other managers. Note the similarity of the two sets of figures. The matrices for the described excellent manager and for the more cognitively complex decision maker are extremely similar, as are the patterns generated by the description of a poor manager and the less cognitively complex decision maker.

For a second comparison, it appeared useful to consider the scores derived from the matrices (see Chapter 6) for the described excellent and poor executives. These scores may be compared to those actually obtained by the same more and less cognitively complex managers who had participated as decision makers in one of our simulations. Score comparisons for the four matrices are presented in Table 7.1 and, graphically, in Figure 7.17.

The similarities between the description of the excellent manager and performance data obtained from the more cognitively complex simulation participant are strikingly evident from both Table 7.1 and Figure 7.17.[7] The same holds for the similarity of the described poor manager and the less complex decision maker. The matrices and scores for the two simulation participants are, incidentally, typical of those generally obtained from more- versus less-cognitively complex persons—no matter whether they are college students, midlevel managers, upper-level managers, or military decision makers. While these various groups would certainly differ in their *specific* content knowledge, they generally do not differ in their range of structural decision-making characteristics.

Managerial and Organizational Performance: Concluding Thoughts

We have seen that, in general, more cognitively complex managers appear to be superior strategists and planners. We have seen that a manager who is viewed as excellent by senior executives is likely to make decisions in a multidimensional fashion. In the process of considering such issues, we have

---

[7]Note, that the Time Weight measure which is most sensitive to length over which integrated strategy is planned appears less useful than measures which emphasize the number of steps across which strategic sequential decisions are developed.

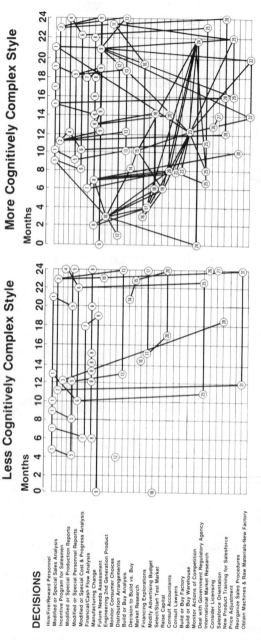

FIGURE 7.15. Senior executive descriptions of a poor and an excellent decision maker. The left matrix, representing a poor decision style reflects poor, the right matrix, representing a more cognitively complex style reflects excellent decision making. (Reprinted (in modified form) from Streufert, S. The dilemma of excellence. *International Management*, 1984, 39, 36–43.)

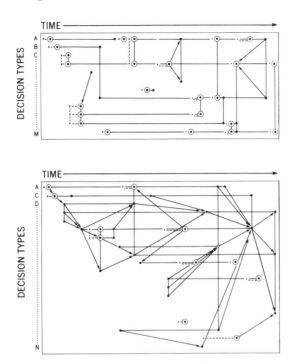

FIGURE 7.16.   Decision making performance of two equivalent executives in a simulation task. The executive represented by the upper matrix was rated as poor in job performance, the executive represented by the lower matrix was rated as excellent in job performance by supervisors and peers. (Reprinted from Streufert, S. The stress of excellence. *Across the Board,* 1983, *20,* 8–16.)

demonstrated that our simulation techniques are appropriate tools for assessment of executive capacities. Yet, a word of caution is again needed. In some situations, there may be little value in strategic decision making. Sometimes, respondent actions are appropriate without concern for secondary or long-term consequences. No final data currently exist that address the capacity of managers to switch from a more differentiative and integrative to a more unidimensional and respondent style of information processing. At present, we are conducting simulation research that requires such a change of orientation. Preliminary data suggest that the ability to shift is present in many but not all cognitively complex managers. On the other hand, that ability seems to be meaningfully related with on-the-job performance ratings of higher executive levels.

The value of differentiated and integrated decision making in organizational settings has also been demonstrated by Schroder and associates and

TABLE 7.1

Matrix-Based Scores for an Excellent and a Poor Manager of a Midsize Company[a]

Scores	Described excellent manager	Described poor manager	Cognitively complex manager (simulation participant)	Less cognitively complex manager (simulation participant)
Number of decisions	34	24	38	36
Number of respondent decisions	9 (26.5)	18 (75.0)	10 (26.3)	23 (63.9)
Number of decision categories	20 (58.8)	15 (62.5)	20 (52.6)	12 (33.3)
Number of integrations	33 (97.1)	8 (33.3)	29 (76.3)	5 (13.9)
Multiplexity F	217 (638.2)	9 (37.5)	235 (618.4)	2 (5.6)
Time weight	219 (644.1)	21 (87.5)	322 (847.4)	10 (27.8)
Number of unintegrated respondent decisions	5 (14.7)	17 (70.8)	6 (15.8)	22 (61.1)
QIS	2156 (6341.2)	31 (129.2)	2008 (5284.2)	20 (55.6)
Weighted QIS	7417 (21814.7)	31 (129.2)	6538 (17205.3)	20 (55.6)
General unintegrated decisions	9 (26.5)	16 (66.7)	8 (21.1)	28 (77.8)

[a]As described by a team of senior executives, and matrix based scores derived from the participation of a cognitively complex (integrating) and a less cognitively complex manager. (Scores are adjusted for the length of simulation participation.) Values in parentheses are proportions of decisions made.

by Driver and associates (see the review chapter). Of particular interest in this regard is the work of Suedfeld and his co-workers, who took their analysis to the *largest* of all organizations—that is, nation states. Suedfeld (e.g., Suedfeld and Rank, 1976; Suedfeld and Tetlock, 1977) has found that speeches by national leaders that reflect a decreased expression of differentiation or integration tend to precede war, and speeches that are characteristic of increased complexity are predictive of periods of peace. Most likely, unidimensional communications, especially where they contain hostility, would generate respondent behavior to perceived challenge that can generate further hostility. In some cases, such hostility may be useful strategy. In other cases, however, it can be counterproductive. On the other hand, refusing the aggressor any intended spoils, but providing the potential to save face tends to reflect a more integrated strategy in response to a serious challenge. If, in fact, greater multidimensionality actually prevents acceleration of conflict into war and, therefore may be employed to aid in the conflict reduction process (cf. Streufert and Streufert, 1979a; Streufert

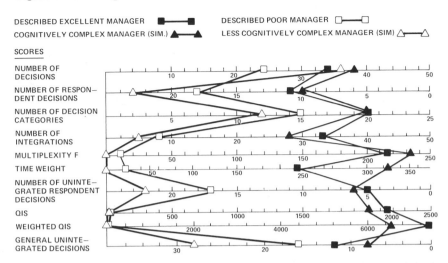

FIGURE 7.17. A graphic representation of matrix based decision making scores derived from descriptions of an excellent and a poor manager of a mid-size company (provided by a team of senior executives) and decision making scores obtained from decisions made by a cognitively complex (integrating) and a less cognitively complex manager who participated in a complex decision making simulation. (Scores are adjusted for length of participation in the simulated decision making task.)

and Streufert, 1985), its application on the international level may be quite valuable.

Many of the theoretical propositions advanced in Chapter 6 are relevant to organizational structure and organizational information flow per se. Our research group, up to this point, has not specifically tested these hypotheses. A reading of the extensive literature on organizations, however, will generate many observations or findings by other authors which may be viewed as more or less directly or indirectly supportive. We hope that some readers of this book will be interested in designing research that will test some of our currently unsupported propositions.

8

Physiological and Health Implications
of Complexity and Other
Managerial Styles

For years, people worried about executives falling prey to the "manager's disease" and early death because of heart attacks. It was thought that this disease occurred with particular frequency among successful managers who are saddled with multiple responsibilities. Several decades of research, however, have shown that managers are not disproportionately subject to heart attacks: Others also experience coronary heart disease with similar frequency. For example, a small craftsman who opens his own shop may be as likely to die from this disease (which physicians term myocardial infarction, or MI for short). Nevertheless, many managers do, in fact, suffer MIs. Their possible death during their productive years is painful to their families, friends, and to their companies alike.

What are the causes of coronary heart disease? How can it be prevented? Millions of dollars have been spent to investigate the major and minor risk factors associated with MIs. The National Institutes of Health have supported several experimental retrospective and prospective research efforts to identify causes and possible intervention techniques. We now know that many of the risk factors are physiological: high blood pressure (both systolic and diastolic), elevated cholesterol in the bloodstream (whether high levels of cholesterol in the food are damaging to persons whose bood level of cholesterol [serum cholesterol] are normal is still under some debate), kidney disease, diabetes, and more. Other major risk factors, however, are behavioral. Smoking (e.g., 20 or more cigarettes per day) can be extremely damaging. Particularly interesting is a phenomenon that has been called "Type A" behavior. We devote considerable space to this concept and its effects on cardiovascular health.

TYPE A CORONARY-PRONE BEHAVIOR

Several years ago, two cardiologists, Rosenman and Friedman, identified a class of behaviors that appeared to be particularly common among heart attack victims. The behaviors appeared to arise from internally generated responses to perceived challenges. More often than not, heart attack victims appear to be time urgent. They tend to set their own deadlines—even when deadlines are not necessary. They often engage in several diverse activities at the same time. They tend to become hostile when challenged by another person, are highly competitive, and view that competitiveness as the foundation of their professional success. Friedman and Rosenman (1974) argued that persons having such behavioral characteristics were predisposed to heart attacks.

At first, Rosenman and Friedman met more skepticism than approval for their behavioral antecedents of heart disease. Physiologists and physicians were accustomed to thinking about failures of physiological systems, about disease, about biochemical and pharmacological agents, and they were not easily persuaded that behavioral (nonpsychiatric, at that) phenomena could be translated into physiological outcomes. However, nearly two decades of research have moved the medical community toward a greater understanding of Type A behavior and its effects, even though cardiovascular physiologists still have no *final* explanation of *how* these behaviors are translated into damage of the heart arteries.

In 1979, the National Heart, Lung and Blood Institute of the National Institutes of Health convened a conference of experts, including cardiovascular physicians, epidemiologists, physiologists, statisticians, and psychologists in what may be described as a "science court." The "court" was convened to determine whether Type A behavior should indeed be considered a major risk factor for heart attacks—a factor of similar importance as high blood pressure, elevated serum cholesterol, and so forth. The expert panel concluded that, at least for working American males, the evidence was clear that Type A behavior *is* a major risk factor. However, the panel also emphasized that additional research was badly needed. They suggested that some components of Type A behavior may well be harmless while others may be detrimental. They also suggested that additional behavioral characteristics that are not included in the Type A conceptualization should be considered as potential candidates for coronary-prone behavior and should be investigated. (With regard to this concern, data presented in the latter part of the present chapter are particularly relevant.)

Let us explore Type A coronary-prone behavior and its implications for the organizational manager. Type A behavior reflects a competitive orientation—that is, a sensitivity to challenge. Challenge and competition however, are typical components of the modern organizational environment, especially at higher levels. In addition, many organizations develop a culture that communicates to its members that Type A behaviors are particularly appropriate and desirable, *and* that they are a foundation of managerial success. It is no wonder, then, that many managers—particularly those striving to advance in companies where internal competition is encouraged, adopt a classic Type A behavioral style. They tend to believe that their particular style of responding is necessary, that it is the basis of their own and their organization's success.

Research, however, suggests otherwise. Our own work (Streufert, Streufert, and Gorson, 1981) has shown that time-urgent behavior, even though it may, at times, be helpful in quite simple tasks where rapid responding is required (e.g., assembly-line operations), it is of no use in complex decision-making tasks that require planning and strategy development. Even simple tasks that require some minimal amount of strategic thought do not favor individuals who display the Type A behavioral style (Streufert, Streufert, and Denson, 1985). Work by David Glass and associates (e.g., Glass, Krakoff, Continda, Hilton, Kehoe, Mannucci, Collins, Snow, and Elting, 1980) has reached quite similar conclusions.

If Type A is a coronary-prone behavior *and* if it is not a likely antecedent of success in complex organizational settings (observation would, for example, suggest that many CEOs are not especially Type As) then we may conclude that one should eliminate this behavioral style from the executive's repertoire of behaviors. Those who have tried (e.g., Rosenman, 1978; Roskies, in press; Suinn and Bloom, 1978) have found this to be a difficult task. For example, the executive who puts away his watch because he does not want to be driven by it any longer often finds it hard to deal with a timeless world where others insist that meetings must start on time. As a result, the executive will likely be peering at other people's wrists—and may remain as time-urgent as ever. In addition, once a Type A executive decides to make the switch to Type B behavior, he or she is likely to want to become a Type B in the hurry that his or her Type A style demands. A lengthy history of intermittent reinforcement for Type A behavior may make this style extremely resistant to extinction.

However, we may not have to be so general in our efforts to eliminate

Type A behaviors. As the NIH panel has suggested, some Type A characteristics may be benign while others are likely dangerous. If we wish to make intervention more successful for executives who want to change toward greater "B'ness," then we should emphasize those Type A components that are *indeed* antecedents of heart disearse. What are these components?

Dembroski, his coworkers, as well as other researchers in the field of behavioral medicine, have analyzed the contributions of various components of Type A behavior to arousal and to subsequent heart disease. Dembroski, MacDougall, Williams, Haney, and Blumenthal (1985) found that only hostility and especially the *anger-in* component of hostility are particularly detrimental. *Anger-in* means that an afflicted person, when challenged, becomes very angry—but does not express that anger overtly. Anger effects may be visible in his or her posture, in the grimace on the face or in a clenched fist. However, speech patterns may remain normal and the challenger may not even notice that he has made the other person furious.

Such internalized anger can generate high levels of physiological arousal—reflected in considerable elevations of blood pressure and heart rate and in the release of catecholamines into the blood stream. A fight-or-flight (i.e., physically active) response to the challenge (which certainly would have been appropriate during our caveman history when we were challenged by that grizzly bear) would serve to diminish or eliminate the circulating catecholamines. However, in today's business world we do not engage in fistfights, and we do not run away from our opponents. Rather, we often just sit there and respond with apparent calm, causing possibly serious damage to our cardiovascular system. We experience what has been termed *stress*. The stressor is the other person and his or her words or actions. The resulting physiological strain initiates a chain of events that—in the long run—can create possible damage to our arteries. To some extent, we may be able to work off the strain effects by jogging or a game of tennis. However, such forms of physical exertion are not always available at the appropriate time.

To summarize, Dembroski would suggest that it is not job involvement or striving for success that represent the antecedents of heart disease, but the intensity of hostility and the tendency to hide one's anger under the surface. We would agree that these characteristics are likely to be quite dangerous. But, why should other components of Type A (e.g., behaviors such as time urgency) be benign—that is, ineffectual in producing heart attacks?

A closer look at the components of Type A appears needed. Together, these components represent a style of behavior. Styles, as we have discussed previously, describe *how* people think and behave, as opposed to *what* they think or which thoughts are translated into behavior. Type A persons generally respond to any challenge, regardless of its content. In other words, they respond to the challenge per se. Their responses are generated by an overall structural style that, in part, governs their perceptions and overt behaviors. Any challenge, for them, is a reason to react overtly or, at least, covertly. The opposite style, Type B, is not easily challenged and often fails to react to interpersonal stressors.

The type A person tends to view information from his or her environment more often as a stressor. He or she is often overly sensitive. As a result, the Type A person may often preceive interpersonal exchange as implying or involving conflict, which, in turn, dictates responses involving overt or covert hostility.

Challenges, however, occur not only in the interpersonal realm. Often we can experience conflicts among our own thought patterns. We are frequently in conflict about decisions we must make. Time urgency may cause conflicts, as may the tendency to simultaneously engage in multiple actions or thoughts. It would, indeed, be surprising if those kinds of conflict would not generate forms of stress and strain, which, in turn, might provide a potential basis for heart disease. We return to that possibility later in this chapter. First, however, let us consider other behavioral characteristics that are related to physiological arousal.

COMPLEXITY, AROUSAL, AND DISEASE

We have indentified Type A as a *style* of behavior. It reflects *how* people respond to challenges and whether they interpret various stimulus information as stressful. In other words, Type A characteristics represent structure, not content. Of course, Type A is not the only style that describes *how* people deal with information. Earlier, we have discussed in some detail the structural characteristics associated with cognitive complexity. We have referred to differentiation and integration as styles of information processing, as cognitive and behavioral processes that address *how* people deal with information. Would, or should, cognitive complexity have similar effects on human cardiovascular physiology as those found in Type A behavior?

Some evidence exists that cognitive styles, in general, relate to physiological response. For example, McCranie, Simpson and Stevens (1981) have demonstrated a relationship between physiological responsivity and field dependence–independence, yet another cognitive style. If styles can relate to arousal, it would only seem reasonable to explore the possible relationship between the style of cognitive complexity and human physiological responsivity. Some research on that relationship has now been completed. While the data available to date are certainly not as extensive as the behavioral data we reported in Chapter 7, they are certainly suggestive. We are reporting these results here, even though each data set may only be based on one or very few studies. We hope that this presentation may motivate other researchers to join us in working on these variables, and to help determine which of these results will be robust and which others may be due to specific intervening variables or may even have been spurious.

The first effort of this kind was reported by Streufert, Streufert, Dembroski, and MacDougall (1978). These authors exposed subjects to challenging tasks and showed that differentiators and integrators generated higher degrees of arousal than their less cognitively complex counterparts ($p < .01$). The arousal levels obtained from differentiators and integrators were similar to those typically obtained from Type A persons. However, the two styles have remained generally uncorrelated. This finding prompted a more detailed exploration of potential effects of cognitive complexity on human cardiovascular physiology and on potential subsequent disease. The resulting research program is currently in its fourth year and has already produced considerable interesting data. Most of those data are concerned with arousal. Minimal (retrospective) data on complexity and heart disease are available as well. We deal initially with research results that are based on physiological responses to various stressor conditions by persons differing in cognitive complexity. Subsequently, we discuss effects of cognitive complexity upon disease.

TASKS

Researchers who investigated the effects of Type A characteristics on arousal and heart disease have typically presented their subjects with *severe* challenges. For example, research participants have been told that they would be asked a few easy questions that most people should be able to answer without difficulty, only to be subjected to questions that they cannot answer even with their best efforts. Others were told that they would be required to submerge their arm for a length of time in ice-cold water, a task that was described as "extremely difficult," and threatened that they would have to submerge their arm "over and over again until they would leave their arm in the ice cold water for the required length of time." Such tasks—or their descriptions by the experimenter as he or she interacts with subjects—can generate very high levels of stress experience. For Type A persons, who feel especially challenged, these tasks tend to generate high levels of arousal.

Typical managers experience high levels of stress only from time to time. Normal job stressor levels are usually lower—yet, in many cases, everpres-

ent. We have felt that our research tasks should reflect more normal managerial stress levels—levels that would be representative of relatively typical
organizational work environments. An understanding of stressor impact at
normal work levels, should provide more detailed insights into the relationships between managerial work and health and into the effects of cognitive complexity as it may moderate these relationships.

We have already discussed our research tasks in a previous chapter. A
concern with planned research on physiological and health effects played a
role in the selection of those tasks. The majority of our research findings
on stress, cognitive complexity, and health have been based on a series of
these tasks which, as the reader will remember, differed considerably from
each other. Participants were exposed (of course, in random order) to the
following tasks or task levels:

1. Resting comfortably alone, while viewing a kaleidoscopic display of
   colors on a videoscreen.
2. Resting comfortably alone, without video (because no arousal differences between conditions (1) and (2) were obtained, data were subsequently combined and employed as a baseline condition to allow the
   calculation of increases in physiological response levels above baseline).
3. Resting in the presence of another person who was occupied with another task. (This condition was defined as a "Social Base Line.")
4. A gentle, nonthreatening interview, based on the Sentence Completion
   (Paragraph Completion) Test of Schroder and Streufert (1962): This
   interview was experienced by most participants as clinical in nature.
   Many participants expressed thoughts and feelings that they had not
   previously communicated to others. In fact, however, the interview
   was designed to assess subjects' complexity level—that is, their ability
   to differentiate and/or integrate. Any statement by participants during the interview that might have implied differentiation and/or integration was gently probed by the interviewer to clarify the presence
   or absence or degree of multidimensionality.
5. Rosenman and Friedman's structured interview (e.g., Rosenman,
   1978) for assessing Type A characteristics: This interview is designed
   to be highly stressful and challenging. The interviewee is continuously
   interrupted, and questioned in somewhat unfriendly and hostile fashion.
6. The visual-motor task that was described previously: Following a low
   stressor warm-up condition, participants were presented with four
   (randomly ordered) load levels varying from moderate to high. The
   same measures of performance discussed in the previous chapter were

employed to compare performance characteristics to physiological responsivity.

Measurement of physiological responsivity under all load conditions was noninvasive. (Invasive measurement would itself have been stressful and would therefore have confounded independent variable manipulations.) Measures of systolic blood pressure (SBP), diastolic blood pressure (DBP), and heart rate (HR) were repeatedly obtained. Unless otherwise specified, repeated measures were averaged within task or load conditions to provide a general indicator of physiological response. For some participants (as additional equipment became available) skin temperature and various electrocardiogram measures were also obtained. The number of data points on these measures are at present insufficient. Nonetheless, these data tend to corroborate other findings that follow.

RESEARCH

Physiological Responsivity (Arousal Levels)

Streufert, Streufert, Lewis, Henderson, and Shields (1982) exposed 26 adult males, varying in age from 24 to 71 to the tasks we have discussed earlier. Increases in SBP, DBP, and HR for the various load and task conditions were compared to nonsocial baseline measurements. For ease of communication, increments in blood pressure and heartrate were expressed as *delta values* (i.e., as differences between mean measured value during a task load and mean baseline value). For the blood pressure measures, the delta values are expressed in terms of millimeters of mercury (Δ mm/Hg); for heartrate as discrepancies in beats per minute (Δ BPM).

Differences between the social baseline condition and the nonsocial baseline (i.e., Δ social baseline) were slight. Some elevation of blood pressure was observed. For the nonthreatening interview (designed to assess cognitive complexity) mean delta values of about 20 mm/Hg were observed for both blood pressure measurements ($p < .01$). Somewhat lower deltas (about 14mm/Hg, $p < .05$) were obtained for the structured interview condition (designed to measure Type A behavior). In both cases, BPM covaried directly with blood pressure changes: a delta of approximately 7 BPM was observed for the nonthreatening complexity interview; a delta of approximately 6 BPM was obtained for the threatening Type A interview. It should be noted that these measures reflect averages—that is, some persons responded with more severe increases in blood pressure and heartrate, and others, of course, with lower elevations. The covariation of SBP, DBP, and

HR for these conditions suggests that a physiologically central process was likely operative: diverse stressors levels resulted in diverse levels of central arousal—producing, in turn, various levels, but no different kinds of physiological strain and stress experience.

A quite different result was obtained for responses to the visual-motor task. For most participants, systolic arousal diminished ($p < .05$), resulting in decreased delta values (particularly when compared to the nonthreatening complexity interview). Diastolic elevations (i.e., delta DBP) however, tended to remain as high as for the structured interview or increased toward or beyond the value observed for the complexity interview. However, for a minority of participants, the physiological reaction was exactly the opposite: They experienced a sharp increase in SBP with a drop in DBP. Heartrate, on the average, tended to rise slightly. Both response tendencies suggest a different *kind* (not just a different level) of stress response than observed for the interviews. The different kind of response occurred for a task that itself was different: In contrast to the interviews, the visual-motor task was nonsocial in nature.

Clearly, the tasks selected for our research proved useful. They were able to generate different levels and different kinds of physiological strain. Based on these findings, we introduced cognitive complexity as an additional variable, primarily to determine whether—and to what degree—a potential capacity to differentiate and/or integrate might moderate physiological arousal. Complexity scores were derived from written responses to the Sentence Completion Test (which correlated highly with scores obtained in the nonthreatening interview). In addition, participants responded to an objective paper and pencil complexity–self description (C × SD) questionnaire that is presently in its developmental stages, and to another developmental measure of cognitive style. That measure, known as General Incongruity Adaptation Level Self-Description Scale (GIAL-SD), is designed to assess the degree to which persons seek or avoid incongruity in their environment.

Subjects in this sample were 42 working adult males. The obtained data replicated the previously obtained results of Streufert, Streufert, & Denson (1983). Again, the greatest arousal level was generated by the nonthreatening complexity interview, with somewhat less arousal obtained during the structured interview. Increases in SBP, DBP, and HR for the two interviews continued to covary, but diverged for the visual-motor task. However, a greater number of persons than previously showed increases in SBP and decreases in DBP.

Only slight effects of cognitive complexity differences on mean arousal deltas were obtained. Significance tests indicated higher levels of arousal by more cognitively complex participants only at $p < .10$. However, a close look at the data suggested that several individual arousal measurements for the cognitively complex participants *within* each series were particularly elevated. Such intermittent elevations were rare for less cognitively complex persons. It appears that some of the questions discussed during the interviews may have generated considerable arousal for differentiators and integrators, while other topics did not. In other words, specific topics turned on a relationship between complexity and arousal. Others did not. In contrast, less cognitively complex individuals apparently responded with general equanimity to all questions in the interviews.

This observation suggested that comparisons of arousal variability rather than level of arousal should be obtained, especially for interview settings where discrepant responses by cognitively complex individuals were especially common. The resulting analysis indicated that arousal variability was higher for cognitively complex persons in both interview situations ($p <$ .01). However, variability also interacted with the Type A behavioral style. Surprisingly, Type B differentiators and integrators generated the highest levels of arousal variability in the complexity interview. Those levels, however, were yet exceeded by arousal variability of cognitively complex individuals identified as Type A when participating in the structured interview. In this interview task, differentiating or integrating Type Bs produced the lowest levels of arousal variability. In other words, arousal variability appears to be an appropriate measure of physiological reactivity (on repeated measurements of noninvasive cardiovascular responses).

Two findings are particularly thought provoking. First of all, only cognitively complex individuals (i.e., differentiators/integrators) generated high but intermittent arousal levels. The global Type A style, by itself, did not predict arousal. A second finding of some interest is the discrepant response by cognitively complex Type As versus cognitively complex Type Bs to the two interviews. Cognitively complex type As responded especially to the structured interview—in other words to *externally* induced challenge. Cognitively complex Type Bs could not be challenged in that fashion, but apparently generated their own *cognitive* conflicts during the nonthreatening complexity interview.

Findings for the visual-motor task were less extensive. Differences in arousal level and in arousal variability across complexity levels were less evident. However, strong performance differences (as discussed in the previous chapter) did emerge. One might expect that performance and arousal would show a common relationship to induced load stressor levels. The obtained relationship, however, was limited to risk-taking behavior and was predicted by differences in Global Type A versus Type B characteristics. Type A persons took greater risks than Type Bs and became more aroused when they did ($p <$ .01). Some greater arousal during risky actions was evident for cognitively complex individuals but that relationship was not strong ($p < .10$). No relationship between risk taking the arousal was obtained for less cognitively complex persons. In general, then, elevated or variable arousal levels were associated with cognitive complexity. Arousal effects were obtained for differentiators and integrators—not for less complex individuals (later in this chapter we consider the potential underlying cause of arousal peaks in these persons: cognitive conflict, generated by the attempt to deal with complex and uncertain environments in a differentiative and integrative strategic fashion). Global Type A style only predicted *which* specific tasks generated elevated physiological responses and only in cognitively complex persons.

Components of Cognitive Complexity

We have already discussed the relationship of Type A to arousal, as well as the differential components of Type A behavior and their likely relationships to heart disease. Cognitive complexity appears similar to Type A in its predictive capacity for arousal. If Type A can be successfully subdivided into components, it might be worthwhile to explore whether cognitive complexity can be subdivided as well. If so, it should be explored whether some components of complexity may be predictors of performance, others of arousal (and possibly disease), yet others of both or neither.

To determine whether the complexity construct can be divided into meaningful components (beyond distinctions between levels of complexity such as the differentiation–integration distinction), we factor analyzed the aforementioned C × SD questionnaire. Six primary factors, accounting for considerably more than half of the total variance in the instrument emerged. They were

1. **Differentiation/integration/hostility.** Persons who scored high on this factor emphasized that other persons apparently fail to understand that the world is multidimensional. They indicated hostility toward those who are unwilling to accept dimensional differences in stimulus fields.
2. **Hasty decision making.** Persons with high scores on this factor appeared to be only vaguely aware of stimulus multidimensionality. They avoided dealing with multidimensional demands by making rapid (often unidimensional) decisions. The time urgency aspect of Type A behavior was also apparent.
3. **Unidimensional authoritarian responding.** Individuals with high scores on this factor were clearly low (unidimensional) in cognitive complexity and emphasized the correctness of their views and perceptions.
4. **High-level integration.** Persons with high scores on this factor tended to view the world in a highly multidimensional fashion and generated

interactive relationships among cognitive dimensions. Planning and strategy development were evident.

5. **Unidimensional rigidity.** Persons with high scores on this factor tended to cling rigidly to unidimensional solutions, even if they were chosen from a partly differentiated group of options.

6. **Differentiation/low-level integration.** Persons with high scores on this factor showed, in general, profiles not unlike those described in Factor 1, however, without the hostility component that was evident in that factor.

Some of these factors (1, 4, 6) appear to reflect cognitively complex styles in cognition or action; others seemed to be associated with less multidimensional orientations (2, 3, 5). While developmental work on the $C \times SD$ instrument continues, the preliminary factor structure appeared sufficiently reasonable to test for physiological arousal implications of the obtained factor scores. All subjects participating in the interview and the visual motor tasks had previously responded to the $C \times SD$ as part of their involvement in the research. Their individual factor scores were calculated. Tests of predictive capacity of the factors for arousal across tasks were performed.

Factor 1 (differentiation/integration/hostility) was a predictor of systolic arousal ($p < .05$). High systolic delta levels were obtained in the complexity interview and (with somewhat lower values) for the visual-motor task. Diastolic delta levels were also elevated, but only for persons who, in addition to high scores on this factor, had been classified as Type A ($p < .01$). The latter group responded with especially high diastolic elevations during the structured interview.

Cognitive complexity, as reflected in Factor 1, does appear to be a reliable predictor of arousal. Particularly interesting was the finding of the joint complexity/Type A/Factor 1 effect on diastolic arousal in the structured interview. Persons who scored high on this factor are not only cognitively complex; they are also hostile. In other words, the combination of hostility, global Type A style, and complexity may have generated arousal levels beyond those that would be obtained on the basis of cognitive complexity or Type A alone. Such a finding may not be surprising, however, if one considers that Dembroski et al. (1985) have specifically related both heart disease and arousal to hostility and internalized anger.

Factor 2 (hasty decision making) reflects cognitions or actions that are not cognitively complex. Nonetheless, persons scoring high on this factor demonstrated considerable arousal (particularly if they had also been classified as Type A) on both the structured interview and the visual-motor task ($p < .005$).

As suggested earlier, hasty decision making is reminiscent of the time-urgency construct that Rosenman and Friedman considered to be a part of the Type A phenomenon (e.g., Friedman and Rosenman, 1974). Yet, research has not generally corroborated the role of time urgency in either arousal or heart disease (e.g., Dembroski et al., in press). One might, therefore, be tempted to question the validity and/or utility of the time urgency component of Type A.

The research discussed here may, however, make a contribution to this issue. Note that the hasty decision-making factor *did* predict physiological arousal in task settings that Type A theorists would view as conducive to increased arousal (i.e., in the socially hostile structured interview and in the challenging video-game represented in our visual-motor task). It appears that differences between our work and the work of Dembroski and others, who did *not* find a relationship between time urgency and physiological arousal, may be a function of the way in which information about people's time orientation was obtained. Where the research of Dembroski and associates relies on the structured interview, with its hostile interpersonal setting, our paper-and-pencil tests did not generate any specific affective responses. It may well be that the obtained hostility in the structured interview overshadows potential time-urgency responses, leading to more pronounced measurement of the former and less sensitivity to the latter (we discuss this issue in more detail later in this chapter).

Factor 4 (high-level integration) served as an excellent predictor of task-related arousal ($p < .01$). An interesting interaction with coronary-prone Type A stylistics was also obtained: Persons classified as Type B with low factor scores (i.e., persons who are not cognitively complex) demonstrated arousal levels that were less than half as high as those of any other group ($p\Delta < .05$). Apparently the combination of Type B stylistics with low complexity levels may function as a protective mechanism. Such a person (because he or she is Type B) may have little reason to feel challenged or upset by environmental events. Because he or she is also classified by a low score on integration, internally generated (and multidimensionally based) cognitive conflicts may also be relatively rare. Such a person may view the world, most of the time, as relatively ordered and unperturbing—even in the event of minor adversity.

The factors reflecting unidimensional authoritarian responding and rigidity did not correlate meaningfully with arousal and are therefore not discussed.

In conclusion, the factors generated substantial evidence for a relationship between cognitive complexity and cardiovascular arousal. The analysis also produced several additional, partly serendipitous, findings. First, complexity, under some conditions, may interact with Type A stylistics or their components. Where both characteristics are present in an individual, arousal levels may be especially elevated. Apparently, task characteristics also affect whether complexity, or Type A, or both, do predict arousal and may also affect the kind (SBP or DBP) of arousal elevation. Secondly, it appears that time urgency, a component characteristic of Type A, may be reindicated by our analysis. In contrast to research that has measured Type A components via the structured interview process, time urgency as assessed via a cognitive paper-and-pencil test *does* appear to preduct arousal.

Complexity and Disease

To date, little is known about the relationship between stylistic facts in human cognition and/or behavior and subsequent disease. A major exception to this statement is, of course, the Type A construct that has been related to the development of heart disease.

What is known about the effects of cognitive complexity on heart disease? Driver (personal communication) has observed that cognitively complex individuals (i.e., differentiators/integrators) are more likely to experience arrhythmias. In a retrospective research effort, Streufert and associates questioned approximately 500 adults about their previous health experience. A modified version of a standard questionnaire often used as an entry interview by family practice physicians was employed. In addition, information about these persons' socioeconomic status, age, gender, et cetera, and Sentence Completion Test scores were obtained.

Responses to all questionnaire items were factor analyzed, yielding, in addition to an expected complexity factor, a number of health-related factors: (1) psychiatric conditions, (2) cardiovascular disease, (3) lung and respiratory disease, and (4) gastrointestinal diseases.

Our interest was, of course, in a potential relationship between cognitive complexity and health. To evaluate effects of complexity as a concomitant of disease, the Sentence Completion Test score was correlated with the various disease factors. It was found that (1) complexity correlated negatively with psychiatric conditions ($p < .05$) (but not with visits to psychiatrists, $p < .01$), (2) less cognitively complex persons tended to be slightly more hypertensive ($p < .10$) and were more often depressed than cognitively complex persons ($p < .05$), (3) cognitively complex individuals experienced more anxiety ($p < .06$) and experienced more categories of gastrointestinal illness ($p < .05$), and (4) the relationships between cognitive complexity and various cardiovascular risk factors (such as hypertension and angina) was generally low but negative (i.e., cognitively complex persons reported fewer heart-related symptons, $p < .10$ and stroke $p < .05$). However, cognitive complexity related positively to the number of reported heart attacks (MI, $p < .05$).

Because only about 7 percent of our sample had actually experienced MIs, standard correlational techniques were not useful as an indicant of any potential relationship. To obtain a better estimate of the relationship of complexity and heart attacks, the 36 persons in our sample who *did* report previous MI's were matched with others of the same age and sex who occupied similar jobs, could be classified as equivalent in socioeconomic status but had remained free of the disease. The difference between the MI and the control group was striking. Heart attack patients scored much higher on the measure of complexity ($p < .001$).

While these data parallel previous findings on complexity and arousal, they should, nonetheless, be considered tentative. First, these data are retrospective. While it is highly unlikely that heart disease could generate complexity (stress usually decreases levels of differentiation and integration), we cannot exclude the possibility of some third factor that might have led to both complexity and heart disease. Prospective research is needed. However, until prospective data are available, we must be concerned about the cardiovascular health of our cognitively complex managers.

AN EXTENSION OF THEORY

Measurement

We have shown that both Type A and cognitive complexity predict arousal. Both Type A and cognitive complexity are apparently predictive of heart disease. Both represent styles of behavior. However, measurement of these styles is widely discrepant. Type A characteristics are best assessed via the structured interview (other measures, such as Jenkins's [1971] Activity Scale are generally less successful). The structured interview represents an unpleasant challenging social situation that often reminds the interviewee of conflicts he or she has previously experienced.

In contrast, cognitive complexity is assessed in a calm or even pleasant setting—either via paper-and-pencil measures that encourage thinking or via the gentle and nonthreatening complexity interview that guides a persons's cognitive efforts. We have seen that the components of the $C \times SD$ measure of complexity do predict arousal where obtained factors reflect a person's capacity to differentiate or integrate.

Quite in contrast, some Type A component scores from the structured interview, which had been expected to predict physiological arousal, have not done so. Two potential reasons for the failure to predict arousal come to mind: (1) a component may indeed be unrelated to physiological responses, or (2) the structured interview may not be an adequate measure of some (theoretical) Type A components. The first possibility appears unlikely because our research obtained time-related arousal effects, while the time urgency component of the structured interview may not do so. In other words, the lack of predictive capacity of some Type A components may be due to measurement problems.

The structured interview technique is primarily social in nature. It is an excellent predictor of hostility-based arousal. Challenge is based on the actions of another person. In Type A individuals, a defensive or aggressive response to the interviewer is generated. One may argue (as did Streufert, 1984) that the experienced social-challenge environment and the potentially resulting hostility experience engenders sufficient interpersonal conflict to overshadow any other, nonsocial, component of Type A responsiveness. In other words, it is possible that the structured interview, especially for Type A individuals, is not an effective means for assessing nonsocial arousal. In contrast, characteristics such as time urgency may reflect an individual's typical response to many task environments that may or may not be interpersonal in nature. From our perspective, such Type A components should probably be measured by techniques that assess an individual's cognitive nonsocial functioning. Such measurement would likely produce a more-accurate representation of their impact on arousal (and, of course, on subsequent behavior).

Theory

We have spent considerable time on the differences of Type A and cognitive complexity. What do the two styles have in common? Are there possible common constructs embedded within these styles that may account for their joint prediction of arousal and disease? Streufert (1984) has suggested that a common construct does exist. A careful analysis of Type A behavior as it is measured by the structured interview points toward one omnipresent phenomenon: *conflict*. For the structured interview situation, that conflict is social in nature. It is generated by the behavior and statements of the interviewer. Anyone who has been trained in administering the structured interview will likely agree that the procedure is characterized by considerable conflict.

What about the interview measuring cognitive complexity? The interviewer is that method behaves very gently. Social conflict is absent. If anything, the interview process is supportive in nature. Where, then, is the conflict?

We would suggest that the interview serves to generate or regenerate conflict in the cognitions of the interviewee. The gentle method of interviewing provides the very basis on which the interviewed persons can generate trust in the interviewer, a trust that permits him or her to expose thoughts and feelings that are unresolved, that reflect previous or concurrent negative experiences. In other words, the technique allows the interviewee to experience and/or express cognitive conflict that, otherwise, may remain hidden. Such conflict, of course, may not be as likely to occur for less cognitively complex persons, and, if it occurs, would probably tend to be less severe.

Arousal and conflict appear to be closely related. We would propose that conflict is a primary antecedent of arousal. Because of its ubiquitous presence and its association with at least two behavioral styles that precede or predict physiological arousal, conflict experience may well be a parsimonious explanation for some behavioral antecedents of heart disease.

We would propose that:

8.1 *Potential behavioral antecedents of cardiovascular disease such as Type A behavior and cognitive complexity induce arousal in response to specific stimulus configurations via the perception and management of social and/or cognitive conflict.*

The presence or absence of conflict may well affect the frequency and the course of other disease states as well. It is now well established that the perception of control over one's environment is related to greater health and loss or absence of control may tend to exacerbate disease. Conflict and control may well be related. For example, Type A persons often feel that conflict with others is a threat to their control of the world (cf. for example, Glass, 1977; Matthews, Glass, Rosenman and Bortner, 1977). On the other hand, greater levels of established control may well diminish the perceived necessity of interpersonal conflict (because others would not dare to initiate a serious challenge to a personal in firm control.

Another research finding suggests that warm physical contact by health care personnel (touching) can shorten the length of hospitalizations. Whether this phenomenon works via some form of identification with the controlling (health care) persons in a perception of concern or caring or merely via the perceived absence of conflict (which is, for most persons, necessarily implied by physical contact warmth), the presence or absence of the conflict component may again play some role. (Note that both the research on control and on touching dealt with disease in general rather than heart disease in specific. In other words, the relationship between conflict and disease may well be general in nature.)

Unfortunately, conflict is common in the organizational world. A manager may experience conflict at home in the morning, with associates and superiors at the office and with competitors and others during the working day. In addition, he or she may generate social or cognitive conflict via Type

A behavior, cognitive complexity, or other personal styles. Although a disease outcome may not be immediate, it may come much too soon for both the manager and for his/her company and family.

THE COMPLEXITY DILEMMA

As we have pointed out earlier, some organizational tasks and situations do not require differentiated and/or integrated approaches to perception, information processing and decision making. However, there are many tasks that clearly do. Particularly, the many complex decision environments with which today's managers are faced on a day-to-day basis are, at least most of the time, better dealt with in an integrative fashion. Surely, an effective manager needs to recognize when multistep planning and strategy are necessary and when they must be modified, either by diminishing the time between steps or by shifting entirely to a respondent mode of decision making.

The manager must also recognize when he or she should again return to a more integrative/strategic mode of information processing and decision making. Yet, to be able to shift back and forth, as required, a manager must, first of all, possess the *capacity* to integrate. We have presented considerable research data that have shown the potential effectiveness of managers who display such an integrative capacity. The conclusion to be drawn from these data is clear: We would want managers to be (or be trained to be) more cognitively complex in general and more integrative in specific. We would also want them to be able to recognize when shifts in their information processing and decision making style are useful or necessary.

We have also provided evidence that points toward increased risk of arousal (and potentially heart disease) for integrative managers. While more data on this topic need to be collected, enough exist to be seriously concerned. An increased risk of heart disease is certainly unacceptable. Costs involved in the loss of any senior executive to illness or death are high.

In other words, we may well be facing a serious dilemma: For managers, particularly responsible senior executives, to be maximally effective, they should be cognitively complex integrators. On the other hand, we would want them to have the lowest possible risk of disease, suggesting, in addition to monitoring of blood pressure and serum cholesterol, regular exercise programs and check-ups, several interventions to decrease *behavioral* risk factors. We would want executives to cease smoking or, at least, to decrease their smoking habits. We would want to intervene, where possible, to diminish the conflict experience generated by their Type A characteristics. But, would we want to intervene to reduce or eliminate managers' integrative multidimensional thought and decision processes, which, as we have shown, are predictive of organizational success? Should we forego our desire for better performance to obtain a reduced risk of heart disease? Or, should performance be our first priority at the cost of potentially increased morbidity and morality? Which choice do we make? What is the rational or moral basis of such a choice? Do we really have to make that choice?

Another Look at Type A and at Complexity

Earlier in this chapter we suggested that conflict is likely the common element in Type A coronary-prone behavior and cognitive complexity. How does the conflict experience generated by Type A behavior and conflict generated by cognitive complexity contribute to managerial performance? If Type A is not productive of managerial (e.g., decision-making) success, while cognitive complexity does predict success, then the two kinds of conflict may themselves be quite different.

Let us first turn to Type A. As currently measured (as described earlier), arousal and heart disease generated by Type A coronary-prone behavior appear to be based on interpersonal hostility and its conscious control (anger-in). Our own research data suggest that Type A may also relate to a time urgency that reflects a cognitive orientation toward rapid elimination of decision conflicts. Such an orientation would not necessarily facilitate executive functioning. While anger-in in executive settings might, at times, be more effective than expressed anger, the generation of hostility toward colleagues, negotiating partners, or competitors (whether or not it is expressed) is generally an ineffective interpersonal strategy. Further, hostility is not conducive to the development of multistep strategies: angry persons, more often than not, tend to behave in respondent or even retaliatory fashion. In other words, any intervention that decreases Type A behavior should be welcome.

The conflict experienced by the cognitively complex integrator is quite different in kind. The latter conflict is more often than not cognitive in nature. We would not argue that the cognitively complex manager will never experience hostility-based interpersonal conflict. Indeed, such a manager might simultaneously demonstrate both Type A and cognitively complex behaviors (although, as discussed previously, the two styles are not meaningfully correlated). However, we suggest that cognitively complex styles by themselves tend to generate substantial cognitive (rather than interpersonal hostility based) conflict patterns.

Cognitive conflict occurs among competing thought patterns and among their perceived implications for action outcomes. It also occurs between competing perceptions of environmental antecedents and competing anticipations of potential consequences of current (considered) decisions. Thus, conflict involves the very essence of integrated thinking and decision making. If we wish to encourage multidimensionality, and especially integrative information processing and decision making, then conflict cannot be eliminated entirely. But, we may be able to reduce its potentially detrimental effects on health.

At the current state of research, we understand only a few of the behavioral effects of conflict experience and we know very little about the physiological outcomes of conflict. We know that conflict can increase physiological arousal (the extensive Type A literature, such as Dembroski, MacDougall, and Shields, 1977, attests to that fact). We also know that some persons (e.g., those at risk for hypertension) are especially subject to conflict-generated physiological responses (e.g., Holroyd and Gorkin, 1983). Nonetheless, until more data become available, our views must remain somewhat global. If, in the long run, research indicates that some cognitive conflicts are more detrimental than other, specifically aimed intervention activities may be identified. At present, however, we can propose only limited procedures for reducing conflict per se.

Let us, however, consider the intervention issue from a different perspective. If conflict is a risk factor that is predictive of heart disease, it joins a number of other risk factors. We know that the major risk factors, at least for heart disease, combine in a fashion that is more than additive (see the U. S. Surgeon General's Report on Smoking, 1983, and, e.g., Brand, Rosenman, Sholtz, and Friedman, 1976). While a single risk factor in an individual may double the chances of MI, the existence of two such factors may increase the risk 6 times. Some researchers have estimated (unpublished) that three risk factors could increase risk as much as 30 times. In other words, it is imperative to minimize the *number* of risk factors that are simultaneously present in any individual. Thus, if conflict is a possible antecedent of cardiovascular disease, we should wish to keep conflict to a minimum. All conflicts that are generally counterproductive should be eliminated. The interpersonal hostility experience generated by the Type A manager is a prime candidate for elimination. Even with regard to cognitive-conflict experiences generated by integrated information processing, something can—at least in some settings—be done. We have seen (Chapter 7) that integration proceeds much more smoothly (and consequently with less sustained conflict experience) when work environments and work (or information) load levels are optimal and when there is a structural match between the organization and its members. Providing such environments where possible (and it certainly may not be possible in all situations) may well reduce some of the undesirable side effects of managerial excellence.

Risk factors, of course, extend much beyond Type A or cognitive-complexity-generated conflict experience. There are a number of physiological risk factors (e.g., elevated blood pressure and high levels of serum cholesterol) that can, where the manager cooperates, be eliminated or, at least, partially controlled. Diets, exercise, and appropriate medications can reduce the risk of heart disease from such factors. But, can one also eliminate the stress that managers experience at their jobs?

There is no question that excessive stress experience is detrimental to both health *and* performance. Nonetheless, many managers are exposed to serious stressor conditions. Biener (1984), for example, reports that of 258 middle and top level managers 8 percent felt very strongly under stress and another 23 percent stated that they were strongly under stress. In other words, about one third of the surveyed managers *admitted* to serious stress problems. Because it is known that managers often deny existing stress experience, the problem may, in fact, be much worse.

Whenever stress experience does exist, it can and often does generate heart disease. In a series of studies in Germany, Siegrist and associates (Siegrist, Dittmann, Matschinger, and Weber, 1982; Siegrist, Dittmann, Rittner, and Weber, 1982; Siegrist, Dittmann, and Weidemann, 1982; Siegrist and Weber, 1983) have shown that unrealistic work demands tend to generate and reinforce styles of unrealistic cognitive appraisals that precede heart disease. In addition, certain *critical experiences*, which Siegrist defines as "active distress," appear to relate to early (premature) heart disease: enhanced efforts due to external demands, threat to achieved position (threat of downward mobility) or to achieved socioeconomic status. Managers, particularly as they achieve higher levels, are quite often under such threat: failure of a venture or even lower profits of a managed division, even if due to a general economic downturn, often leads to the firing of the supposedly responsible manager.

Siegrist points toward two other experiences that tend to be predictive of heart disease: acute life changes and lack of social support. A number of other researchers have studied the effects of these variables on heart disease as well. Undesirable major life events often occur in the year that precedes heart attacks (e.g., Magni, Corfini, Berto, Rizzardo, Bombardelli, and Miraglia, 1983). Major life events have a number of negative effects, from excessive secretion of norepinephrine (e.g., Kohn, Sleet, Caron, and Gray, 1983) to emotional changes, fatigue and weakness, all of which seem to precede heart disease (Falger, 1982). In addition, these negative life events complicate potential recovery from heart attacks (Ell, de Guzman, and Haywood, 1983).

The danger of subsequent heart disease is even greater when managers believe that they are unable to control those events (Magni, et al., 1983). Yet, at least every 10th manager believes that he/she has no control whatsoever over experienced stressors (Biener, 1984). Further, preceived lack of social support exacerbates these problems (e.g., Siegrist et al., 1982 a, b, c) and the combined effect of several stressors is particularly detrimental. Even such standard managerial problems as role conflict (e.g., as we stated, being both hard and soft with one's subordinates) adds into the multiple risk factors that threaten managers (Orpen, 1982). Without question, these demands increase conflict experience, create "worries" (Crisp, Queenan, and Souza, 1984) and anxiety (Marquand and Hughes, 1982). Where the manager is not hardy (Kobasa, Maddi, and Zola, 1983), his coronary-prone characteristics may combine with experienced work stressors to generate physiological heartbeat abnormalities (e.g., Cook and Cashman, 1982), which are frequently the precursors of a coming heart attack.

Unfortunately, experienced anxiety, worries, lack of social support can, in turn, generate other behaviors that, in and of themselves, are likely detrimental. Overeating and excessive smoking are good examples of stress-related compensatory behaviors that exacerbate the problem of potential disease. Overeating often implies greater intake of cholesterol that can speed the onset of heart disease. Smoking under stress may be even worse. For example, MacDougall, Dembroski, Staats, Herd, and Eliot (1983) have shown that either stressors *or* smoking will result in considerably increased physiological responsivity. However if one smokes *during* a stress experience, the physiological (cardiovascular) reaction is likely twice as great.

Intervention

With various risk factors combining to create physiological damage, with the unavoidable stress that managers experience, what can be done to intervene? Some evidence, however limited, for successful interventions does exist (see Johnston, 1982). Of course, we have already suggested that risk factors such as smoking and excessive cholesterol *can* be reduced if the individual cooperates. However, that may not be enough. It may well be worthwhile to consider what an organization may be able to do to aid managers in avoiding disease—especially those managers who are cognitively complex and, consequently, of special value to their company.

A short digression may be useful. Generally, we know that heart disease tends to be high in Western developed nations. It is especially high in some Scandinavian locations and generally low in Japan. While some of these differences may be due to characteristic food intake in those countries, part of these differences may also be explained by the culture in which people live. Japan, for example, has a particularly low rate of heart disease and a culture that is close-knit and provides an excellent social support system. Many Western countries do not generate much social support (Marmot, 1983). Yet, where considerable social support does exist, heart disease tends to be low (e.g., the town of Roseto, PA; see Bruhn, Philips, and Wolf, 1982).

On the other hand, where conflict is present and support is absent, the likelihood of heart disease is considerably greater, no matter whether the person with whom potential conflict may exist is one's spouse (e.g., Haynes, Eaker, and Feinleib, 1983) or one's co-workers or subordinates. It is interesting to note that while heart disease is very high in locations like Finland (Volkonen, 1982) and Norway, countries that are often mentioned in discussions of the epidemiology of heart disease, it is even higher among managers in South Africa. Why? With the limited number of whites in that country, managers reach higher levels of responsibility much earlier in their careers and supervise 5 to 10 times as many persons as they would in most other countries. Control under those conditions is continuously threatened. Conflict, including interracial conflict is enhanced. In other words, stress is excessive. While such high stress levels are not typically present in North America or European organizations, they are nonetheless sufficiently present to consider interventions.

An intervention procedure open to organizations is the intentional reduction of control- and conflict-based stress. The Japanese corporation avoids these problems by more reliable employment and matched organization–individual structures. In contrast, where the Western executive is viewed as an expendable resource, security and the needed support are certainly not provided. It is interesting to note that the cognitively complex manager (unless he or she is at the presidential or CEO level where considerable control is given) may be even more subject to the problems of control and lacking support. Such a manager would necessarily be more aware of control problems. The cognitively complex management style may, itself, be a generator of perceived lacking control: The complex manager is cognizant of uncertain decision outcomes, of potential inaccuracies in predictions, and so forth. In other words, where cognitive complexity and high levels of responsibility come together in persons who cannot be sure of their organizational future, perceived conflict is likely exaggerated, resulting in possibly increased physiological arousal responses and potential subsequent disease. Providing such a person with greater control and security experiences and with the needed support (even if a specific task happens to fail!) should diminish experienced stress, decrease the likelihood of disease and, most likely, increase the quality of task performance.

9

Contributions of Complexity Theory
to Organizations

THEORY AND RESEARCH

In Chapters 4 and 5 (and to some extent in later chapters as well), we presented our theoretical views. Those views have been summarized as Propositions. Most, if not all of these propositions are testable—many with laboratory and field research, others by carefully designed and controlled observational methods. Chapter 7 presented many of the data that we have collected to test and advance complexity theory. At this point in the book, it may be important to consider whether those data support our views. Even more important may be another question: How much of the theory has been supported?

By necessity, the focus of our past research efforts has been somewhat selective. As the reader has probably recognized, specific groups of theoretical propositions have been tested extensively; others remain supported only by observations drawn from manned simulations, from recording behavior of actual groups and/or from relevant observations or research data obtained by other scientists. In part, our *own* research efforts have been restricted as a result of our earlier focus on the determinants of *performance* by individuals, especially managers. We have spent relatively little time testing complexity theory predictions for managerial differences in perceptual variables: Extensive research, reviewed in detail by Streufert and Streufert (1978) had already done that. Another area where we have collected few data is represented by many of the propositions contained in Chapter 5: the functioning of organizations as entities. There simply has been insufficient time and manpower to test all of the propositions we have advanced.

A third group of variables, which has not yet been extensively tested, concerns the acquisition of cognitive complexity by managers, the training methods that may be used to transfer cognitive complexity (where it is already present in other domains) to new task settings or to train the capacity to apply these structural processes to specific task demands. These deficits contrast sharply with the considerable research efforts completed by other scientists as well as by our own research teams with regard to at least three sets of variables: individual (including managerial) perceptual complexity, effects of individual differences in complexity (differentiation and integration) on performance variables, and effects of task environments on performance quality and quantity. Much of the research accomplished in these areas has also considered the interactive effects of environment, individual differences in perceptual complexity, and individual differences in complexity-based task performance.

On the basis of obtained data, there remains little question that managers who display a cognitively complex (differentiative and/or integrative) style differ widely from their less cognitively complex counterparts. For example, such persons tend to hold more multiply determined (and consequently often more moderated) attitudes than do less complex individuals. They are more open to disconfirming information and tend to adjust their thinking accordingly. They engage in more effective information search. They tend to perceive co-workers, as well as opponents, more accurately and are effective in discerning those persons' intents and strategies. They interrelate decisions better, develop more appropriate strategies and are typically more flexible in their consideration of distant goals. They do not over- or underplan. Their strategy development tends to proceed in stepwise fashion and they are open to feedback. In general, they are more effective managers.

Complexity theory predictions about the effects of various task and task-environment (e.g., work load) levels on complex managerial functioning have also been confirmed. We know, for instance, that intermediate levels of environmental input tend to produce optimal levels of differentiation and integration where required. Environmental input variables such as load, challenge, threat, and failure experience all have been shown to generate specific optimal levels that predict maximal differentiative and integrative functioning both in perceptual and in performance tasks. In addition, obtained perceptual and performance differences between complex and less complex managers tend to be greatest at or near these optima. Research has also confirmed that degrees of environmental optimality tend to affect such behaviors as information search, information utilization, and risk taking.

Other propositions involving different kinds and distributions of leadership characteristics in cognitively complex managers, when compared to their less complex counterparts, have also been supported. We know that cognitively complex managers are less likely to attribute cause-and-effect relationships erroneously. Our research has shown that cognitively complex managers function differently, and often much more effectively than do less complex managers, especially when task conditions are at, or near, optimal levels.

This knowledge allows us to predict the extent to which managers (or candidates for a managerial job) are likely to do well in specific job situations. Jobs and task demands can be analyzed to determine the degree to which differentiation and/or integration are useful or essential. The knowledge we have gained may be applied to assessment techniques to find the best managerial talent for various jobs. However, that may not be enough. The reader may ask, "What do we know about the origins of individual differences in managerial complexity? How can we train existing managers to function in more complex fashion? How can we generate the flexibility that permits a manager to employ differentiation and integration, when appropriate, but switch to simpler unidimensional, decisive, actions when those actions are more useful?"

At present, hard data that would support our propositions on the development of cognitive complexity and on managerial training for flexible complexity are scarce. Some research on the development of cognitive complexity (e.g., by Hunt, 1966, 1975, and associates) has been reported in the literature. However, most of that work is concerned with children and teens, not managers. At present, we are involved in a research project on the development of techniques for training adults (including managers) in cognitively complex functioning. The work is based on training simulation methodologies at The Pennsylvania State University, College of Medicine, in Hershey, Pennsylvania. Tests of several of our theoretical propositions on acquiring cognitive complexity and on training for complexity should be completed by the end of 1986.

As mentioned, complexity-oriented research data concerned with organizational functioning are presently limited. It is difficult, if not impossible, to meaningfully manipulate organizations of considerable size in a laboratory setting. Even field research that seeks to control independent variables is often difficult. One can simulate small organizations or segments of organizations, but extrapolations from such simulations to large organizations with multiple units is at best risky. In the face of such difficulties, many organizational researchers have relied on observations of naturally occurring organizational events. However, observations, especially if they are carried out in casual fashion, are often misleading or incomplete. Carefully planned and systematic observational work remains the only alternative. Excellent observational efforts in organizations, such as those by Isenberg (1984), tend to agree with our own observations in simulated organizational settings and lend support to many of the hypotheses advanced in Chapter 5. However, confirming observations do not absolve us from engaging in relevant possible research that is designed to test those propositions in the most rigorous way possible. Such efforts are planned.

COMPLEXITY IN MANAGERIAL AND ORGANIZATIONAL SCIENCE

In the beginning of this book, we considered the differences between "what" people (especially managers) think and "how" they think. We defined the *what* of managerial thinking as relevant to the content of their jobs. We considered *how* they think as reflective of their structural functioning. We suggested that most senior-level managers are generally expert at dealing with job content. They have survived the long process of weeding out those who are less competent. When promoted, transferred, or changing jobs, they are likely to acquire the relevant equivalent content knowledge. To achieve content-based excellence, standard intelligence, motivation, and similar individual difference characteristics are of significance. Structural concerns such as complexity would contribute less to content competence.

The fact that *senior* executives show relatively few differences in their capacity to deal with job content suggests that other phenomena must determine the degree of skill with which they handle their complex tasks. The difference between excellent and not-so-excellent senior executives appears to be based in their structural functioning and specifically in their cognitive complexity.

Most organizational employees do not yet function at senior levels. For a newly hired and aspiring junior executive, mastery of job content is clearly of importance. As long as he or she must merely follow relatively precise instructions, existing structural characteristics may not determine much of the attained success. However, structural concerns appear to take on greater and greater significance as a manager's responsibility increases, as more complicated and contradictory information is encountered, as immediate and particularly long-range outcomes of decisions are less predictable, and as strategy and tentative planning increase in importance. Until such a job level is reached, and until there is certainty that a particular manager understands and handles specific job content very well, the manager must be evaluated in terms of both content and structural abilities.

Below senior levels, managerial assessment must consider whether a manager's inherent intelligence and motivation are sufficient to acquire and handle content knowledge. Does a manager possess the requisite interpersonal skills, attitudes, training, and leadership to allow him or her to survive in and contribute adequately to the organization? Are these and similar characteristics a sufficient part of the person's repertoire of abilities? If they are, or if they exist in sufficient numbers for a specific job, then we may turn to a consideration of a manager's structural characteristics. In summary, we must consider the abilities of managers from the simultaneous vantage points of both content and structurally based capability.

It has often been suggested that managers are frequently promoted until they reach their personal level of incompetence (e.g., the "Peter Principle"). Although that statement has typically focused on content, it holds equally well when one considers structure. Consider a military example. In the military, increases in structurally determined performance requirements tend to be greater at certain promotions than they are at others. For an officer who entered the services as a second lieutenant, promotion up the ranks to lieutenant colonel may have been smooth. The officer received excellent ratings and recommendations because all instructions, even those requiring complicated task performance, have been carried out to the satisfaction of superiors. Independent planning, novel strategy development, and consideration of the implications of multiple uncertainities may, however, not have been necessary. As the officer is promoted to full colonel or even to brigadier general, task requirements may suddenly change. He or she may be faced with making independent decisions that could have major consequences, that must be weighted in the light of considerable uncertainty and that must be integrated into a complex set of interrelated strategies.

Whether or not the officer is able to perform the new task adequately will depend to a great extent on structural characteristics, many of which may not have been required during assignments at previous military levels. Unfortunately, the officer may not know how to differentiate or integrate. He or she may be completely unaware that his or her structurally based performance is inadequate. This lack of awareness points toward major differences between performance based on content characteristics and performance based on structure. People who do not differentiate or integrate (either generally or within a relevant domain) are most often not aware that task-relevant differentiative and/or integrative processes are possible, meaningful, or needed. Quite in contrast, a person whose content knowledge is lacking typically does understand that he or she needs to obtain more information or skill before proceeding.

To summarize, the complexity approach to managerial effectiveness is an important one, yet it is *not* a replacement for more familiar content-based approaches, at least not at junior management levels. Both structural *and* content variables must be considered in managerial assessment and selection. At lower managerial and at nonmanagerial levels (such as assembly-line operations), content considerations may far outstrip the importance of structural considerations. However, in selecting personnel who may later be considered for advancement to higher levels, content variables alone will likely turn out to be insufficient when those persons are considered for advanced positions. However, once higher management positions have been attained, the ability to deal adequately with content may often be considered as a given, and structural complexity variables may emerge as the major predictors of task performance.

It is important to reemphasize that the capacity to differentiate and integrate alone is not necessarily always of value. Without question, responsible managers must be able to apply such capabilities to relevant task areas. However, they must also be able to recognize *when* and *to what extent* differentiative and integrative processes are appropriate at a given time and in response to a given task. Flexibility to apply or not to apply structural capacities, as appropriate, represents a form of ability that reflects another determinant of managerial excellence.

So far, we have discussed the place of complexity in managerial settings on the basis of the data that were presented in Chapter 7. Earlier in this chapter, we stated that data on acquisition of cognitive complexity, on training for differentiation and integration, and on complexity-theory-based predictions of organizational functioning are still limited. As a consequence, we must also limit our discussion of these areas. However, we already know that people can be taught task-relevant differentiative and integrative functioning *if* they do possess the basic capacity to differentiate and integrate in some other domain. We also know that *hierarchical* complexity can be acquired. Other data that may confirm relevant propositions presented in Chapter 4 must await future research. Yet, on the basis of research data that are available, we are aware that the structural performance of many (but not all) managers can, in fact, be modified. In our view, any increase in managerial capacity to differentiate and integrate can be of value, *if* it is associated with the flexibility to use those processes when they are appropriate, retaining, however, the capacity to shift toward more unidimensional functioning as required. Some managers have experienced these training procedures in our simulation setting. Preliminary data suggest improved performance, both in subsequent (training) simulations and on the job.

In the last few pages, we have made a number of suggestions about applying complexity theory to managerial assessment and training. These suggestions, in many cases, were based on data we reported in Chapter 7 and/ or direct observations of managerial task performance in simulated settings. We have not yet presented detailed suggestions for applying the complexity approach to organizational functioning *per se*. At present, very little *experimental* research has tested those of our propositions that are concerned with organizational functioning (Chapter 5). In this area we must, at present, rely heavily on *observations* drawn either from simulation procedures or from observations of actual organizations. Of course, observational data are "soft" in comparison to experimental data. Nonetheless, these observations (by our own research groups and by a number of other researchers) provide at least some support for many of the propositions presented in Chapter 5.

Wherever strong experimental support for our views has been presented or where observations clearly suggest that our propositions are likely valid, we may apply complexity theory to improve managerial and organizational functioning. Within the managerial area, the complexity-based approach permits

1. Assessment of a manager's ability to optimize information flow and to avoid information overload
2. Assessment of a manager's ability to perceive information in differentiated and integrated fashion (e.g., to accurately recognize an opponent's intent and strategy)
3. Assessment of a manager's ability to maximize interpersonal effectiveness via differentiated and integrated attitudinal, leadership, and related processes
4. Assessment of a manager's ability to conceive and apply flexible and contingent strategies
5. Assessment of a manager's approach to planning (e.g., avoidance of overplanning and underplanning)
6. Assessment of a manager's capacity to use and integrate apparently independent or contradictory information toward appropriate interactive decision sequences
7. Assessment of a manager's capacity to shift from one structural mode of information processing to another as task demands shift
8. Training of managers to apply existing differentiative and integrative complexity to additional domains in the task environment

9. Training of managers to understand differences between content and structure to increase available alternative actions and to provide more understanding of task conditions and more alternative decision choices

10. Increasing the level of managers' cognitive complexity toward, at a minimum, a hierarchical and partially integrated approach to strategy development (where appropriate)

11. Training managers to recognize which task demands require cognitively complex responses and which may require (at least temporarily) rapid decision responses.

12. Training managers to search for and deal with information more effectively so that information processing is optimized and overload is, when possible, avoided

13. Training managers to consider risk taking from an integrated perspective to generate risk levels that are determined by task optimization rather than by stressor effects or psychological limitations.

Similarly, from an organizational perspective, the complexity-based approach permits

1. Designing organizational information flow characteristics to optimize load

2. Designing organizational information flow characteristics to be compatible with individual managerial characteristics

3. Designing organizational planning processes to facilitate downstream decision requirements

4. Developing placement strategies for allocating managers to organizational subunits with complexity characteristics that are compatible with those of the managers

5. Developing ways to minimize information uncertainty among upper-level managers (except as uncertainty is required for optimal decision making)

6. Designing goal-oriented strategic approaches to specific task requirements

7. Matching structural information-processing characteristics among organizational subunits

8. Developing organizational design strategies that emphasize multidimensional integrated information processing

9. Minimizing information disparities among organizational subunits where such disparities are inappropriate

10. Optimizing projection and anticipation of future conditions on the basis of integrated information-processing activities

11. Devolping integrated management and leadership strategies

12. Designing flexible strategic planning techniques
13. Developing techniques that minimize excessive organizational differentiation (permitting managers to have adequate overviews of relevant units)
14. Developing means to permit and encourage optimal levels of organizational experimentation and creativity
15. Developing approaches to organizational problems that integrate information load levels with appropriate time spans needed to process the information
16. Designing appropriate information flow strategies among organizational levels and organizational subunits
17. Designing optimal organizational communication techniques, including information filtering strategies across organizational levels.

Certainly, additional interventions based on complexity are possible. Again, future research and evaluation is required to advance complexity-based views and techniques beyond their current level.

We will certainly continue to design research that will investigate the propositions presented in this book. We will also continue to collect data in organizational settings, as appropriate. Our own efforts, however, will not be sufficient. There is too little time available for us to test all of the propositions we have advanced. We invite present and future colleagues to join us in the task of testing complexity theory propositions for managerial and for organizational functioning. We will be delighted if future research supports our views. Yet, we will be equally delighted when research may find those views lacking: Theory improves only when theorists are willing to modify their views as required. Theory improves only when the theorists are willing to grow with their theory. In advance, we thank those scientists who will contribute to that growth process.

Measurement Via the Time–Event Matrix

In Chapter 6, we have discussed measurement in some detail. Time–event matrices that can be derived from simulation research techniques or, where appropriate, from observation of managerial behavior within organizational environments, have been introduced. Whether actually drawn by hand or by computer or represented in terms of numerical values, these matrices may be used to calculate a large number of values that can describe the organizational functioning (e.g., decision making) of a manager, a team of decision makers, or an organization. This appendix presents details about several measures that have been employed in research, in assessment of managerial or organizational performance and/or in training techniques. The measures presented here are not considered exhaustive. Time–event-matrix technology permits the development and validation of a wide variety of additional measurement systems that may be specifically designed with the research, assessment, or training intents of interested investigators or trainers in mind.

It should be noted that the measures suggested in this appendix are *structural* in orientation—that is, they are not concerned with quality of a manager's ability to deal with job content. Procedures for an evaluation of content can, however, be built into specific simulation designs or into our procedures for performance analysis and scoring. Such scores would, of course, have to be obtained in *addition* to the measures that are considered in this appendix. The measurement systems discussed here have, in research by Streufert and associates, been shown to be reliable and valid (criterion validity) for a number of task settings. Additional measures can be developed and calculated if useful for a specific task or setting. Calculation of the measures assumes either that a time–event matrix has been drawn or that measures have been calculated by computer on the basis of data that would be used to generate such a matrix. The various measures reflect different *kinds* of task performance. In and of themselves, scores on any one measure cannot be considered a reflection of good versus bad performance with regard to any particular criterion without knowledge of the momentary situational demands (e.g., environmental conditions). Without question, there are situations where extensive sequential planning is of considerable value, and there are other situations where such planning may be superfluous and inappropriate. In the next pages, each measure and its purpose are discussed. For convenience of communication, we again focus on decision making as one of the two dimensions of a time–event matrix. It should be remembered, however, that numerous other action categories may have been selected instead (or, in addition, in the case of 3- or *n*-dimensional matrices).

NUMBER OF DECISION
CATEGORIES (MEASURE 3)[1]

This measure is a simple count of the number of decision categories that decision makers use during a specified time period. Any category that is part of the count may have been used once or more than once. The measure reflects the extent to which a decision maker is likely to select small or large numbers of action types. In addition, further analysis could reveal whether decision maker(s) are likely to select certain specific actions and eliminate others from consideration. The basic measure may be written as

$$\sum_{1}^{P} C$$

where C is the number of categories employed and 1 through P is the time of participation.

---

[1]For the convenience of those who use the microcomputer-based simulations developed by Streufert, Swezey, and associates, the measure number printed by the computerized scoring program is provided in parentheses.

NUMBER OF DECISIONS (MEASURE 1)

This measure reflects the amount of decision-making activity. It consists of a count of the number of decisions made: the number of points in the matrix.

NUMBER OF INTEGRATIONS
(MEASURES 4 AND 7)

The number of integrations may be computed as

$$\sum_{1}^{P} i_f \quad \text{or} \quad \sum_{1}^{P} i_b \quad \text{or} \quad \sum_{1}^{P} (i_b + i_f) = \sum_{1}^{P} i$$

where i_f are forward integrations (i.e., connections among decision-making points with diagonal arrows pointing forward)

i_b are backward integrations (i.e., connections among decision-making points with diagonal arrows pointing backward), and

i are integrations (i.e., relationships where directionality cannot be established).

As discussed earlier, some decision-making tasks (particularly real-world decision-making settings where the researcher or observer cannot interfere) do not lend themselves to questioning the decision maker(s) about their intent concerning future decisions. Consequently, it may be impossible to determine whether a connection (relationship) among decisions reflects forward integrations (planning a later decision at the time an earlier decision has been made), or backward integration, (using a previous decision to advantage, although the connection was not considered at the time the earlier decision did occur).

Translation of diagonals into integration scores is achieved on a one-to-one basis—that is counting the number of diagonals of a specific type produces the relevant integration score. Where no distinction between forward and backward diagonals can be made, integrations are counted without concern for the direction of the arrows.

Example

For simplicity's sake, let us return to the example matrix in Figure 6.2. The upper matrix contains two forward diagonals, i.e., a score of 2 for i_f (forward integrations). It contains three backward diagonals (i.e., a score of 3 for i_b [backward integrations]). The score of i ($i_f + i_b$) would be 5. Obviously the score for the lower matrix in Figure 6.2 is considerably higher.

Where an entire decision matrix is analyzed, simple counting or statistical processing of the number of diagonals (number of integrations) is sufficient. However, if an experimenter or observer is concerned with a limited time period that represents a part of a larger decision time sequence (e.g., if different conditions are introduced into an experimental simulation across time or if artificial or natural probes are used in a free simulation), diagonals will often cross the time lines that describe a period of interest. In that case, diagonals are credited to the time period during which they originate. If distinctions between backward and forward integrations (diagonals with backward and forward arrows) can be made, then backward integrations will be credited to the period of the second of two decisions. Forward integrations will be credited to the period of the initial of two interconnected decisions. If no distinctions between forward and backward diagonals can be made, all diagonals are credited as integrations to the initial decision.

INTEGRATION TIME WEIGHT (MEASURE 6)

Integration time weight (often simply listed as "Weight") may be computed as

$$\sum_{1}^{P} W$$

Where the measure for number of integrations is concerned merely with the frequency with which connections (i.e., strategic relationships) occur among decisions, the time weight measure addresses the length of time involved in future planning. The measure focuses on individual integrations (diagonals) but measures each diagonal on the time dimension (in units chosen by the experimenter or observer) and replaces the value of 1 (for the occurrence of the diagonal) with the time length value.[2] Consider the example from Figure A.1.

In Figure A.1, the time weight for forward integrations (diagonal connections) between initial decisions B and H, which are connected to decision C, represent two time units each. The connection between C and D rep-

---

[2]Where performance is measured in real-world planning and decision making environments, the Integration Time Weight measure should be applicable to the theory of Jaques (1977) and associates while the measure for forward integrations is not. In the same vein the QIS measure (below) and its sequels may have some meaning for Jaques' theory while Multiplexity and Multiplexity F would not. All of these measures are, however, relevant to complexity theory.

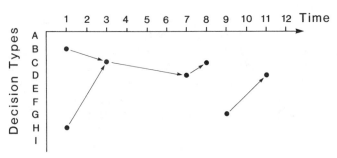

FIGURE A.1.

resents four time units. The connection between D and C represents one time unit, and finally the connection between G and D represents two time units. The total score for integration time weight in this matrix is then $2 + 2 + 4 + 1 + 2 = 11$.

QUALITY OF INTEGRATED STRATEGIES (QIS) (MEASURE 9)

The QIS measure is concerned with the degree to which planning (strategic behavior) follows an overall pattern or is composed of a number of separate unrelated plans. While the score for number of integrations may, for example, be the same in either case, existence of an overall plan connecting all components of the decision-making sequence in a combined strategy would result in a higher QIS score, while separate strategic plans would result in lower QIS scores. QIS measures tend to distinquish between decision-making quality when decision makers operate at advanced decision-making levels. QIS scores cannot exceed integration time weight scores when integrations are made without reference to each other—that is, where an overall strategic plan does not exist or is not developed. The QIS measure reflects, in part, the length of time across which decisions are planned.

QIS may be calculated as

$$\sum_{1}^{P} W(1 + n_{\mathrm{p}} + n_{\mathrm{f}})$$

where W represents the length of the time dimension for any forward integration (or any integration, if distinctions between forward and backward integrations cannot be made). Note, that W is the aforementioned measure (i.e., integration time weight)

n_{p} is the number of additional forward integrations (or any integration, if distinctions between forward and backward integrations cannot be made) connecting to the initial decision in a diagonal connection between two decisions, and

n_f is the number of forward integrations (or any integrations, if distinctions between forward and backward integrations cannot be made) connecting to the decision point representing the subsequent decision in a diagonal connection between two decisions.

The number of integrations n_p and n_f here include only those integrations that are directly connected to either the initial (n_p) or subsequent (n_f) decision points.

Example

Let us again return to Figure A.1. A QIS value is established for each diagonal in the matrix. Let us initially take the diagonal which connects B with C. We have already shown that its weight (W) score is 2.

There are no diagonals connecting to its beginning point. On the other hand, there are two diagonals connecting directly to its end point. It QIS score for this diagonal would be

$$2(1 + 0 + 2) = 6.$$

The same value of 6 would also be obtained for the H to C diagonal. The C to D diagonal, with a W value of 4, connects to two other diagonals at its beginning point and to one other diagonal at its end point. Its score would therefore be

$$4(1 + 2 + 1) = 16.$$

In turn the D to C connection is

$$1(1 + 1 + 0) = 2.$$

Finally, the G to D diagonal maintains its W value because there are no diagonals connected to either the initial or to the subsequent decisions:

$$2(1 + 0 + 0) = 2.$$

For this matrix, thus, the total QIS score then would be

$$6 + 6 + 16 + 2 + 2 = 32.$$

MULTIPLICITY OF INTEGRATION

The multiplicity measure is similar to the previous (QIS) measure. It does *not*, however, take *time* between the original decision and the planned future decision into account. While this measure is not considered to be entirely orthogonal to QIS, it is designed to be supplemental and, possibly, more appropriate than QIS in situations where responding (including strategic integrated responding) occurs quite rapidly or where the time delay between an original and a subsequent decision is more a function of task demands than of long-range decision-planning characteristics. In other words, the measure is sensitive to planning across multiple steps, independent of the time delay between steps. The formula for multiplicity can be directly derived from the formula for quality of integrated strategies (QIS) by removing the time weight term W:

$$\sum_{1}^{P} (1 + n_p + n_f)$$

WEIGHTED QIS (MEASURE 10)

Weighted quality of integrated strategies (WQIS) is an extension of the QIS measure and is designed to obtain scores for sequential chains of interconnections among integrated decisions over long periods of time (i.e., multiple long-term strategic actions that are coordinated). Where the QIS formula calculates time weight for an integration (diagonal connection between decision points differing in time) and multiplies that weight value by the number of other diagonals connected *directly* to the beginning point (initial decision) and to the end point (later integrated decisions) of an integration, the WQIS measure considers *all* integrations (diagonals) that lead in chain sequence to the decision that represents the beginning point of any one integration, *and all* integrations (diagonals) that follow the decision that represents the end of the diagonal connections relfecting an integrated decision, as long as there is no interruption in diagonal (integration) links. Diagonals pointing forward to any decision point in a chain but not connected in any fashion to that chain at their own beginning point are counted. However, other diagonals that are more than one step removed (e.g., those connected to the beginning point of a diagonal that meets the strategic chain only at its endpoint) are ignored. Because of the multiplicative nature of this measure, high scores can be obtained as additional links are added to any strategic chain of decisions. Where no more than three decision points (differing in time) are connected with diagonals (integrations), the WQIS measure will not differ from the QIS measure. Where four decision points (three sequential diagonals) are involved, the measure will not differ for the middle integration, but will differ for the outer two integration diagonals. With an even greater number of diagonal connections in chain sequence, the score for WQIS will exceed the QIS score considerably. The formula for WQIS can be written as

$$\sum_{1}^{P} W (1 + n_{pp} + n_{ff})$$

where n_{pp} is the number of forward integrations reflected in the term n_p for the QIS measure plus all other forward integrations connecting to these integrations, until all integrations (diagonals in the matrix) that connect to each other and that can be traced forward, or maximally one step backward, without interruption, to the beginning point of the forward integration of interest, have been exhausted,

n_{ff} is the number of forward integration reflected in the term n_f for the QIS measure plus all other forward integrations connecting to these integrations, unitl all integrations (diagonals in the matrix) that connect to each other and can be traced forward or maximally one step backward without interruption to the later decision, have been exhausted.

All other terms are the same used in previous formulas.

For the example in Figure A.1, the WQIS score would be calculated as $2(1 + 0 + 3) + 2(1 + 0 + 3) + 4(1 + 2 + 1) + 1(1 + 3 + 0) + 2(1 + 0 + 0) = 38$.

NUMBER OF RESPONDENT DECISIONS

Respondent decision making reflects responses that are made subsequent to and/or are determined in their nature by incoming information. In the time–event matrix, respondent decisions are preceded by a star, representing information to which a decision is relevant. Respondent decision making can be calculated as

$$\sum_{1}^{P} r$$

where r is any decision made within a given time period (discussed later) after receipt of relevant information, if that decision is made in direct response to the information.

Whether a decision is made in response to previously received information should ideally (as discussed earlier) be determined by asking the decision maker to indicate the rationale for a decision as it is made, but may have to be determined by competent judges if access to the decision maker(s) for questioning is not possible.

Different decision-making situations require different timeframes for processing information and for making subsequent decisions. Respondent decisions are most often made quickly in response to incoming information. The potential decision is usually not pondered extensively and may not be considered in terms of existing or emerging strategy. For example, a respondent decision to the intrusion of enemy aircraft into friendly airspace may involve immediate defensive action. Although the reasons for the intrusion may be subsequently considered and may, in some cases, be reflected in future strategic activities, the initial action may represent a one-to-one response to incoming formation. Where an external time limitation between receipt of information and response is imposed to determine whether decision was made quickly enough (after receipt of information) to qualify as a respondent decision, the specific constraints of the decision-making situation must be considered. In other words, such a time frame must be determined individually for each *group* of decision-making *settings* of interest. Obviously, that time frame cannot be changed from one decision-making measurement to the next, if comparisons are to be made.

Received information that leads to respondent decisions is located in the time–event matrix in front of *all* relevant actions (on all relevant horizontals) as asterisks or star points. Where measurement of the length of time between input and decision is of interest, it follows the same time scale that is used to determine the weight of diagonals. All decisions that respond to information are counted in determining the value of the number-of-respondent-decisions score, even if they were made in response to a single item of information.

Note that two variants of respondent decision making exist. One is termed "retaliatory decision making." In this measure, those decisions that are part of a strategic sequence (i.e., are interconnected with other decisions by a forward or backward diagonal) are *not* included in the value of "r." In other words, the measure of retalitory decision making provides an estimate of nonstrategic respondent behavior. Another modification of the respondent decision making measure involves elimination of the time constraint on the information–decision sequence. Here, all decisions made in response to information (regardless of delay) are counted. Such a measure assesses the overall amount of respondent activity. It may be further modified by dividing its value by the total number of decisions in the matrix, to assess the degree to which reactive rather than proactive decisions are made. Note, however, that these modifications of the respondent decision-making measure are not statistically independent. Nonetheless they can be useful for specific research or observation intents.

AVERAGE RESPONSE SPEED (MEASURE 11)

The response speed measure reflects the rapidity with which decision maker(s) respond to incoming information with respondent decisions. The elapsed time between each input and the subsequent decision is measured; the sum of those measures is divided by the number of responses made to that information. For this measure, r (number of respondent decisions) is not constrained by a time limitation between receipt of information and a subsequent decision.

The formula for average response Speed is

$$\frac{\sum\limits_{1}^{P} t_r}{r_p},$$

where t_r is the elapsed time between information receipt and subsequent respondent decision, and

r_p is the number of respondent decisions made in the time period between 1 and p.

SERIAL CONNECTIONS (MEASURE 12)

The serial connection measure is similar to the number of integrations measure. However, it counts interconnections between decisions from the *same* decision category. These interconnections were not considered in any of the preceeding measures. For example, if a decision maker decides to move troop unit A and plans to subsequently move troop unit B (and, when movement of B is accomplished, indicates that the movement of A was accomplished as an antecedent to the movement of B), then a forward serial connection is established. Both decisions fall into a single decision category (i.e., troop movement). They are, by themselves, not likely to reflect an ongoing strategy (as defined) unless they are also interconnected with other decisions from different categories (to which they would be connected by diagonals in the matrix). Serial connections without integrations often reflect a stagnating series of moves that may fail to take complexities of the task environment (i.e., other dimensions and categories) into account. If associated with strategic moves (as reflected in high scores on such measures as number of integrations or QIS), they may, nevertheless, be part of a general (e.g., in the military, an encircling) strategy.

Serial connections may (as were number of integrations) be measured in terms of forward, backward, or general connections between decisions of a single category:

$$\sum_1^P i_{sf} \quad \text{or} \quad \sum_1^P i_{sb} \quad \text{or} \quad \sum_1^P (i_{sf} + i_{sb}) \quad = \quad \sum_1^P i_s,$$

where i_{sf} are forward serial connections, and i_{sb} are backward serial connections and i_s are total $(i_{sf} + i_{sb})$ connections.

PLANNED INTEGRATIONS (MEASURE 13)

Not all actions (here, decisions) that are planned as a follow-up to current actions are actually carried out. Time demands, changed situations, forgetfulness, new strategies, and more may be the reasons for lacking implementation of planned actions. In some settings, an incomplete connection between a current action and a planned future action may indicate lacking strategy. In other settings (e.g., those with considerable uncertainty) a number of contingent actions may have been planned as alternatives and only one (depending on subsequent events) may be carried out as most appropriate. In that case, the ratio of number of actual to planned integrations would necessarily decrease. In other words, evaluation of performance associated with this measure must be based on specific situational and task characteristics. The planned integrations measure reflects the number of times decision makers fail to carry out a previously planned action. The formula for planned integrations can be written as

$$\sum_1^P i_{pf} ,$$

where i_{pf} is a planned forward integration that was not carried out.

Planned integrations that were not completed may be compared with the number of integrations that were completed, to obtain an estimate of the degree to which decision makers do, in fact, operationalize their plans. This score would be reflected by the formula

$$\sum_{1}^{P} i_f - \sum_{1}^{P} i_{pf}$$

or, if a proportion is desired,

$$\frac{\sum_{1}^{P} i_f}{\sum_{1}^{P} i_{pf}}$$

finally, the planned integration measure may be used to estimate the assumed time value for number of integrations that would have occurred in a situation where measurement is artificially truncated by the end of a measurement or observation sequence (e.g., during final participation periods in experimental simulations, or at the retirement of an executive or officer prior to final completion of a task). Under such conditions, it may not be possible to complete all future decisions that were planned when a given action was initiated. A· a result, the uncorrected measure for number of integrations would underestimate the actual strategic planning sequence of a decision maker. This correction may be calculated as

$$1 - \frac{\sum_{1}^{c} i_{pf}}{\sum_{1}^{c} i_f + \sum_{1}^{c} i_{pf}} = \gamma,$$

where 1 through C is any prior time period (or periods) to which a time period under analysis is to be compared.

The obtained value of this correction is then multiplied with the total number of intended integrations plus the number of integrations that were completed

$$\gamma \left(\sum_1^P i_{pf} + \sum_1^P i_f \right),$$

to obtain an estimated value for a corrected number of integrations. Unless the corrected value is less than the actually obtained value for number of integrations, the number of integrations score may be replaced by the corrected score. Similar calculations may be employed to correct other measures that are based on forward or backward integrations.

MULTIPLEXITY F (MEASURE 5)

The multiplexity F measure, although similar in concept to the weighted QIS measure, differs from that measure in two ways: (1) as is the case with the multiplicity of integration calculation, it does not take into account time between an original decision and a planned future decision, and (2) it focuses only on plans that are related to, or are subsequent to, a planned future decision (i.e., the endpoint of a diagonal). In other words, the measure is concerned with the complexity of future strategies as viewed from any given point in time only. By necessity, this measure is truncated by limitations imposed by time: where a paticipant in a task is forcibly removed from the setting or where a task is almost complete, multiplexity F will produce a lower score. In other words, where this measure is to stand representative for general performance at any point in a task, it is useful to divide multiplexity F by time remaining in the task.

Multiplexity F may be written as

$$\sum_1^P (1 + n_{ff}),$$

where n_{ff} is the number of forward integrations reflected in the term n_f of the QIS measure plus all other forward integrations connecting in continuing sequence to these integrations. The use of the term n_{ff} and its limits are the same as previously discussed for the weighted QIS measure. To measure general multiplexity, the formula may be modified,

$$\frac{\sum\limits_{1}^{P} (1 + n_{ff})}{t_r}$$

where t_r is the time remaining in the task.

MEASURES OF PERFORMANCE QUALITY

Performance quality measures that are oriented toward content variables are not directly obtained from a time–event matrix. While the matrix reflects utilization of decision-making styles, it does not in-and-of-itself generate values reflecting performance quality *unless* validated for a given decision-making setting. While validation has occurred in various research-based and applied settings (e.g., executive decision making), we do not wish to argue for the generalization of this validity to any and all decision-making tasks and settings. The various measures obtained via the time–event matrix indicate whether and to what degree specific decision-making behavior occur. Where, for example, strategy is of value, the demonstration of strategic activity will typically reflect performance quality. If, however, a task is quite simple, and only immediate responding is vital, planning and strategy may be useless. In that case, strategic actions (as reflected in the integration measures) may be counterproductive. In addition, task characteristics and performance requirements may change. In one of our experimental simulations, a decision maker is placed in charge of an emergency preparedness team. As he or she enters the simulation, a potential emergency is in the offing, requiring both preparations and planning—that is, strategic action. At this point, a high score for integration, QIS, and multiplexity F may be reflective of performance excellence. As a disaster actually hits, however, planning activity must be replaced by decisive, immediate, and responsive action (now making good use of earlier strategic planning). At this point, high scores on respondent measures, possibly elevated scores on backward integrations and low scores on average response speed are vital. Planning is now of marginal importance and possibly useless if it interferes with the immediate needs to which a decision maker must attend. Once the immediate problems with the disaster are resolved, however, planning—although not necessarily as complex as was previously appropriate—may again be required.

Measuring quality of performance via stylistic time–event matrix variables thus requires consideration of what kind of response is apropriate for specific situations, specific points in a task, and persons with specific responsibility. In addition, scores obtained by persons whose performance is evaluated may tell us (1) whether they are capable of employing a particular performance style (as reflected in some specific measure), and (2) whether (if and when task demands change) they are capable of shifting from one style to another to effectively deal with changes in the task itself.

References

Adorno, T. W., Frenkel-Brunswick, E., Levinson, D. J., and Sanford, R. N. *The authoritarian personality*. New York: Harper, 1950.

Allison, G. T. *Essence of decision*. Boston: Little, Brown, 1971.

Anderson, N. H., and Barrios, A. A. Primacy effects in personality impression formation. *Journal of Abnormal and Social Psychology*, 1961, *63*, 346-350.

Arnett, M. D. Least preferred co-worker score as a measure of cognitive complexity. *Perceptual and Motor Skills*, 1978, *47*, 567-574.

Asch, S. E. Forming impressions of personality. *Journal of Abnormal and Social Psychology*, 1946, *41*, 258-290.

Attneave, F. *Applications of information theory to psychology*. New York: Holt, 1959.

Barnard, C. I. *The functions of the executive*. Cambridge, MA: Harvard University Press, 1968.

Beagles-Roos, J., and Greenfield, P. M. Development of structure and strategy in two-dimensional pictures. *Developmental Psychology*, 1979, *15*, 483-494.

Bhutani, K. A. study of the effect of some cognitive and personality factors on attitude change. *Indian Educational Review*, 1977, *12*, 50-60.

Biener, K. Stress load of management personnel: Results of a survey. *Fortschritt der Medizin*, 1984, *102*, 259-262.

Bieri, J. Cognitive complexity-simplicity and predictive behavior. *Journal of Abnormal and Social Psychology*, 1955, *51*, 263-268.

Bieri, J. Complexity-simplicity as a personality variable in cognitive and preferential behavior. In D. W. Fiske and S. R. Maddi (Eds.), *Functions of varied experience*. Homewood, IL: Dorsey, 1961.

Bieri, J. Cognitive complexity and personality development. In O. J. Harvey (Eds.), *Experience, structure, and adaptability*. New York: Springer, 1966.

Bieri, J. Cognitive complexity and judgment of inconsistent information. In R. P. Abelson, E. Aronson, W. J. McGuire, T. M. Newcombe, M. J. Rosenberg, and P. H. Tannenbaum (Eds.), *Theories of cognitive consistency*. Chicago: Rand McNally, 1968, pp. 633–640.

Bieri, J., Atkins, A. L., Briar, S., Leaman, R. L., Miller, H., and Tripodi, T. *Clinical and social judgment: The discrimination of behavioral information*. New York: Wiley, 1966.

Brand, R. J. , Rosenman, R. H., Scholtz, R. I., and Friedman, M. Multivariate prediction of coronary heart disease in the Western Collaborative Group Study compared to the findings of the Framingham Study. *Circulation*, 1976, *53*, 348–355.

Bruch, M. A., Heisler, B. D., and Conroy, C. G. Effects of conceptual complexity on assertive behavior. *Journal of Counseling Psychology*, 1981, *28*, 377–385.

Bruhn, J. G., Philips, Jr., B. U., and Wolf, S. Lessons from Roseto 20 years later: A community study of heart disease. *Southern Medical Journal*, 1982, *75*, 575–580.

Burns, J. M. *Leadership*. New York: Harper & Row, 1978.

Chandler, M. Siegel, M., and Boyes, M. The development of moral behavior: Continuities and discontinuities. *International Journal of Behavioral Development*, 1980, *3*, 323–332.

Cohen, H. S., and Feldman, J. M. On the domain specificity of cognitive complexity: An alternative approach. *Proceedings of the Annual Convention of the American Psychological Association*, 1975.

Cioata, E. Relationship between cognitive complexity and integrative constants of personality: Emotional stability and affective meaning of stimulation. *Revista de Psichologie*, 1977, *23*, 331–348.

Cook, T. C., and Cashman, P. M. Stress and ecotopic beats in ship's pilots. *Journal of Psychosomatic Research*, 1982, *26*, 559–569.

Crisp, A. H., Queenan, M., and Souza, M. F. Myocardial infarction and the emotional climate. *Lancet*, 1984, *17*, *1* 8377, 616–619.

Crockett, W. H. Cognitive complexity and impression formation. In B. A. Maher (Ed.), *Progress in experimental personality research* (Vol. 2). New York: Academic Press, 1965, pp. 47–90.

Cronen, V. E., and laFleur, G. Inoculation against persuasive attacks: A test of alternative explanations. *Journal of Social Psychology*, 1977, *102*, 255–265.

Daft, R. L., and Weick, K. E. *Toward a model of organizations as interpretation systems*. Texas A&M University: Technical Report ONR No. DG-04, September, 1983.

Davis, C. S., Cook, D. A., Jennings, R. L., and Heck, E. J. Differential client attractiveness in a counseling analogue. *Journal of Counseling Psychology*, 1977, *24*, 472–476.

Delia, J. G., and Clark, R. A. Cognitive complexity, social perception, and the development of listener-adapted communication in six-, eight-, ten-, and twelve-year old boys. *Communication Monographs*, 1977, *44*, 326–345.

Dembroski, T. M., MacDougall, J. M., and Shields, J. L. Physiological reactions to social challenge in persons evidencing the Type A coronary prone behavior pattern. *Journal of Human Stress*, 1977, *3*, 2–10.

Dembroski, T. M., MacDougall, J. M., Williams, R. B., Haney, T. L., and Blumenthal, J. A. Components of Type A, hostility and anger-in: Relationships to angiographic findings. *Psychosomatic Medicine*, 1985, *47*, 219–233.

Dickson, D. N. *Using logical techniques for making better decisions*. Harvard Buisiness Review. New York: John Wiley & Sons, 1983.

Domangue, B. A. Decoding effects of cognitive complexity, tolerance of ambiguity, and verbal–nonverbal inconsistency. *Journal of Personality*, 1978, *46*, 519–535.

Driver, M. J. *Conceptual structure and group process in an internation simulation. Part One: The perception of simulated nations.* Princeton, NJ: Princeton University and Educational Testing Service, ONR Technical Report No. 9, 171-055, and AF Technical Report AF 49(638)-742, and Research Report NIMH Grant M 4186, 1962.

Driver, M. J., and Mock, T. J. *Human information processing, decision style theory and accounting information systems.* Working paper No. 39, Graduate School of Business, University of Southern California, May, 1974.

Driver, M. J., and Steufert, S. *Group composition, input load and group information processing* (Institute Paper, 142). Institute for Research in the Behavioral, Economic and Management Sciences, Purdue University, 1966.

Driver, M. J., and Steufert, S. Integrative complexity: An approach to individuals and groups as information processing systems. *Administration Science Quarterly*, 1969, *14*, 272-285.

Drucker, P. F. *The age of discontinuity: Guidelines to our changing society.* New York: Harper & Row, 1969, pp. 56-57.

Dunnette, M. D. *Handbook of organizational and industrial psychology.* Chicago: Rand McNally, 1976.

Dunnette, M. D. *Handbook of organizational and industrial psychology.* New York: Wiley, 1983.

Durand, R. M. Cognitive complexity, attitudinal affect, and dispersion in affect ratings for products. *Journal of Social Psychology*, 1979, *107*, 209-212.

Durand, R. M. The effect of cognitive complexity on affect ratings in retail stores. *Journal of Social Psychology*, 1980, *110*, 141-142.

Durand, R. M., and Lambert, Z. V. Cognitive differentiation and alienation of consumers. *Perceptual and Motor Skills*, 1979, *49*, 99-108.

Edwards, W. Probability preferences among bets with differing expected values. *American Journal of Psychology*, 1954a, *67*, 56-57.

Edwards, W. Variance preferences in gambling. *American Journal of Psychology*, 1954b, *67*, 441-452.

Edwards, W. Optimal strategies for seeking information: Models for statistics, choice reaction times, and human information processing. *Journal of Mathematical Psychology*, 1965, *2*, 312-329.

Ell, K. L., de Guzman, M., and Haywood, L. J. Stressful life events: A predictor in recovery from heart attacks. *Health Social Work*, 1983, *8*, 133-142.

Falger, P. Factors contributing to the development of vital exhaustion and depression in male MI patients. *Acta Nerv Super* (Praha), 1982, *S3*, 151-156.

Fiedler, F. *Effects of intellectual ability and military experience on leadership performance.* Paper presented at the ARI Conference, Georgetown University, September, 1984.

Fiedler, F. E. A contingency model of leadership effectiveness. In L. Berkowitz (ed.), *Advances in experimental social psychology*, New York: Academic Press, 1964, pp. 149-190.

Fiedler, F. E. The contingency model: A theory of leadership effectiveness. In H. Proshansky and B. Seidenbert (Eds.), *Basic studies in social psychology*. New York: Holt, Rinehart & Winston, 1965, pp. 538-551.

Fishbein, M. An investigation of the relationships between beliefs about an object and the attitude toward that object. *Human Relations*, 1963, *16*, 233-240.

Fishbein, M. Attitude and the prediction of behavior. In M. Fishbein (Ed.), *Readings in attitude theory and measurement*. New York: Wiley, 1967a, 477-492.

Fishbein, M. A behavior theory approach to the relations between beliefs about an object and the attitude toward the object. In M. Fishbein (Ed.), *Readings in attitude theory and measurement*. New York: Wiley, 1967b, 389-400.

Fishbein, M., and Ajzen, I. Attitudes and opinions. In P. Mussen and M. Rosenweig (Eds.), *Annual review of psychology 1972*, Palo Alto, CA: Annual Reviews, 1972, pp. 487–544.

Friedman, M., and Roseman, R. H. *Type A behavior and your heart*. New York: Knopf, 1974.

Fromkin, H. L., and Streufert, S. Laboratory experimentation. In M. Dunnette (Ed.), *Handbook of organizational and industrial psychology*. Chicago: Rand McNally, 1976, pp. 415–465.

Fromkin, H. L., and Steufert, S. Laboratory experimentation. In M. Dunnette (Ed.), *Handbook of organizational and industrial psychology*. New York: Wiley, 1983.

Glass, D. C. *Behavior patterns, stress, and coronary disease*. Hillsdale, NJ: Erlbaum, 1977.

Glass, D., Krakoff, L. R., Continda, R., Hilton, W. F., Kehoe, K., Mannucci, E. G., Collins, C., Snow, B., and Elting, E. Effect of harassment and competition upon cardiovascular and plasma catecholamine responses in Type A and Type B individuals. *Psychophysiology*, 1980, *17*, 453–463.

Guetzkow, H. A use of stimulation in the study of international relations. *Behavioral Science*, 1959, *4*, 183–191.

Hale, C. L. Cognitive complexity–simplicity as a determinant of communication effectiveness. *Communication Monographs*, 1980, *47*, 304–311.

Harvey, O. J., Hunt, D. E., and Schroder, H. M. *Conceptual systems and personality organization*. New York: Wiley, 1961.

Harvey, O. J., Reich, J. W., and Wyer, R. S. Effects of attitude direction, attitude intensity and structure of beliefs upon differentiation. *Journal of Personality and Social Psychology*, 1968, *10*, 472–478.

Haynes, S. G., Eaker, E. D. & Feinleib, M. Spouse behavior and coronary heart disease in men. *American Journal of Epidemiology*, 1983, *118*, 1–22.

Heider, F. Attitudes and cognitive organizations. *Journal of Psychology*, 1946, *21*, 107–112.

Hendrick, H. W. Differences in group problem solving behavior and effectiveness as a function of abstractness. *Journal of Applied Psychology*, 1979, *64*, 518–525.

Higbee, K. L., and Streufert, S. Perceived control and riskiness. *Psychonomic Science*, 1969, *17*, 105–106.

Holloway, E. L., and Wolleat, P. L. Relationship of counselor conceptual level to clinical hypothesis formation. *Journal of Counseling Psychology*, 1980, *27*, 539–545.

Holroyd, K. A., and Gorkin, L. Young adults at risk for hypertension. *Journal of Psychosomatic Research*, 1983, *27*, 131–138.

Horike, K. Studies on person perception (1): The relationship of cognitive complexity to social interaction. *Tohoku Psychologica, Folia*, 1978, *37*, 102–115.

Hunt, D. E. A conceptual systems change model and its application to education. In O. J. Harvey (Ed.), *Experience, structure, and adaptability*. New York: Springer, 1966, pp. 277–302.

Hunt, D. E. Person–environment interaction: A challenge found wanting before it was tried. *Review of Educational Research*, 1975, *2*, 209–230.

Huse, E. F., and Bowditch, J. L. *Behavior in organizations: A systems approach to managing*. (2nd ed.). Reading, MA: 1977.

Hussy, W. Analysis of the need for information during a modified prisoner's dilemma game. *Zeitschrift für Experimentelle und Angewandte Psychologie*, 1979, *26*, 561–572.

Hussy, W., and Scheller, R. Predictive value of cognitive variables in information processing. *Archiv für Psychologie*, 1977, *129*, 226–241.

Isenberg, D. J. How senior managers think (and what about). *Harvard Business Review*, 1984, *Nov/Dec*, 80–90.

Jackson, P. W., and Messick, S. The person, the product and the response: Conceptual problems in the assessment of creativity. *Journal of Personality*, 1965, *33*, 309–329.

James, L. R., and Jones, A. P. Organizational structure: A review of structural dimensions and their conceptual relationships with individual attitudes and behavior. *Organizational Behavior and Human Performance*, 1976, *16*, 74–113.

Jaques, E. *Progression handbook*. Carbondale, IL: Southern Illinois University Press, 1968.

Jaques, E. *A general theory of bureaucracy*. London: Heinemann Educational Books, 1976.

Jaques, E. *A general theory of bureaucracy*. New York: Halsted Division, John Wiley and Sons, 1977.

Jaques, E. *Development of intellectual capability*. Paper presented at the ARI Conference, Georgetown University, September, 1984.

Jaques, E., Gibson, R. O., and Isaac, D. J. *Levels of abstraction in logic and human action*. London: Heinemann, 1978.

Jenkins, C. D. Psychologic and social precursors of coronary disease: II. *New England Journal of Medicine*, 1977, *284*, 307–317.

Johnston, D. W. Behavioral treatment in the reduction of coronary risk factors. *British Journal of Clinical Psychology*, 1982, *21*, 281–294.

Jones, A. P., and Butler, M. C. Influence of cognitive complexity on the dimensions underlying perceptions of the work environment. *Motivation and Emotion*, 1980, *4*, 1–19.

Karlins, M., and Lamm, H. Information search as a function of conceptual structure in a complex problem solving task. *Journal of Personality and Social Psychology*, 1967, *5*, 456–459.

Kenn, P. G. W., and Scott-Morton, M. S. *Decision support systems: An organizational perspective*. Reading, MA: Addison-Wesley, 1978.

Kelly, G. A. *The psychology of personal constructs. Volume 1: A theory of personality*. New York: W. W. Norton, 1955.

Kobasa, S. C., Maddi, S. R., and Zola, M. A. Type A and hardiness. *Journal of Behavioral Medicine*, 1983, *6*, 41–51.

Kohn, L. M., Sleet, D. A., Carson, J. C., and Gray, R. T. Life changes and urinary norepinephrine in myocardial infarction. *Journal of Human Stress*, 1983, *9*, 38–45.

Lawrence, P. R., and Dyer, D. *Renewing American industry*. New York: Free Press, 1983.

Lawrence, P. R., and Lorsch, J. W. Differentiation and integration in complex organizations. *Administrative Science Quarterly*, 1967a, *12*, 1–47.

Lawrence, P. R., and Lorsch, J. W. *Organization and environment*. Cambridge, MA: Harvard University Press, 1967b.

Levi, A., and Tetlock, P. E. A cognitive analysis of Japan's 1941 decision for war. *Journal of Conflict Resolution*, 1980, *24*, 195–211.

Lewin, K. *Principles of topological psychology*. New York: McGraw-Hill, 1936.

Linville, P. W., and Jones, E. E. Polarized appraisals of out-group members. *Journal of Personality and Social Psychology*, 1980, *38*, 689–703.

Lorsch, J. W. *Handbook of organizational behavior*. New Jersey: Prentice-Hall, in press.

Lorsch, J. W., and Lawrence, P. R. The diagnosis of organizational problems. In W. G. Bennis, D. K. Benne, and R. Chin (Eds.): *The planning of change*. (2nd ed.). New York: Holt, Rinehart and Winston, 1969, pp. 468–477.

Luchins, A. S. Primacy-recency in impression information. In C. I. Hovland (Ed.), *The order of presentation in persuasion*. New Haven: Yale University Press, 1957, pp. 33–61.

Luchins, A. S. Definitiveness of impressions and primary–recency in communication. *Journal of Social Psychology*, 1958, *48*, 275–290.

MacDougall, J. M., Dembroski, T. M., Staats, S., Herd, J. A., and Eliot, R. S. Selective cardiovasuclar effects of stress and cigarette smoking. *Journal of Human Stress*, 1983, *9*, 13-21.

Maddi, S. R. Motivational aspects of creativity. *Journal of Personality*, 1965, *33*, 330-347.

Magni, G., Corfini, A., Berto, F., Rizzardo, R., Bombardelli, S., and Miraglia, G. Life events and myocardial infarction. *Australian and New Zealand Journal of Medicine*, 1983, *13*, 257-260.

March, J. G. The technology of foolishness. In H. J. Leavitt, L. R. Pondy, and D. M. Boje (Eds.), *Readings in managerial psychology* (3rd ed.). Chicago: University of Chicago Press, 1980, pp. 628-639.

March, J. G., and Simon, H. A. *Organizations*. New York: Wiley, 1958.

Margerison, C., and Kakabadse, A. *How American chief executives succeed: Implications for developing high potential employees*. New York: American Management Associations, 1984.

Marmot, M. G. Stress, social and cultural variations in heart disease. *Journal of Psychosomatic Research*, 1983, *27*, 377-384.

Marquand, C. J., and Hughes, R. N. Psychosocial characteristics of coronary prone personality. *New Zealand Medical Journal*, 1982, *9*, 376-379.

Matthews, K. A., Glass, D. C., Rosenman, R. H., and Bortner, R. W. Competitive drive, pattern A, and coronary heart disease: A further analysis of some data from the Western Collaborative Group Study. *Journal of Chronic Disease*, 1977, *30*, 489-498.

McCranie, E. W., Simpson, M. E., and Stevens, J. S. Type A behavior, field dependence, and serum lipids. *Psychosomatic Medicine*, 1981, *43*, 107-116.

Mednick, S. A. The associate basis of the creative process. In M. T. Mednick and S. A. Mednick (Eds.), *Research in personality*. New York: Holt, Rinehart and Winston, 1963.

Mihevc, N.T. Information valence and cognitive complexity in the political domain. *Journal of Psychology*, 1978, *99*, 163-177.

Miller, G. A. The magical number seven plus or minus two: Some limits on our capacity to process information. *Psychological Review*, 1956, *63*, 81-97.

Miller, J. G. *Living systems*. New York: McGraw-Hill, 1978.

Mintzberg, H. Planning on the left side and managing on the right. *Harvard Business Review*, July-August, 1976, p. 53.

Mitchell, T. R. The construct validity of three dimensions of leadership research. *Journal of Social Psychology*, 1970, *80*, 89-94.

Mizerski, R. W. Causal complexity: A measure of consumer causal attribution. *Journal of Marketing Research*. 1978, *15*, 220-228.

Neimeyer, G. J., and Banikiotes, P. G. Flexibility of disclosure and measures of cognitive integration and differentiation. *Perceptual and Motor Skills*, 1980, *50*, 907-910.

Nogami, G. Y., and Streufert, S. The dimensionality of attributions of causality and responsibility for an accident. *European Journal of Social Psychology*, 1983, *13*, 433-436.

O'Keefe, D. J., and Brady, R. M. Cognitive complexity and the effects of thought on attitude change. *Social Behavior and Personality*, 1980, *8*, 49-56.

O'Keefe, B.J., and Delia, J. G. Construct comprehensiveness and cognitive complexity. *Perceptual and Motor Skills*, 1978, *46*, 548-550.

Orpen, C. Type A personality as a moderator of role overload and individual strain. *Journal of Human Stress*, 1982, *8*, 8-14.

Osgood, C. E., Suci, G. J., and Tannenbaum, P. H. *The measurement of meaning*. Urbana IL: University of Illinois Press, 1957.

Peters, J. J., and Waterman, R. H., Jr. *In search of excellence*. New York: Harper & Row, 1982.

Peterson, C., and Scott, W. A. *Generality and topic specificity of cognitive styles*. Unpublished manuscript, University of Colorado, 1974.

Pettigrew, A. M. *The politics of organizational decision making*. London: Tavistock, 1973.

Pettigrew, A. M. On studying organizational cultures. *Administrative Science Quarterly*, 1979, *24*, 570–581.

Pfeffer, J., and Salancik, G. R. *The external control of organizations: A resource dependence perspective*. New York: Harper & Row, 1978.

Pogash, R. M., Streufert, S. C., Denson, A. L., and Streufert, S. A player's manual for a complex disaster decision simulation. Pennsylvania State University College of Medicine: Technical Report ONR No. 17, 1984.

Pomerleau, O. F., and Brady, J. P. *Behavioral medicine: Theory and practice*. Baltimore, MD: Williams & Wilkins Company, 1979.

Porter, C. A., and Suedfeld, P. Integrative complexity in the corresponding of literary figures: Effects of personal and societal stress. *Journal of Personality and Social Psychology*, 1981, *40*, 321–330.

Porter, L. W., Lawler, E. E., and Hackman, J. R. *Behavior in organizations*. New York: McGraw-Hill, 1975.

Prokop, C. K., and Bradley, L. A. *Medical psychology*. New York: Academic Press, 1981.

Quinn, E. Creativity and cognitive complexity. *Social Behavior and Personality*, 1980, *8*, 213–215.

Raiffa, H., and Schlaiffer, R. *Applied statistical decision theory*. Cambridge, MA: Harvard University, 1961.

Raphael, T. D. Integrative comlexity theory and forecasting international crises: Berlin 1946–1962. *Journal of Conflict Resolution*, 1982, *26*(3), 423–450.

Raphael, D., Moss, S. W., and Rosser, M. E. Evidence concerning the construct validity of conceptual level as a personality variable. *Canadian Journal of Behavioural Science*, 1979, *11*, 327–339.

Rokeach, M. *The open and closed mind*. New York: Basic Books, 1960.

Rosenman, R. H. The interview method of assessment of the coronary-prone behavior pattern. In T. M. Dembroski, S. M. Weiss, J. L. Shields, S. G. Haynes, and M. Feinleib (Eds.), *Coronary prone behavior*. New York: Springer-Verlag, 1978, pp. 83–10.

Roskies, E. Modification of coronary risk behavior. In D. Krantz, A. Baum, and J. E. Singer (Eds.), *Handbook of psychology and health*. Hillsdale, Erlbaum, in press.

Rotton, J., Olszewski, D., Charleton, M., and Soler, E. Loud speech, conglomerate noise, and behavioral aftereffects. *Journal of Applied Psychology*, 1978, *63*, 360–365.

Rubin, J. Z. *Dynamics of third party intervention*. New York: Praeger, 1981.

Sauser, W. I., and Pond, S. B. Effects of rater training and participation on cognitive complexity: An exploration of Schneier's cognitive reinterpretation. *Personal Psychology*, 1981, *34*, 563–577.

Schneier, C. E. The contingency model of leadership: An extension to their emergent leadership and leader's sex. *Organizational Behavior and Human Performance*, 1978, *21*, 220–239.

Schroder, H. M. The measurement and development of information processing systems. *Management Information Systems*, 1971, *14*, 811–829.

Schroder, H. M. *Conceptual complexity and managerial performance*. Paper presented to International Congress of Applied Psychology, Edinburgh, Scotland, 1982.

Schroder, H. M., Driver, J. J., and Streufert, S. *Human information processing*. New York: Holt, Rinehart, and Winston, 1967.

Schroder, H. M., and Streufert, S. *The measurement of four systems of personality structure varying in level of abstractness: Sentence completion method.* Princeton University: ONR Technical Report No. 11, 1962.

Scott, W. A. Cognitive structure and social structure: Some concepts and relationships. In N. F. Washburne (Ed.), *Decision, values and groups.* New York: Pergamon Press, 1962.

Scott, W. A. Conceptualizing and measuring structural properties of cognition. In O. J. Harvey (Ed.), *Motivation and social interaction.* New York: Ronald Press, 1963, pp. 266–288.

Scott, W. A. Structure of natural cognitions. *Journal of Personality & Social Psychology,* 1969, *12,* 261–278.

Scott, W. A. Varieties of cognitive integration. *Journal of Personality and Social Psychology,* 1974, *30,* 563–578.

Scott, W. A., Osgood, D. W., and Peterson, C. *Cognitive structure: Theory and measurement of individual differences.* Washington, DC and New York: V. H. Winston & Sons and Halsted Division, Wiley, 1979.

Sells, S. B. Toward a taxonomy of organizations. In W. W. Cooper, H. J. Leavitt, and M. W. Shelly (Eds.), *New perspectives in organization research.* New York: Wiley, 1964, pp. 515–532.

Selznick, P. *Leadership in administration: A sociological interpretation.* New York: Harper & Row, 1957.

Shalit, B. Structural ambiguity and limits to coping. *Journal of Human Stress,* 1977, *3,* 32–45.

Siegrist, J., Dittman, K., Matschinger, H., and Weber, I. Towards a cognition–performance model of coronary prone behavior. *Acta Nerv Super* (Praha), 1982, *S32,* 139–143.

Siegrist, J., Dittman, K., Rittner, K., and Weber, I. The social context of active distress in patients with early myocardial infarction. *Social Science and Medicine,* 1982, *12,* 443–453.

Siegrist, J., Dittmann, K., and Weidemann, H. The role of psychosocial risks in patients with early myocardial infarction. *Acta Nerv Super* (Praha), 1982, *24,* 14–24.

Siegrist, J., and Weber, I. Status threat in mid-adulthood and its health consequences. *Zeitschrift für Gerontologie,* 1983, *16,* 100–106.

Simon, H. A. Information processing models of cognition. *Annual Review of Psychology,* *30,* Palo Alto, CA: Annual Reviews, 1979.

Simons, R. C., and Pardes, H. *Understanding human behavior in health and illness.* Baltimore: Williams & Wilkins, 1981.

Sokal, R. R., and Sneath, P. H. *Principles of numerical taxonomy.* San Francisco: Freeman, 1963.

Stabell, C. B. Integrative complexity of information environment perception and information use: An empirical investigation. *Organizational Behavior and Human Performance,* 1978, *22,* 116–142.

Stamp, G. Levels and types of managerial capability. *Journal of Management Studies,* 1981, *18*(3).

Sternberg, R. J. Toward a triarachic theory of human intelligence. *The Behavioral and Brain Sciences,* 1984, *7,* 269–315.

Stogdill, R. M. Methods for determining patterns of leadership behavior in relation to organization structure and objectives. *Journal of Applied Psychololgy,* 1948, *32,* 286–291.

Stogdill, R. M. New leadership description subscales. *Journal of Psychology,* 1962, *54,* 259–569.

Streufert, S. Conceptual structure, communicator importance and interpersonal attitudes toward deviant and conforming group members. *Journal of Personality and Social Psychology,* 1966, *4,* 100–103.

Streufert, S. Complexity and complex decision making: Convergences between differentiation and integration approaches to the prediction of task performance. *Journal of Experimental Social Psychology*, 1970, *6*, 494–509.

Streufert, S. The human component in the decision-making situation. In B. King, S. Streufert, and F. E. Fiedler (Eds.), *Managerial control and organizational democracy.* Washington, DC: V. H. Winston and Sons and John Wiley, 1978, pp. 215–230.

Streufert, S. *Measurement of task performance on the basis of the time/event matrix: An extension of methods.* Pennsylvania State University College of Medicine: Technical Report ONR NO. 12, 1983a.

Streufert, S. The stress of excellence. *Across the Board*, 1983, *20*(9), 8–11.

Streufert, S. The dilemma of excellence: How strategic decision-making can kill you. *International Management*, 1984, *39*, 36–40.

Streufert, S., Bushinsky, R. C., and Castore, C. H. Conceptual structure and social choice: A replication under modified conditions. *Psychonomic Science*, 1967, *9*, 227–228.

Streufert, S., and Castore, C. H. Information search and the effects of failure: A test of complexity theory. *Journal of Experimental Social Psychology*, 1971, *7*, 125–143.

Streufert, S., Clardy, M. A., Driver, M. J., Karlins, M., Schroder, H. M., and Suedfeld, P. A tactical game for the analysis of complex decision making in individuals and groups. *Psychological Reports*, 1965, *17*, 723–729.

Streufert, S., and Driver, M. J. Conceptual structure, information load and perceptual complexity. *Psychonomic Science*, 1965, *3*, 249–250.

Streufert, S., and Driver, M. J. Impression formation as a measure of the complexity of conceptual structure. *Educational and Psychological Measurement*, 1967, *27*, 1025–1039.

Streufert, S., Driver, M. J., and Haun, K. W. Components of response rate in complex decision-making. *Journal of Experimental Social Psychology*, 1967, *3*, 286–295.

Streufert, S., and Fromkin, H. L. Complexity and social influence. In James Tedeschi (Ed.), *Social influence processes.* Chicago: Aldine Publishing Company, 1972.

Streufert, S., and Ishibashi-Sandler, S. I. Perceived success and competence of the opponent, or the laboratory Dien-Bien-Phu. *Journal of Applied Social Psychology*, 1973, *3*, 84–93.

Streufert, S., Kliger, S. C., Castore, C. H., and Driver, M. J. Tactical and negotiations game for analysis of decision integration across decision areas. *Psychological Reports*, 1967, *20*, 155–157.

Streufert, S., and Nogami, G. Y. Misattributions in attribution research: Choices of scientific certainty vs. understanding of reality: A rejoinder. *European Journal of Social Psychology*, 1984, *14*, 227–230.

Streufert, S., and Streufert, S. C. Information load, time spent and risk taking in complex decision making. *Psychonomic Science*, 1968, *13*, 327–330.

Streufert, S., and Streufert, S. C. Effects of conceptual structure, failure and success on attributions of causality and interpersonal attitudes. *Journal of Personality and Social Psychology*, 1969, *11*, 138–147.

Streufert, S., and Streufert, S. C. *Behavior in the complex environment.* Washington, DC: V. H. Winston and Sons, and John Wiley, 1978.

Streufert, S., and Streufert, S. C. The development of inter-nation conflict. In W. G. Austin and S. Worchel (Eds.), The *social psychology of intergroup relations.* Monterey, CA: Brooks/Cole, 1979, pp. 103–120.

Streufert, S., and Streufert, S. C. *Stress and the measurement of task performance: Decision making in complex tasks.* Pennyslvania State University College of Medicine: Technical Report ONR No. 3, 1981a.

Streufert, S., and Streufert, S. C. *Stress and information search in complex decision making:*

Effects of load and time urgency. Pennsylvania State University College of Medicine: Technical Report ONR No. 4, 1981b.

Streufert, S., and Streufert, S. C. The development of inter-nation conflict. In W. G. Austin and S. Worchel (Eds.), *The psychology of intergroup relations.* Chicago: Nelson Hall, 1985, 134–152.

Streufert, S., Streufert, S. C., Brink, J., Cafferty, T. P., Kreiger, W., Nogami, G. Y., and Turner, W. *Simulation as a technique for analyzing campus unrest.* Office of Education Final Report, Purdue University, 1972.

Streufert, S., Streufert, S. C., and Castore, C. H. Leadership in negotiations and the complexity of conceptual structure. *Journal of Applied Psychology,* 1968, *52,* 218–223.

Streufert, S., Streufert, S. C., and Castore, C. H. Complexity, increasing failure and decision making. *Journal of Experimental Research in Personality,* 1969, *3,* 293–300.

Streufert, S., Streufert, S. C., Dembroski, T. M., and MacDougall, J. M. Complexity, coronary prone behavior and physiological response. In D. J. Oborne, M. M. Gruneberg, and J. R. Eiser (Eds.), *Research in psychology and medicine* (Vol. 1). London: Academic Press, 1979, pp. 206–218.

Streufert, S., Streufert, S. C., and Denson, A. L. *Effects of four task stressors on blood pressure responses in persons differing in Type A Coronary Prone Behavior and cognitive complexity.* Pennsylvania State University College of Medicine: Technical Report ONR No. 11, 1983.

Streufert, S., Streufert, S. C., and Denson, A. L. Information load stress, risk taking and physiological responsitivity in a visual–motor task. *Journal of Applied Social Psychology,* 1983, *13,* 145–163.

Streufert, S., Streufert, S. C., and Denson, A. L. Effects of load stressors, cognitive complexity and Type A coronary prone behavior on visual-motor task performance. *Journal of Personality and Social Psychology,* 1985, *48,* 728–739.

Streufert, S., Streufert, S. C., and Gorson, D. M. Time urgency and coronary prone behavior: The effectiveness of a behavior pattern. *Basic and Applied Social Psychology,* 1981, *2,* 161–174.

Streufert, S., Streufert, S. C., Lewis, J., Henderson, R., and Shields, J. L. *Differential effects of four stressors on blood pressure and heart rate.* Pennsylvania State University of College of Medicine, Technical Report ONR No. 5, 1982.

Streufert, S., Suedfeld, P., and Driver, M. J. Conceptual structure, information search and information utilization. *Journal of Personality and Social Psychology,* 1965, *2,* 736–740.

Streufert, S., and Swezey, R. Simulation and related research methods in environmental psychology. In J. Singer and A. Baum (Eds.), *Advances in environmental psychology,* 1985, *5,* 99–117.

Streufert, S. C. Effects of information relevance on decision making in complex environments. *Memory and Cognition,* 1973, *1,* 224–228.

Suedfeld, P., Corteen, R. S., and McCormick, C. The role of integrative complexity in military leadership: Robert E. Lee and his opponents. *Journal of Applied Social Psychology,* Special Issue on Military Psychology, 1985, in press.

Suedfeld, P., and Piedrahita, L. E. Intimations of mortality: Integrative simplification as a precursor of death. *Journal of Personality and Social Psychology,* 1984, *47,* 848–852.

Suedfeld, P., and Rank, A. D. Revolutionary leaders: Long-term success as a function of changes in conceptual complexity. *Journal of Personality and Social Psychology,* 1976, *34,* 169–178.

Suedfeld, P., and Streufert, S. Information search as a function of conceptual and environmental complexity. *Psychonomic Science*, 1966, *4*, 351-352.

Suedfeld, P., and Tetlock, P. E. Integrative complexity of communications in international crisis. *Journal of Conflict Resolution*, 1977, *21*, 169-184.

Suinn, R. M., and Bloom, L. J. Anxiety management training for pattern A behavior. *Journal of Behavioral Medicine*, 1978, *1*, 25-35.

Swezey, R. W., Davis, E., Baudhuin, E. S., Streufert, S., and Evans, R. Organizational and systems theories: An integrated review. *Psychological Documents*, 1983, *13*, 2, 29.

Swezey, R. W., Streufert, S., Criswell, E. L., Unger, K. W., and Van Rijn, P. *Development of a computer simulation for assessing decision-making style using cognitive complexity theory*. (SAI Report No. SAI-84-04-178). McLean, VA: Science Applications, Inc., 1984.

Swezey, R. W., Streufert, S., and Mietus, J. Development of an empirically derived taxonomy of organizational systems. *Journal of the Washington Academy of Sciences*, *73*(1), 27-42, March 1983.

Swezey, R. W., and Unger, K. W. *Establishing a basis for the simulation system*. Paper presented at the Annual Convention of the American Psychological Association, Washington, DC, August 1982.

U. S. Surgeon General's Report on Smoking, 1983.

Valkonen, T. Psychosocial stress and sociodemographic differentials in mortality. *Acta Med Scandinavia*, 1982, *660*, 152-164.

Vancil, R. F. Strategy formation in complex organizations. *Sloan Management Review*, 1976, *17*, 1-18.

VanMaanen, J., and Schein, E. H. Toward a theory of organizational socialization. In B. Staw (Ed.), *Research in organizational behavior* (Volume 1). Greenwich, CT: JAI Press, 1979.

Vecchio, R. A test of the cognitive complexity interpretation of the least preferred co-worker scale. *Educational and Psychological Measurement*, 1979, *39*, 523-526.

Vetter, M. Ego development and cognitive complexity. *Zeitschrift für Entwicklungspsychologie und Pädagogische Psychologie*, 1980, *12*, 126-143.

Von Eye, A., and Hussy, W. On the contribution of variables of cognitive complexity to the identification of risk groups in traffic. *Schweizerische Zeitschrift für Psychologie und ihre Anwendungen*, 1979, *38*, 58-70.

Wald, A. *Sequential analysis*. New York: Wiley, 1947.

Warriner, C. K. *Organizational types: Notes on the "organizational species" concept*. University of Kansas working papers in sociology. Lawrence, KS: Charles K. Warriner, 1980.

Weick, K. E. *The social psychology of organizing* (2nd ed.). Reading, MA: Addison-Wesley, 1979.

Weiss, H. M., and Adler, S. Cognitive complexity and the structure of implicit leadership theories. *Journal of Applied Psychology*, 1981, *66*, 69-78.

Weiss, S. M., Herd, J. A., and Fox, B. H. *Perspectives on behavioral medicine*. New York: Academic Press, 1981.

Werner, H. *Comparative psychology of mental development*. New York: International Universities Press, 1957.

White, C. M. Cognitive complexity and completion of social structures. *Social Behavior and Personality*, 1977, *5*, 305-310.

Witkin, H. A., Dyk, R. B., Faterson, H. F., Goodenough, D. R., and Karp, S. A. *Psychological differentiation*. New York: Wiley, 1962.

Wohl, J. H. Force management decision requirements for Air Force tactical command and control. *IEEE Transactions on Systems, Man, and Cybernetics, SMC-11*(9), September, 1981.

Wojciszke, B. Affective factors in organization of cognitive structures in the context of interpersonal perception. *Polish Psychological Bulletin*, 1979, *10*, 3–13.

Wolfe, J., and Chacko, T. I. Cognitive structures of business game players. *Simulation and Games*, 1980, *11*, 461–476.

Wrapp, H. E. Don't blame the system, blame the managers. *Dun's Review*, September, 1980, p. 88.

Wyer, R. S. Assessment and correlates of cognitive differentiation and integration. *Journal of Personality*, 1964, *32*, 395–509.

Zajonc, R. B. The process of cognitive tuning in communication. *Journal of Abnormal and Social Psychology*, 1960, *32*, 395–509.

Zalot, G., and Adams, W. J. Cognitive complexity in the perception of neighbors. *Social Behavior and Personality*, 1977, *5*, 281–283.

Index*

*This book is concerned with the impact of cognitive complexity on managers and orga-
nizations. Where specialized terms such as differentiation, integration, multidimensionality,
and unidimensionality are used to describe complexity, they are listed in the subject index.
The reader should assume that those listings are not exclusive. Where effects of cognitive
complexity are considered *without* special terminology, listings are not provided. Listings of
that kind would have required an inclusion of every page in this book.